Ellyn Kaschak, PhD
Leonore Tiefer, PhD
Editors

A New View
of Women's Sexual Problems

A New View of Women's Sexual Problems has been co-published simultaneously as *Women & Therapy*, Volume 24, Numbers 1/2 2001.

Pre-publication
REVIEWS,
COMMENTARIES,
EVALUATIONS . . .

"This USEFUL, COMPLEX, AND VALID critique of simplistic notions of women's sexuality will be ESPECIALLY VALUABLE FOR WOMEN'S STUDIES AND PUBLIC HEALTH COURSES. An important compilation representing many diverse individuals and groups of women."

Judy Norsigian and Jane Pincus,
Co-Founders,
Boston Women's Health Collective;
Co-Authors, Our Bodies, Ourselves for the New Century

The Haworth Press, Inc.

A New View
of Women's Sexual Problems

A New View of Women's Sexual Problems has been co-published simultaneously as *Women & Therapy*, Volume 24, Numbers 1/2 2001.

The *Women & Therapy* Monographic "Separates"

Below is a list of "separates," which in serials librarianship means a special issue simultaneously published as a special journal issue or double-issue *and* as a "separate" hardbound monograph. (This is a format which we also call a "DocuSerial.")

"Separates" are published because specialized libraries or professionals may wish to purchase a specific thematic issue by itself in a format which can be separately cataloged and shelved, as opposed to purchasing the journal on an on-going basis. Faculty members may also more easily consider a "separate" for classroom adoption.

"Separates" are carefully classified separately with the major book jobbers so that the journal tie-in can be noted on new book order slips to avoid duplicate purchasing.

You may wish to visit Haworth's website at . . .

http://www.HaworthPress.com

. . . to search our online catalog for complete tables of contents of these separates and related publications.

You may also call 1-800-HAWORTH (outside US/Canada: 607-722-5857), or Fax 1-800-895-0582 (outside US/Canada: 607-771-0012), or e-mail at:

getinfo@haworthpressinc.com

A New View of Women's Sexual Problems, edited by Ellyn Kaschak, PhD, and Leonore Tiefer, PhD (Vol. 24, No. 1/2, 2001). *"This USEFUL, COMPLEX, AND VALID critique of simplistic notions of women's sexuality will be ESPECIALLY VALUABLE FOR WOMEN'S STUDIES AND PUBLIC HEALTH COURSES. An important compilation representing many diverse individuals and groups of women"* (Judy Norsigian and Jane Pincus, Co-Founders, Boston Women's Health Collective; Co-Authors, Our Bodies, Ourselves for the New Century)

Intimate Betrayal: Domestic Violence in Lesbian Relationships, edited by Ellyn Kaschak, PhD (Vol. 23, No. 3, 2001). *"A groundbreaking examination of a taboo and complex subject. Both scholarly and down to earth, this superbly edited volume is an indispensable resource for clinicians, researchers, and lesbians caught up in the cycle of domestic violence."* (Dr. Marny Hall, Psychotherapist; Author of The Lesbian Love Companion, Co-Author of Queer Blues)

The Next Generation: Third Wave Feminist Psychotherapy, edited by Ellyn Kaschak, PhD (Vol. 23, No. 2, 2001). *Discusses the issues young feminists face, focusing on the implications for psychotherapists of the false sense that feminism is no longer necessary.*

Minding the Body: Psychotherapy in Cases of Chronic and Life-Threatening Illness, edited by Ellyn Kaschak, PhD (Vol. 23, No. 1, 2001). *Being diagnosed with cancer, lupus, or fibromyalgia is a traumatic event. All too often, women are told their disease is 'all in their heads' and therefore both 'unreal and insignificant' by a medical profession that dismisses emotions and scorns mental illness. Combining personal narratives and theoretical views of illness,* Minding the Body *offers an alternative approach to the mind-body connection. This book shows the reader how to deal with the painful and difficult emotions that exacerbate illness, while learning the emotional and spiritual lessons illness can teach.*

For Love or Money: The Fee in Feminist Therapy, edited by Marcia Hill, EdD, and Ellyn Kaschak, PhD (Vol. 22, No. 3, 1999). *"Recommended reading for both new and seasoned professionals . . . . An exciting and timely book about 'the last taboo' . . . . "* (Carolyn C. Larsen, PhD, Senior Counsellor Emeritus, University of Calgary; Partner, Alberta Psychological Resources Ltd., Calgary, and Co-editor, Ethical Decision Making in Therapy: Feminist Perspectives)

Beyond the Rule Book: Moral Issues and Dilemmas in the Practice of Psychotherapy, edited by Ellyn Kaschak, PhD, and Marcia Hill, EdD (Vol. 22, No. 2, 1999). *"The authors in this important and timely book tackle the difficult task of working through . . . conflicts, sharing their moral struggles and real life solutions in working with diverse populations and in a variety of clinical settings. . . . Will provide psychotherapists with a thought-provoking source for the stimulating and essential discussion of our own and our profession's moral bases."* (Carolyn C. Larsen, PhD, Senior Counsellor Emeritus, University of Calgary, Partner in private practice, Alberta Psychological Resources Ltd., Calgary, and Co-editor, Ethical Decision Making in Therapy: Feminist Perspectives)

Assault on the Soul: Women in the Former Yugoslavia, edited by Sara Sharratt, PhD, and Ellyn Kaschak, PhD (Vol. 22, No. 1, 1999). *Explores the applications and intersections of feminist therapy, activism and jurisprudence with women and children in the former Yugoslavia.*

Learning from Our Mistakes: Difficulties and Failures in Feminist Therapy, edited by Marcia Hill, EdD, and Esther D. Rothblum, PhD (Vol. 21, No. 3, 1998). *"A courageous and fundamental step in evolving a well-grounded body of theory and of investigating the assumptions that unexamined, lead us to error." (Teresa Bernardez, MD, Training and Supervising Analyst, The Michigan Psychoanalytic Council)*

Feminist Therapy as a Political Act, edited by Marcia Hill, EdD (Vol. 21, No. 2, 1998). *"A real contribution to the field. . . . A valuable tool for feminist therapists and those who want to learn about feminist therapy." (Florence L. Denmark, PhD, Robert S. Pace Distinguished Professor of Psychology and Chair, Psychology Department, Pace University, New York, New York)*

Breaking the Rules: Women in Prison and Feminist Therapy, edited by Judy Harden, PhD, and Marcia Hill, EdD (Vol. 20, No. 4 & Vol. 21, No. 1, 1998). *"Fills a long-recognized gap in the psychology of women curricula, demonstrating that feminist theory can be made relevant to the practice of feminism, even in prison." (Suzanne J. Kessler, PhD, Professor of Psychology and Women's Studies, State University of New York at Purchase)*

Children's Rights, Therapists' Responsibilities: Feminist Commentaries, edited by Gail Anderson, MA, and Marcia Hill, EdD (Vol. 20, No. 2, 1997). *"Addresses specific practice dimensions that will help therapists organize and resolve conflicts about working with children, adolescents, and their families in therapy." (Feminist Bookstore News)*

More than a Mirror: How Clients Influence Therapists' Lives, edited by Marcia Hill, EdD (Vol. 20, No. 1, 1997). *"Courageous, insightful, and deeply moving. These pages reveal the scrupulous self-examination and self-reflection of conscientious therapists at their best. An important contribution to feminist therapy literature and a book worth reading by therapists and clients alike." (Rachel Josefowitz Siegal, MSW, retired feminist therapy practitioner; Co-Editor, Women Changing Therapy; Jewish Women in Therapy; and Celebrating the Lives of Jewish Women: Patterns in a Feminist Sampler)*

Sexualities, edited by Marny Hall, PhD, LCSW (Vol. 19, No. 4, 1997). *"Explores the diverse and multifaceted nature of female sexuality, covering topics including sadomasochism in the therapy room, sexual exploitation in cults, and genderbending in cyberspace." (Feminist Bookstore News)*

Couples Therapy: Feminist Perspectives, edited by Marcia Hill, EdD, and Esther D. Rothblum, PhD (Vol. 19, No. 3, 1996). *Addresses some of the inadequacies, omissions, and assumptions in traditional couples' therapy to help you face the issues of race, ethnicity, and sexual orientation in helping couples today.*

A Feminist Clinician's Guide to the Memory Debate, edited by Susan Contratto, PhD, and M. Janice Gutfreund, PhD (Vol. 19, No. 1, 1996). *"Unites diverse scholars, clinicians, and activists in an insightful and useful examination of the issues related to recovered memories." (Feminist Bookstore News)*

Classism and Feminist Therapy: Counting Costs, edited by Marcia Hill, EdD, and Esther D. Rothblum, PhD (Vol. 18, No. 3/4, 1996). *"Educates, challenges, and questions the influence of classism on the clinical practice of psychotherapy with women." (Kathleen P. Gates, MA, Certified Professional Counselor, Center for Psychological Health, Superior, Wisconsin)*

Lesbian Therapists and Their Therapy: From Both Sides of the Couch, edited by Nancy D. Davis, MD, Ellen Cole, PhD, and Esther D. Rothblum, PhD (Vol. 18, No. 2, 1996). *"Highlights the power and boundary issues of psychotherapy from perspectives that many readers may have neither considered nor experienced in their own professional lives." (Psychiatric Services)*

Feminist Foremothers in Women's Studies, Psychology, and Mental Health, edited by Phyllis Chesler, PhD, Esther D. Rothblum, PhD, and Ellen Cole, PhD (Vol. 17, No. 1/2/3/4, 1995). *"A must for feminist scholars and teachers . . . These women's personal experiences are poignant and powerful." (Women's Studies International Forum)*

Women's Spirituality, Women's Lives, edited by Judith Ochshorn, PhD, and Ellen Cole, PhD (Vol. 16, No. 2/3, 1995). *"A delightful and complex book on spirituality and sacredness in women's lives." (Joan Clingan, MA, Spiritual Psychology, Graduate Advisor, Prescott College Master of Arts Program)*

Psychopharmacology from a Feminist Perspective, edited by Jean A. Hamilton, MD, Margaret Jensvold, MD, Esther D. Rothblum, PhD, and Ellen Cole, PhD (Vol. 16, No. 1, 1995). *"Challenges readers to increase their sensitivity and awareness of the role of sex and gender in response to and acceptance of pharmacologic therapy." (American Journal of Pharmaceutical Education)*

Wilderness Therapy for Women: The Power of Adventure, edited by Ellen Cole, PhD, Esther D. Rothblum, PhD, and Eve Erdman, MEd, MLS (Vol. 15, No. 3/4, 1994). *"There's an undeniable excitement in these pages about the thrilling satisfaction of meeting challenges in the physical world, the world outside our cities that is unfamiliar, uneasy territory for many women. If you're interested at all in the subject, this book is well worth your time." (Psychology of Women Quarterly)*

Bringing Ethics Alive: Feminist Ethics in Psychotherapy Practice, edited by Nanette K. Gartrell, MD (Vol. 15, No. 1, 1994). *"Examines the theoretical and practical issues of ethics in feminist therapies. From the responsibilities of training programs to include social issues ranging from racism to sexism to practice ethics, this outlines real questions and concerns." (Midwest Book Review)*

Women with Disabilities: Found Voices, edited by Mary Willmuth, PhD, and Lillian Holcomb, PhD (Vol. 14, No. 3/4, 1994). *"These powerful chapters often jolt the anti-disability consciousness and force readers to contend with the ways in which disability has been constructed, disguised, and rendered disgusting by much of society." (Academic Library Book Review)*

Faces of Women and Aging, edited by Nancy D. Davis, MD, Ellen Cole, PhD, and Esther D. Rothblum, PhD (Vol. 14, No. 1/2, 1993). *"This uplifting, helpful book is of great value not only for aging women, but also for women of all ages who are interested in taking active control of their own lives." (New Mature Woman)*

Refugee Women and Their Mental Health: Shattered Societies, Shattered Lives, edited by Ellen Cole, PhD, Oliva M. Espin, PhD, and Esther D. Rothblum, PhD (Vol. 13, No. 1/2/3, 1992). *"The ideas presented are rich and the perspectives varied, and the book is an important contribution to understanding refugee women in a global context." (Comtemporary Psychology)*

Women, Girls and Psychotherapy: Reframing Resistance, edited by Carol Gilligan, PhD, Annie Rogers, PhD, and Deborah Tolman, EdD (Vol. 11, No. 3/4, 1991). *"Of use to educators, psychotherapists, and parents–in short, to any person who is directly involved with girls at adolescence." (Harvard Educational Review)*

Professional Training for Feminist Therapists: Personal Memoirs, edited by Esther D. Rothblum, PhD, and Ellen Cole, PhD (Vol. 11, No. 1, 1991). *"Exciting, interesting, and filled with the angst and the energies that directed these women to develop an entirely different approach to counseling." (Science Books & Films)*

Jewish Women in Therapy: Seen But Not Heard, edited by Rachel Josefowitz Siegel, MSW, and Ellen Cole, PhD (Vol. 10, No. 4, 1991). *"A varied collection of prose and poetry, first-person stories, and accessible theoretical pieces that can help Jews and non-Jews, women and men, therapists and patients, and general readers to grapple with questions of Jewish women's identities and diversity." (Canadian Psychology)*

Women's Mental Health in Africa, edited by Esther D. Rothblum, PhD, and Ellen Cole, PhD (Vol. 10, No. 3, 1990). *"A valuable contribution and will be of particular interest to scholars in women's studies, mental health, and cross-cultural psychology." (Contemporary Psychology)*

Motherhood: A Feminist Perspective, edited by Jane Price Knowles, MD, and Ellen Cole, PhD (Vol. 10, No. 1/2, 1990). *"Provides some enlightening perspectives. . . . It is worth the time of both male and female readers." (Comtemporary Psychology)*

Diversity and Complexity in Feminist Therapy, edited by Laura Brown, PhD, ABPP, and Maria P. P. Root, PhD (Vol. 9, No. 1/2, 1990). *"A most convincing discussion and illustration of the importance of adopting a multicultural perspective for theory building in feminist therapy. . . . This book is a must for therapists and should be included on psychology of women syllabi." (Association for Women in Psychology Newsletter)*

Monographs "Separates" list continued at the back

A New View of Women's Sexual Problems

Ellyn Kaschak, PhD
Leonore Tiefer, PhD
Editors

A New View of Women's Sexual Problems has been co-published simultaneously as *Women & Therapy*, Volume 24, Numbers 1/2 2001.

The Haworth Press, Inc.
New York • London • Oxford

A New View of Women's Sexual Problems has been co-published simultaneously as *Women & Therapy*™, Volume 24, Numbers 1/2 2001.

The development, preparation, and publication of this work has been undertaken with great care. However, the publisher, employees, editors, and agents of The Haworth Press and all imprints of The Haworth Press, Inc., including The Haworth Medical Press® and Pharmaceutical Products Press®, are not responsible for any errors contained herein or for consequences that may ensue from use of materials or information contained in this work. Opinions expressed by the author(s) are not necessarily those of The Haworth Press, Inc.

The Haworth Press, Inc., 10 Alice Street, Binghamton, NY 13904-1580 USA

Cover design by Anastasia Litwak

Cataloging-in-Publication Data

A new view of women's sexual problems / Ellyn Kaschak, Leonore Tiefer, editors.
       p. cm.
"Co-published simultaneously as Women & therapy, volume 24, numbers 1/2 2001."
Includes bibliographical references and index.
       ISBN 0-7890-1681-8 (alk. paper) – ISBN 0-7890-1682-6 (pbk. : alk. paper)
    1. Psychosexual disorders. 2. Women–Mental health. 3. Women–Sexual behavior. I. Kaschak, Ellyn, 1943- II. Tiefer, Leonore. III. Women & therapy.
 RC556 .N395 2002
 616.85'83'0082–dc21

                                                    2002001575

Indexing, Abstracting & Website/Internet Coverage

This section provides you with a list of major indexing & abstracting services. That is to say, each service began covering this periodical during the year noted in the right column. Most Websites which are listed below have indicated that they will either post, disseminate, compile, archive, cite or alert their own Website users with research-based content from this work. (This list is as current as the copyright date of this publication.)

Abstracting, Website/Indexing Coverage . . . . Year When Coverage Began

- *Academic Abstracts/CD-ROM* **1995**
- *Academic ASAP <www.galegroup.com>* **1992**
- *Academic Index (on-line)* **1992**
- *Academic Search Elite (EBSCO)* **1994**
- *Alternative Press Index (print, online & CD-ROM from NISC)*
  <www.altpress.com> **1982**
- *Behavioral Medicine Abstracts* **1996**
- *BUBL Information Service, an Internet-based Information*
  Service for the UK higher education community
  <URL: http://bubl.ac.uk/> **1995**
- *Child Development Abstracts & Bibliography (in print & online)*
  <www.ukans.edu> **1994**
- *CINAHL (Cumulative Index to Nursing & Allied Health*
  Literature) <www.cinahl.com> **2000**
- *CNPIEC Reference Guide: Chinese National Directory*
  of Foreign Periodicals **1996**
- *Contemporary Women's Issues* **1998**
- *Current Contents: Social & Behavioral Sciences*
  <www.isinet.com> **1995**

(continued)

(continued)

Special Bibliographic Notes related to special journal issues (separates) and indexing/abstracting:

- indexing/abstracting services in this list will also cover material in any "separate" that is co-published simultaneously with Haworth's special thematic journal issue or DocuSerial. Indexing/abstracting usually covers material at the article/chapter level.
- monographic co-editions are intended for either non-subscribers or libraries which intend to purchase a second copy for their circulating collections.
- monographic co-editions are reported to all jobbers/wholesalers/approval plans. The source journal is listed as the "series" to assist the prevention of duplicate purchasing in the same manner utilized for books-in-series.
- to facilitate user/access services all indexing/abstracting services are encouraged to utilize the co-indexing entry note indicated at the bottom of the first page of each article/chapter/contribution.
- this is intended to assist a library user of any reference tool (whether print, electronic, online, or CD-ROM) to locate the monographic version if the library has purchased this version but not a subscription to the source journal.
- individual articles/chapters in any Haworth publication are also available through the Haworth Document Delivery Service (HDDS).

A New View
of Women's Sexual Problems

CONTENTS

ABOUT THE EDITORS

Ellyn Kaschak, PhD, is Professor of Psychology at San Jose State University in San Jose, California. She is author of *Engendered Lives: A New Psychology of Women's Experience*, as well as numerous articles and chapters on feminist psychology and psychotherapy. Dr. Kaschak is editor of *Minding the Body: Psychotherapy in Cases of Chronic and Life-Threatening Illness* and *The Next Generation: Third Wave Feminist Psychotherapy*, and co-editor of *Assault on the Soul: Women in the Former Yugoslavia; Beyond the Rule Book: Moral Issues and Dilemmas in the Practice of Psychotherapy*, and *For Love or Money: The Fee in Feminist Therapy*. She has had more than thirty years of experience practicing psychotherapy, is past Chair of the Feminist Therapy Institute and of the APA Committee on Women and is Fellow of Division 35, the Psychology of Women, Division 12, Clinical Psychology, Division 45, Ethnic Minority Issues and Division 52, International Psychology, of the American Psychological Association. She is co-editor of the journal *Women & Therapy*.

Leonore Tiefer, PhD, is Clinical Associate Professor of Psychiatry at New York University School of Medicine and Albert Einstein College of Medicine, both in New York City. She is the author of *Sex Is Not a Natural Act, and Other Essays* and *Human Sexuality: Feelings and Functions* in addition to dozens of empirical and theoretical chapters and articles and scores of book reviews. She is a licensed clinical psychologist, and has been active in sexuality education and research for the past 30 years. From her dissertation on hamsters and hormones to her current work on the medicalization of theory and practice in sexology, Dr. Tiefer has gained an international reputation as lecturer, author, activist, and theorist in her field. She has served as National Coordinator of the Association for Women in Psychology, President of the International Academy of Sex Research, and Secretary of the Society for the Scientific Study of Sexuality, and is currently a member of the Board of Directors of the National Coalition Against Censorship and a Fellow of several American Psychological Association divisions.

PART I:
A NEW VIEW
OF WOMEN'S SEXUAL PROBLEMS

A New View of Women's Sexual Problems

The Working Group for A New View
of Women's Sexual Problems

SUMMARY. This document was written by a group of 12 clinicians and social scientists and released at a press conference on October 25, 2000. The first part criticizes current American Psychiatric Association nomenclature for women's sexual problems because of false equivalency between men and women, erasing the relational contact of sexuality, and ignoring differences among women. The second part offers guidance for new nomenclature from international sexual rights documents. The third part offers our new classification system. It begins with a woman-centered definition of sexual problems, "discontent or dissatisfaction with any emotional, physical, or relational aspect of sexual experience," and provides four categories of causes: socio-cultural, political, or economic factors, partner and relationship factors, psychological factors, and medical factors. The document is designed for researchers, educators, clinicians, and the public. *[Article copies available for a fee from The Haworth Document Delivery Service: 1-800-*

[Haworth co-indexing entry note]: "A New View of Women's Sexual Problems." The Working Group for A New View of Women's Sexual Problems. Co-published simultaneously in *Women & Therapy* (The Haworth Press, Inc.) Vol. 24, No. 1/2, 2001, pp. 1-8; and: *A New View of Women's Sexual Problems* (ed: Ellyn Kaschak, and Leonore Tiefer) The Haworth Press, Inc., 2001, pp. 1-8. Single or multiple copies of this article are available for a fee from The Haworth Document Delivery Service [1-800-HAWORTH, 9:00 a.m. - 5:00 p.m. (EST). E-mail address: getinfo@haworthpressinc.com].

HAWORTH. E-mail address: <getinfo@haworthpressinc.com> Website: <http://www.HaworthPress.com> © 2001 by The Haworth Press, Inc. All rights reserved.]

KEYWORDS. Women's sexuality, women's sexual problems, nomenclature, medicalization, feminist politics

A NOTE ABOUT AUTHORSHIP

This document is presented, slightly reformatted for publication, exactly as it was released in a press conference on October 25, 2000. The authors of this document, The Working Group on A New View of Women's Sexual Problems, in alphabetical order, are: Linda Alperstein, MSW, Carol Ellison, PhD, Jennifer R. Fishman, BA, Marny Hall, PhD, Lisa Handwerker, PhD, MPH, Heather Hartley, PhD, Ellyn Kaschak, PhD, Peggy Kleinplatz, PhD, Meika Loe, MA, Laura Mamo, BA, Carol Tavris, PhD, and Leonore Tiefer, PhD.

INTRODUCTION

In recent years, publicity about new treatments for men's erection problems has focused attention on women's sexuality and provoked a competitive commercial hunt for "the female Viagra." But women's sexual problems differ from men's in basic ways which are not being examined or addressed.

We believe that a fundamental barrier to understanding women's sexuality is the medical classification scheme in current use, developed by the American Psychiatric Association [APA] for its *Diagnostic and Statistical Manual of Disorders (DSM)* in 1980, and revised in 1987 and 1994. It divides (both men's and) women's sexual problems into four categories of sexual "dysfunction": sexual desire disorders, sexual arousal disorders, orgasmic disorders, and sexual pain disorders. These "dysfunctions" are disturbances in an assumed universal physiological sexual response pattern ("normal function") originally described by Masters and Johnson in the 1960s (Masters and Johnson, 1966, 1970). This universal pattern begins, in theory, with sexual drive, and proceeds sequentially through the stages of desire, arousal, and orgasm.

In recent decades, the shortcomings of the framework, as it applies to women, have been amply documented (Tiefer, 1991; Basson, 2000).

The three most serious distortions produced by a framework that reduces sexual problems to disorders of physiological function, comparable to breathing or digestive disorders, are:

1. A false notion of sexual equivalency between men and women. Because the early researchers emphasized similarities in men's and women's physiological responses during sexual activities, they concluded that sexual disorders must also be similar. Few investigators asked women to describe their experiences from their own points of view. When such studies were done, it became apparent that women and men differ in many crucial ways. Women's accounts do not fit neatly into the Masters and Johnson model; for example, women generally do not separate "desire" from "arousal," women care less about physical than subjective arousal, and women's sexual complaints frequently focus on "difficulties" that are absent from the *DSM* (cf. Frank, Anderson, and Rubinstein, 1978; Hite, 1976; Ellison, 2000).

Furthermore, an emphasis on genital and physiological similarities between men and women ignores the implications of inequalities related to gender, social class, ethnicity, sexual orientation, etc. Social, political, and economic conditions, including widespread sexual violence, limit women's access to sexual health, pleasure, and satisfaction in many parts of the world. Women's social environments thus can prevent the expression of biological capacities, a reality entirely ignored by the strictly physiological framing of sexual dysfunctions.

2. The erasure of the relational context of sexuality. The American Psychiatric Association's *DSM* approach bypasses relational aspects of women's sexuality, which often lie at the root of sexual satisfactions and problems–e.g., desires for intimacy, wishes to please a partner, or, in some cases, wishes to avoid offending, losing, or angering a partner. The *DSM* takes an exclusively individual approach to sex, and assumes that if the sexual parts work, there is no problem; and if the parts don't work, there is a problem. But many women do not define their sexual difficulties this way. The *DSM*'s reduction of "normal sexual function" to physiology implies, incorrectly, that one can measure and treat genital and physical difficulties without regard to the relationship in which sex occurs.

3. The levelling of differences among women. All women are not the same, and their sexual needs, satisfactions, and problems do not fit neatly into categories of desire, arousal, orgasm, or pain. Women differ in their values, approaches to sexuality, social and cultural backgrounds, and current situations, and these differences cannot be smoothed over into an identical notion of "dysfunction"–or an identical, one-size-fits-all treatment.

Because there are no magic bullets for the socio-cultural, political, psychological, social or relational bases of women's sexual problems, pharmaceutical companies are supporting research and public relations programs focused on fixing the body, especially the genitals. The infusion of industry funding into sex research and the incessant media publicity about "breakthrough" treatments have put physical problems in the spotlight and isolated them from broader contexts. Factors that are far more often sources of women's sexual complaints–relational and cultural conflicts, for example, or sexual ignorance or fear–are downplayed and dismissed. Lumped into the catchall category of "psychogenic causes," such factors go unstudied and unaddressed. Women with these problems are being excluded from clinical trials on new drugs, and yet, if current marketing patterns with men are indicative, such drugs will be aggressively advertised for all women's sexual dissatisfactions.

A corrective approach is desperately needed. We propose a new and more useful classification of women's sexual problems, one that gives appropriate priority to individual distress and inhibition arising within a broader framework of cultural and relational factors. We challenge the cultural assumptions embedded in the *DSM* and the reductionist research and marketing program of the pharmaceutical industry. We call for research and services driven not by commercial interests, but by women's own needs and sexual realities.

SEXUAL HEALTH AND SEXUAL RIGHTS:
INTERNATIONAL VIEWS

To move away from the *DSM*'s genital and mechanical blueprint of women's sexual problems, we turned for guidance to international documents. In 1974, the World Health Organization [WHO] held a unique conference on the training needs for sexual health workers. The report noted: "A growing body of knowledge indicates that problems in human sexuality are more pervasive and more important to the well-being and health of individuals in many cultures than has previously been recognized." The report emphasized the importance of taking a positive approach to human sexuality and the enhancement of relationships. It offered a broad definition of "sexual health" as "the integration of the somatic, emotional, intellectual, and social aspects of sexual being" (WHO, 1975).

In 1999, the World Association of Sexology, meeting in Hong Kong, adopted a Declaration of Sexual Rights (Ng, Borras-Valls, Perez-Conchillo, and Coleman, 2000). "In order to assure that human beings and societies develop healthy sexuality," the Declaration stated, "the following sexual rights must be recognized, promoted, respected, and defended":

- The right to sexual freedom, excluding all forms of sexual coercion, exploitation and abuse;
- The right to sexual autonomy and safety of the sexual body;
- The right to sexual pleasure, which is a source of physical, psychological, intellectual and spiritual well-being;
- The right to sexual information . . . generated through unencumbered yet scientifically ethical inquiry;
- The right to comprehensive sexuality education;
- The right to sexual health care, which should be available for prevention and treatment of all sexual concerns, problems, and disorders.

WOMEN'S SEXUAL PROBLEMS: A NEW CLASSIFICATION

Sexual problems, which The Working Group on A New View of Women's Sexual Problems defines as discontent or dissatisfaction with any emotional, physical, or relational aspect of sexual experience, may arise in one or more of the following interrelated aspects of women's sexual lives.

I. SEXUAL PROBLEMS DUE TO SOCIO-CULTURAL, POLITICAL, OR ECONOMIC FACTORS
   A. Ignorance and anxiety due to inadequate sex education, lack of access to health services, or other social constraints:
      1. Lack of vocabulary to describe subjective or physical experience.
      2. Lack of information about human sexual biology and life-stage changes.
      3. Lack of information about how gender roles influence men's and women's sexual expectations, beliefs, and behaviors.
      4. Inadequate access to information and services for contraception and abortion, STD prevention and treatment, sexual trauma, and domestic violence.
   B. Sexual avoidance or distress due to perceived inability to meet cultural norms regarding correct or ideal sexuality, including:
      1. Anxiety or shame about one's body, sexual attractiveness, or sexual responses.

    2. Confusion or shame about one's sexual orientation or identity, or about sexual fantasies and desires.
- C. Inhibitions due to conflict between the sexual norms of one's subculture or culture of origin and those of the dominant culture.
- D. Lack of interest, fatigue, or lack of time due to family and work obligations.

II. SEXUAL PROBLEMS RELATING TO PARTNER AND RELATIONSHIP

- A. Inhibition, avoidance, or distress arising from betrayal, dislike, or fear of partner, partner's abuse or couple's unequal power, or arising from partner's negative patterns of communication.
- B. Discrepancies in desire for sexual activity or in preferences for various sexual activities.
- C. Ignorance or inhibition about communicating preferences or initiating, pacing, or shaping sexual activities.
- D. Loss of sexual interest and reciprocity as a result of conflicts over commonplace issues such as money, schedules, or relatives, or resulting from traumatic experiences, e.g., infertility or the death of a child.
- E. Inhibitions in arousal or spontaneity due to partner's health status or sexual problems.

III. SEXUAL PROBLEMS DUE TO PSYCHOLOGICAL FACTORS

- A. Sexual aversion, mistrust, or inhibition of sexual pleasure due to:
  1. Past experiences of physical, sexual, or emotional abuse.
  2. General personality problems with attachment, rejection, co-operation, or entitlement.
  3. Depression or anxiety.
- B. Sexual inhibition due to fear of sexual acts or of their possible consequences, e.g., pain during intercourse, pregnancy, sexually transmitted disease, loss of partner, loss of reputation.

IV. SEXUAL PROBLEMS DUE TO MEDICAL FACTORS

Pain or lack of physical response during sexual activity despite a supportive and safe interpersonal situation, adequate sexual knowledge, and positive sexual attitudes. Such problems can arise from:

A. Numerous local or systemic medical conditions affecting neurological, neurovascular, circulatory, endocrine or other systems of the body;

B. Pregnancy, sexually transmitted diseases, or other sex-related conditions.

C. Side effects of many drugs, medications, or medical treatments.

D. Iatrogenic conditions.

CONCLUSION

This document is designed for researchers desiring to investigate women's sexual problems, for educators teaching about women and sexuality, for medical and nonmedical clinicians planning to help women with their sexual lives, and for a public that needs a framework for understanding a rapidly changing and centrally important area of life.

REFERENCES

American Psychiatric Association (1980). *Diagnostic and Statistical Manual of Mental Disorders* (3rd ed.). Washington, DC: author.

American Psychiatric Association (1987). *Diagnostic and Statistical Manual of Mental Disorders* (3rd ed. rev.). Washington, DC: author.

American Psychiatric Association (1994). *Diagnostic and Statistical Manual of Mental Disorders*, (4th ed.) Washington, DC: author.

Basson, R. (2000). The female sexual response revisited. *Journal of the Society of Obstetrics and Gynecology of Canada, 22*, 383-387.

Ellison, C. (2000) *Women's Sexualities*. Oakland, CA: New Harbinger.

Frank, E., Anderson, C., & Rubinstein, D. (1978). Frequency of sexual dysfunction in "normal" couples. *New England Journal of Medicine*, 299, 111-115.

Hite, S. (1976). *The Hite Report: A nationwide study on female sexuality*. New York: Macmillan.

Masters, W. H. & Johnson, V. E. (1966). *Human Sexual Response*. Boston: Little, Brown, and Co.

Masters, W. H. & Johnson, V. E. (1970). *Human Sexual Inadequacy*. Boston: Little, Brown, and Co.

Ng, E. M. L., Borras-Valls, J. J., Perez-Conchillo, M. & Coleman, E. (Eds.) (2000) *Sexuality in the New Millenium*. Bologna, Editrice Compositor: also on the World Association of Sexology website <www.tc.umn.edu/~coleman001/was/wdecla/htm>.

Tiefer, L. (1991). Historical, scientific, clinical and feminist criticisms of the "Human Sexual Response Cycle" model. *Annual Review of Sex Research*, *2*, 1-23.

World Health Organization (1975). *Education and treatment in human sexuality: The training of health professionals*. Technical Report, series Nr. 572. Full text available on the Robert Koch Institute Sexuality Archive website <www.rki.de/ GESUND/ARCHIV/HOME.HTM>

PART II:
COMMENTARIES ON THE DOCUMENT:
A NEW VIEW
OF WOMEN'S SEXUAL PROBLEMS

"A New View
of Women's Sexual Problems"–
A Family Physician's Response

Lucy M. Candib

SUMMARY. Sexual problems arise frequently in women's lives and are intertwined with all aspects of their social, family, personal, and psychological situations. In the past, physicians have under-recognized or medicalized patients' sexual problems. Moreover, family physicians have been limited to the DSM-IV taxonomy of sexual dysfunction to describe patients' sexual problems. This classification system does not address the need for a patient-centered model, nor does it fit with the biopsychosocial approach of family medicine. In contrast, "The New View

Lucy M. Candib, MD, is Professor, Department of Family Medicine and Community Health, University of Massachusetts Medical School and Family Health Center of Worcester.

Address correspondence to: 26 Queen Street, Worcester, MA 01610 (E-mail: lcandib@massmed.org).

[Haworth co-indexing entry note]: " 'A New View of Women's Sexual Problems'–A Family Physician's Response." Candib, Lucy M. Co-published simultaneously in *Women & Therapy* (The Haworth Press, Inc.) Vol. 24, No. 1/2, 2001, pp. 9-15; and: *A New View of Women's Sexual Problems* (ed: Ellyn Kaschak, and Leonore Tiefer) The Haworth Press, Inc., 2001, pp. 9-15. Single or multiple copies of this article are available for a fee from The Haworth Document Delivery Service [1-800-HAWORTH, 9:00 a.m. - 5:00 p.m. (EST). E-mail address: getinfo@haworthpressinc.com].

of Women's Sexual Problems" is compatible with the biopsychosocial approach because it places the woman and her experience at the center of interest. The "New View" would be strengthened by explicit recognition of the influence of the clinician's own perspective and experience on the process of diagnosis and treatment. *[Article copies available for a fee from The Haworth Document Delivery Service: 1-800-HAWORTH. E-mail address: <getinfo@haworthpressinc.com> Website: <http://www.HaworthPress.com> © 2001 by The Haworth Press, Inc. All rights reserved.]*

KEYWORDS. Family physicians, female sexual dysfunction, sexuality, biopsychosocial model, nosology, relationship-centered care

Specialized physicians take for granted the authority of other specialized physicians to speak the truth about their own area of expertise. Although the validity of the DSM categorization schema for mental health problems has been questioned by feminists for almost twenty years (Caplan, 1991; Kaplan, 1983; Ritchie, 1989), medical physicians have largely been unaware of that controversy. Thus it is not surprising that medical practitioners have not questioned the legitimacy of the DSM-IV diagnostic categories on sexuality. On the other hand, medical physicians are more tolerant than psychiatrists that day-to-day clinical presentations of sexual concerns do not need to match any categorical diagnostic schema, perhaps because medical clinicians do not need to apply a DSM diagnostic code for billing purposes. A revised version of the DSM-IV designed especially for use in primary care, which happens to use the identical sexual dysfunction categories of the DSM-IV, is not widely known or used (APA, 1995). The reality is that many primary care physicians would blandly accept the DSM-IV categorization of sexual dysfunctions but would also make little use of it.

Despite the high prevalence of sexual disorders among primary care patients around the world (Read, King, & Watson, 1997; Shahar, Lederer, & Herz, 1991), and despite exhortations to do so, primary care physicians have not usually addressed patients' sexual issues. Even with increasing public comfort with discussions about sexual issues–from sexual abuse to sexual functioning–increasing time pressures in primary care make it likely that primary care physicians will spend as little time addressing sexuality as they have in the past. Moreover, medical approaches to all symptoms, including sexual ones, typically begin with an attempt to "rule out" biomedical factors. For instance, the DSM-IV-PC for primary care conditions tells the clinician that sexual dysfunctions due to a general medical condition "should be considered and ruled out before a primary Sexual Dysfunction diagnosis is made" (APA, 1995, p. 113). Typically only after the exclusion of medical causes (meaning diagnosable disease processes) does the physician then move on to consider possible psychological factors, and only after that to etiologies perceived as less relevant to medical practice. As a result, articles on sexual dysfunction in medical journals focus disproportionately on the disease model (diabetes) or the hormone deficiency model as a way of explaining women's sexual problems. Conversely, sexual pain is categorized as a sexual dysfunction when in fact it has multifactorial causation (Steege, Stout, & Somkuti, 1993) and may be better addressed as a pain syndrome that affects sex rather than a sexual problem (Meana, Binik, Khalife, & Cohen, 1997).

Family physicians have begun to develop a more integrated approach that builds in attention to psychosocial factors and recognizes the complexity of the relationship between desire, arousal, and orgasm. "Unsatisfying encounters" can lead to decreased desire, decreased arousal, decreased orgasm, and painful sex; inadequate stimulation can contribute to this cycle by limiting lubrication and arousal (Phillips, 2000). Nevertheless, such approaches are still grounded in the DSM classification system of disorders of desire, arousal, orgasm, and sexual pain, and still lack a taxonomy to make the connection to wider social and political causes of sexual problems.

CASE PRESENTATION

A 32-year-old Salvadoran married woman, a documented immigrant, works 40 hours cleaning houses, looking after her two children and her husband's aging mother, cares for the house, and does all the housework and cooking. She presents to her family physician with an urgent concern about sex. She reports that for the last few months she has not been interested in having sexual relations and she worries that her husband will seek sex elsewhere. Family history reveals that her mother died when she was young. She was raised by an older brother in whose home she was a servant. She was never sexually abused, but felt neglected and poorly treated by her brother and sister-in-law. She became pregnant on the first episode of intercourse, married promptly, immigrated to the U.S., and never had any further partners. Further inquiry reveals that communication between her and her husband about sex or the relationship is minimal, and that he is not affectionate. Nevertheless, she finds him to be a good provider and good father. She has no interest in other partners nor in divorce. She reports that although she used to become sexually aroused, she has never had orgasm. She takes oral contraceptives and wonders if they are the cause of her lack of interest. She does not feel depressed although sometimes she is tired for days on end, but she wonders if her husband could be depressed.

This patient is typical of the women from the multicultural population at the urban community health center where I practice. Under a DSM-IV classification of women's sexual dysfunctions, this patient can be viewed as suffering from disorders of sexual desire, arousal, and orgasmic dysfunction. Oral contraceptives or depression may be contributing factors. Alternatively, under the taxonomy proposed by the "New View," her problems can be dissected in the following ways:

I. Sociocultural, political or economic factors

1. The patient herself lacks information about sexual functioning, and we can presume that her husband is similarly uninformed about human sexuality, and women's sexual responses.
2. Culturally she believes that she should make herself available to him whether or not she is interested as she feels it is his right to have sexual relations with his wife.
3. She has been raised in a culture where there is a strict division of labor in the home along gender lines; even though she is now also working outside the home, she still believes that all the household work is her sole responsibility.
4. She works hard and is often overtired; the economic situation prevents her from reducing her workload.

II. Sexual problems relating to partner and relationship

5. Although she accepts rather rigid gender roles in her home, she acknowledges her unhappiness that he does not communicate much, is unaffectionate, and does not even try to share in the work of the house or the children.
6. She does not recognize the contribution of his lack of communication or affection to her lack of interest.
7. She does not recognize the power imbalance in their relationship.
8. She worries about the repercussions of not having sex.
9. Her partner may be depressed, exacerbating his lack of communication.

III. Sexual problems due to psychological factors

10. She fears loss of her partner's fidelity if she does not comply with his needs.
11. Her unrecognized resentment may interfere with interest in sexual activity.
12. She herself may have a masked depression. Perpetuation of the current dynamic may also lead to clinical depression.

IV. Medical factors

13. Oral contraceptives may contribute to lack of sexual interest and/or depression.

Clearly the "New View" provides a much richer and more ample framework for viewing this patient's sexual concerns. The majority of the relevant factors are well outside the biomedical arena, and most fall into the social and partner/relationship realm. This woman's sexual symptoms are typical of the many women seen by family physicians. Fatigue, overwork, and lack of sexual interest are typical problems that women patients will bring to family physicians. In addition, women's experience of men's beliefs about sex and men's own sexual problems often are a cause of women's symptoms. Many clinicians recognize that responsibility for home and childcare double women's workload and strongly contribute to fatigue (Hall, 1992; Tierney, Romito, & Messing, 1990), resulting in women's lack of interest in sex. In short, if she's mad at him for not doing his share, why would she want to have sex with him? The DSM categorization labels this symptom as a "sexual dysfunction"–a disorder of sexual desire. Yet feminist practitioners may recognize this symptom as a byproduct of male privilege: the wife as cook, cleaner, childminder, and bed partner. Add to this the high frequency of physical and emotional abuse in marital relationships, not to mention sexual abuse. Practitioners may attempt to address the anger that women hold about both the division of labor and the experiences of abuse, but such anger is usually chronic, and many women develop symptoms in relation to it–headaches, chronic pain, fatigue, or depression–especially when the relationship appears to be an inescapable trap. Inequities and oppression become translated into individual clinical diagnoses like depression and sexual dysfunction, when the real problem lies outside of the woman herself. In this climate, the "New View" offers welcome respite from a pathologizing approach to women's sexuality that does not look beyond the "dysfunctions" to the realities of women's lives.

Family physicians are trained to think in terms of the individual life cycle, the family life cycle, and the family system. Ideally, family practice assessments are based on the biopsychosocial model, a comprehensive approach in which symptoms are not strictly limited to biomedical etiologies. The "New View" provides an open framework that can be integrated within the biopsychosocial model to address the sexual problems of women in family practice. As the case above demonstrates, the practicing family physician will rarely see an isolated biomedical condition causing a sexual problem; rather, a combination of interrelated factors is usually at work. Using this framework we can avoid locating the problem as a matter of individual pathology and together with the patient make a detailed examination of the factors that are contributing to the problem. Our usual skills of asking, listening, and empathizing can be amplified and strengthened by a structural framework that places the woman and her experiential concerns at the center, rather than focusing primarily on the physiology of sex. With this advance, family physicians working together with women and their partners can begin to make some headway in this common and distressing arena, knowing that there are no magic potions for making these problems better.

All diagnostic classification systems are limited by those who use them. The "New View" is not explicit about the role of the clinician in the use of the taxonomy. A relational approach to medical practice recognizes that clinicians as well as patients are shaped by cultural norms and that the perspective and experience of the clinician her/himself influence what concerns will be recognized and addressed. Women clinicians may be more attuned to nuances in a woman patient's description of her concerns. Older practitioners may not only have seen more problems, they may also have personally experienced a range of sexual changes as they have aged, and are familiar with the variations in sexual energy across the lifecycle. Practitioners with experience in a family systems approach may know that a married woman's concerns about sexuality may be more likely to surface when her husband starts having some sexual difficulty or when her teenage daughter becomes sexually active. The sexual orientation of the clinician may be critical. Heterosexual clinicians may be uncomfortable or uninformed in raising, recognizing and addressing sexual concerns as they arise among lesbian patients. Hence practitioners themselves are integral to the application of any diagnostic system. The "New View" would be strengthened by the explicit recognition of the need for clinicians to re-examine continuously their own assumptions about gender roles, sexual functioning, and sexual orientation as they go about the work of addressing women's sexual problems.

REFERENCES

American Psychiatric Association. (1995). *Diagnostic and Statistical Manual of Mental Disorders, Fourth Edition, Primary Care Version. DSM-IV-PC.* Washington, D.C.: APA.

Caplan, P. J. (1991). Delusional Dominating Personality Disorder (DDPD). *Feminism & Psychology, 1(1),* 171-174.

Hall, E. M. (1992). Double exposure: The combined impact of the home and work environments on psychosomatic strain in Swedish women and men. *International Journal of Health Services, 22,* 239-260.

Kaplan, M. (1983). A Woman's View of DSM-III. *American Psychologist, 38,* 786-792.

Meana, M., Binik, Y. M., Khalife, S., & Cohen, D. (1997). Dyspareunia: Sexual dysfunction or pain syndrome? *Journal of Nervous and Mental Disease, 185,* 561-569.

Phillips, N. A. (2000). Female sexual dysfunction: Evaluation and treatment. *American Family Physician, 62,* 127-136, 141-142.

Read, S., King, M., & Watson, J. (1997). Sexual dysfunction in primary medical care: Prevalence, characteristics and detection by the general practitioner. *Journal of Public Health Medicine, 19,* 387-391.

Ritchie, K. (1989). The little woman meets son of DSM-III. *Journal of Medicine and Philosophy, 14,* 695-708.

Shahar, E., Lederer, J., & Herz, M. J. (1991). The use of a self-report questionnaire to assess the frequency of sexual dysfunction in family practice clinics. *Family Practice, 8,* 206-212.

Steege, J. F., Stout, A. L., & Somkuti, S. G. (1993). Chronic pelvic pain in women: Toward an integrative model. *Obstetrical and Gynecological Survey, 48,* 95-110.

Tierney, D., Romito, P., & Messing, K. (1990). She ate not the bread of idleness: Exhaustion is related to domestic and salaried working conditions among 539 Quebec hospital workers. *Women & Health, 16,* 21-42.

The Taming of the Screw:
Reflections on "A New View
of Women's Sexual Problems"

Gina Ogden

SUMMARY. The DSM IV's medical classification of women's sexual dysfunction pathologizes women who fail to perform according to a genital, orgasmic norm. The "New View of Women's Sexual Problems" provides a more complex instrument for assessing sexual problems women experience. It includes a broad enough sexual framework to allow for multi-level clinical evaluation, an outline of cultural factors that contribute to women's sexual problems, an emphasis on sex education, and relationship-friendly descriptors. The New View's assumption is that women's sexual problems manifest as defense and withdrawal; it would be strengthened by also addressing problems caused by socio-cultural, political, economic, relational, psychological, or medical discounting of women's positive sexual energy. *[Article copies available for a fee from The Haworth Document Delivery Service: 1-800-HAWORTH. E-mail address: <getinfo@ haworthpressinc.com> Website: <http://www.HaworthPress.com> © 2001 by The Haworth Press, Inc. All rights reserved.]*

Gina Ogden, PhD, is a Visiting Scholar at the Wellesley College Center for Research on Women and author of *Women Who Love Sex: An Inquiry into the Expanding Spirit of Women's Erotic Experience.*

Address correspondence to: Gina Ogden, PhD, 36 Shepard Street, Cambridge, MA 02138 (E-mail: womanspirit@ earthlink.net).

[Haworth co-indexing entry note]: "The Taming of the Screw: Reflections on 'A New View of Women's Sexual Problems.'" Ogden, Gina. Co-published simultaneously in *Women & Therapy* (The Haworth Press, Inc.) Vol. 24, No. 1/2, 2001, pp. 17-21; and: *A New View of Women's Sexual Problems* (ed: Ellyn Kaschak, and Leonore Tiefer) The Haworth Press, Inc., 2001, pp. 17-21. Single or multiple copies of this article are available for a fee from The Haworth Document Delivery Service [1-800-HAWORTH, 9:00 a.m. - 5:00 p.m. (EST). E-mail address: getinfo@haworthpressinc.com].

KEYWORDS. Communication, emotions, pleasure, relationship, satisfaction, spirituality

The DSM IV classification of women's sexual dysfunction belongs to a time-honored tradition of pathologizing women who fail to perform according to a genital, orgasmic norm. Labels for these dysfunctions have changed with the times. Yesterday's "frigidity" and "nymphomania" are today's "aversion disorder" and "paraphilia." Such depersonalized labels have helped keep the national consciousness about sex focused on a heterosexual intercourse model, and most women well tamed–locked, in fact, into a kind of cultural missionary position, man on top. "A New View of Women's Sexual Problems" is a radical attempt to expand this national consciousness by taking back the definitions of sexual experience, or at least the definitions of some of the sexual problems women encounter. I am honored to be asked to provide some personal reflections.

As a marriage, family, and sexuality therapist since 1974, I applaud the New View's well-researched effort to create a broader clinical framework for understanding women's sexual problems. I have long felt the limitations of the "doing it" theory of sexual normality and the "didja come?" theory of sexual satisfaction, in which I was meticulously trained–and about which documentation is required for insurance reimbursement. Clearly, if you listen closely to women describe their sexual experiences, you will find many more than the one normal cycle of sexual response Masters and Johnson outlined almost 40 years ago. And just as clearly you will find more than the six categories of sexual distress the DSM IV presently categorizes. In my clinical experience, women's sexual responses are infinitely individual, as are their sexual problems. Moreover, both sexual responses and problems are multidimensionally complex, with biological, sensual, emotional, cognitive, spiritual, relational, and cultural interrelationships.

As a woman born in 1935 (and as a feminist since I discovered the term), I applaud the New View's emphasis on cultural factors as primary contributors to women's sexual problems. My personal sexual history embodies the sociosexual movements since before World War II–the repression, depression, liberation, backlash, and empowerment; the gender imbalances; the expectations and control; the racism, violence, and censorship. I remember these tides of change at a cellular level in my body and brain–the shame of early sexual abuse, the outrage in acknowledging myself as a lesbian, the terrifying need for emotional commitment. I have been able to relieve much personal relationship angst by understanding sexual dysfunction as a manifestation of cultural dysfunction. I know I am not unique. Many women tell a similar story. Including the culture as an agent of sexual problems is a crucial diagnostic tool for women who are still blaming themselves or their partners.

As a mother and grandmother, I applaud the New View's emphasis on sex education and development of relationship-friendly descriptive language. My fervent hope is that my brand new granddaughter and my grandson, an 11-year-old jock with the old soul of a Tibetan lama, will never be subjected to the deep humiliation I felt as a young person–first at not knowing what to ask for as a sexual being, and then at knowing no language with which to communicate it. May they never feel sick or immoral for craving sexual pleasure. And may they never have to seek advice from doctors whose sexual wisdom is limited to DSM diagnoses.

As a researcher presently coordinating a national survey on sexuality, spirituality, and the multidimensionality of meaningful sexual relationship, I do want to register one reservation about the perspective of the New View. I cannot help feeling there must be a way to reframe the national understanding of women's sexuality other than by recategorizing women's sexual problems. After all, pointing out women's shortcomings has been an effective method of controlling us for centuries. Moreover, the New View's assumption is that women's sexual problems manifest only as defense and withdrawal: "ignorance," "anxiety," "inhibition," "avoidance," "distress," "aversion," "mistrust," "pain," or "lack of physical response." If we must recategorize women's sexual problems, let us consider adding one more category. This category would include the problems caused by socio-cultural, political, economic, relational, psychological, or medical discounting of women's *positive* sexual energy. My research since 1980 has focused on women whose sexual response remains a rich source of power and vitality despite all society can do to leach it away. The problems of these women are not defense and withdrawal. They are quite the opposite, stemming from openheartedness, altruism, nurturance, and generative thinking and behavior. These women possess too much desire, too much intuition, too much joy to squeeze into the sexual molds devised by the culture. Because they often allow themselves to be wide open emotionally, they are easily taken advantage of by needy, manipulative, or predatory partners. Because their sexual consciousness resides well outside and beyond cultural missionary position, they are labeled society's outsiders–"sluts," "addicts," "seducers," "ball-busters," "bad women," "women who love too much." In my opinion, these women are victimized along with the women who numb out and knuckle under in order to survive.

In its totality, the "New View of Women's Sexual Problems" is a courageous effort to counteract the prevailing medical model of sexual dysfunction that stereotypes and pathologizes women. I urge every clinician to get behind it, especially if it can be expanded to address the problems that accompany high sexual energy. By get behind this document, I mean use it actively and literally. When you talk with clients and colleagues about sexual desire and behavior, emphasize that sex is more than biology and performance. Broaden your sexual discourse to include emotional, spiritual, and cultural elements. Find your own heartfelt ways of saying: "Sex is more than intercourse. It's more than physical. It's part of your personality. It involves all of you–body, senses, emotions, thoughts, memories, meanings, relationship." By taking this proactive stance, you breathe life into the ideas professed in the New View, and begin to embed them in the national conversation about sex. You challenge the gender stereotypes and power imbalances that narrow too many women's sexual choices and keep too many women trapped in passionless or abusive relationships. You call into question performance-based standards of intercourse and orgasm. You argue against the creation of sexual norms through research financed by pharmaceutical companies invested in products that prolong the mechanics (but not the desire) for penis-vagina intercourse. Above all, you encourage women to define their own sexual problems rather than deferring to medical authorities. And once women can successfully articulate their sexual problems, it is only a small conceptual leap for women to articulate the positive aspects of sexual energy, thus opening a potential flood of collective creativity and power.

REFERENCES

Angier, Natalie (1999). *Woman: An intimate geography*. Boston: Houghton-Mifflin.

Damasio, Antonio (1999). *The feeling of what happens: Body and emotion in the making of consciousness*. San Diego, Calif.: Harcourt.

Eisler, Riane (1995). *Sacred pleasure: Sex, myth, and the politics of the body*. San Francisco: Harper Collins.

Eriksen, Julia A. (1999). *Kiss and tell: Surveying sex in the twentieth century*. Cambridge, Mass.: Harvard University Press.

Espin, Oliva (1997). *Latina realities: Essays on healing, migration, and sexuality*. Boulder, Colo.: Westview Press.

Giddings, Paula (1984). *When and where I enter: The impact of black women on race and sex in America.* New York: William Morrow.

Heyward, Carter (1989). *Touching our strength: The erotic as power and the love of God.* New York: Harper Collins.

Lorde, Audre (1978). *Uses of the erotic.* Trumansburg, N.Y.: Out and Out Books/Crossing Press.

McCormick, Naomi (1994). *Sexual salvation: Affirming women's rights and pleasures.* Westport Conn.: Praeger.

Ogden, Gina (2001-in press). Sexuality overview. In Gamer, Susan et al. (Eds.) *International encyclopedia of women.* New York: Routledge.

_____(2001). Integrating sexuality and spirituality: A group approach to women's sexual dilemmas. In Kleinplatz, Peggy J. (Ed.). *New directions in sex therapy: Innovations and alternatives.* Philadelphia: Brunner-Routledge. 322-346.

_____(1999). *Women who love sex: An inquiry into the expanding spirit of women's erotic experience.* (Rev. Ed.). Cambridge, Mass.: Womanspirit Press.

_____(1999, December). Vibrators 'r' us: Women in search of sexual control. *Sojourner.* 27-28.

_____(1999, January-February). Sex and spirit: The healing connection. *New Age.* 78-81, 128-130.

_____(1998, July). How sex can be spiritual. *New Woman.* 105-109.

_____(1997). No more Dr. nice-gal. Finding a public voice as a feminist sexologist. In Allgeier, Elizabeth, Richard Allgeier, and Gary Brannigan (Eds.). *The sex scientists.* New York: Addison-Wesley. 201-214.

_____(1995, November/December). Media interruptus: Sexual politics on the book-tour circuit. *Ms.* 86-87.

_____(1988). Women and sexual ecstasy: How can therapists help? *Women & Therapy* 7, 2/3, 43-56.

Evidence for the Importance
of Relationship Satisfaction
for Women's Sexual Functioning

E. Sandra Byers

SUMMARY. The *New View of Women's Sexual Problems* proposes "Sexual Problems Relating to Partner and Relationship" as a major context for understanding women's sexual problems. This commentary summarize s some quantitative research on heterosexual women's (and men's) sexual satisfaction based on the Interpersonal Exchange Model of Sexual Satisfaction. The research provides strong empirical support for the importance of including the relational context in any discussion or definition of women's sexual problems, sexual functioning and/or sexual satisfaction. *[Article copies available for a fee from The Haworth Document Delivery Service: 1-800-HAWORTH. E-mail address: <getinfo@haworthpressinc.com> Website: <http://www.HaworthPress.com> © 2001 by The Haworth Press, Inc. All rights reserved.]*

KEYWORDS. Interpersonal Exchange Model of Sexual Satisfaction, sexual satisfaction

---

E. Sandra Byers, PhD, is affiliated with the University of New Brunswick.

Address correspondence to: E. Sandra Byers, Department of Psychology, University of New Brunswick, Fredericton, NB E3B 6E4 (E-mail: byers@unb.ca).

The author would like to thank Sheila MacNeil for her helpful comments on an earlier draft of this manuscript.

[Haworth co-indexing entry note]: "Evidence for the Importance of Relationship Satisfaction for Women's Sexual Functioning." Byers, E. Sandra. Co-published simultaneously in *Women & Therapy* (The Haworth Press, Inc.) Vol. 24, No. 1/2, 2001, pp. 23-26; and: *A New View of Women's Sexual Problems* (ed: Ellyn Kaschak, and Leonore Tiefer) The Haworth Press, Inc., 2001, pp. 23-26. Single or multiple copies of this article are available for a fee from The Haworth Document Delivery Service [1-800-HAWORTH, 9:00 a.m. - 5:00 p.m. (EST). E-mail address: getinfo@haworthpressinc.com].

The *New View of Women's Sexual Problems* criticizes existing classification schemes for women's sexual problems on a number of grounds including their failure to include the relational context in which interpersonal sexual expression occurs. In contrast, the New View proposes "Sexual Problems Relating to Partner and Relationship" as a major context for understanding women's sexual problems. Certainly, women's reports of their experiences of their sexuality support the importance of relationship to the understanding of women's sexual functioning. However, in this commentary, I would like to summarize some of the quantitative research carried out by members of the Sexuality Research Group at the University of New Brunswick on heterosexual women's (and men's) sexual satisfaction based on the Interpersonal Exchange Model of Sexual Satisfaction (IEMSS) (Lawrance & Byers, 1995).[1] Our research provides empirical support for the importance of including the relational context in any discussion of women's sexual functioning in general and their sexual satisfaction in particular.

As a social exchange model, the IEMSS takes the interpersonal context in which sexuality occurs into account. The IEMSS proposes that sexual satisfaction is affected by four factors: the balance of sexual rewards and costs in the relationship, how these rewards and costs compare to the expected level of rewards and costs, the perceived equality of sexual rewards and costs between partners, and relationship satisfaction. Sexual rewards are exchanges between partners that are gratifying and pleasing to the individual; sexual costs are exchanges between partners that demand physical or mental effort or cause pain, embarrassment, anxiety or other negative effect. We have demonstrated the validity of the IEMSS in a number of studies, including studies of individuals in dating relationships and in long-term cohabiting and marital relationships in Canada, and married individuals in China (Lawrance & Byers, 1995; Byers, Demmons & Lawrance, 1998; Renaud, Byers & Pan, 1997). These studies show that women (and men) are more sexually satisfied if they experience a more favourable balance of sexual rewards and costs in their relationship, this balance compares favorably to their expectations, they perceive themselves and their partners to experience approximately equal levels of rewards and costs, and they are satisfied with the nonsexual aspects of the relationship. Thus, consistent with traditional classification schemes for women's sexual problems, sexual exchanges such as oral sex, consistency of orgasm, and expression of affection are important components of women's sexual satisfaction. However, our results show that relationship satisfaction is the most important contributor to sexual satisfaction–more important than the nature of the sexual exchanges. That is, although it is important for women to find their sexual interactions positive and their perceptions of the relative levels of sexual rewards and costs contribute significantly to their sexual satisfaction, women's overall feelings about their relationship and their partner have a greater influence on their sexual satisfaction than do sexual rewards and costs. Similarly, greater relationship satisfaction is associated with experiencing fewer sexual problems and concerns (Byers & Demmons, 1997). These data provide clear support for the argument that women's sexual problems and concerns cannot be separated from their feelings about the relationship in general. Further these results suggest that women's sexual satisfaction can be increased by improving the quality of the nonsexual aspects of the relationship, as well as by improving the sexual script (Byers, 1999).

The intimacy of the relationship, as measured by the extent of self-disclosure, is also important for women's sexual satisfaction. For example, we have found that both self-disclosure about specific sexual likes and dislikes as well as being in a generally disclosing romantic relationship contributes to sexual satisfaction (MacNeil & Byers, 1997). Further, men's understanding of women's sexual preferences is related both to their female partner's sexual self-disclosure and to her sexual satisfaction (MacNeil & Byers, 1999). Incidentally, we observed similar relationships between self-disclosure and sexual satisfaction for men. Thus, being in a relationship that fosters sharing of both sexual and nonsexual intimate information and results in greater partner understanding is important for women's (and men's) sexual satisfaction.

We have also used the IEMSS to study specific types of rewards and costs in the sexual relationship. We found that men and women do not differ in their overall levels of sexual satisfaction, sexual rewards or sexual costs—on average, women and men are equally satisfied with their sexual relationships (Lawrance & Byers, 1995; Byers et al., 1998). In contrast, we found that men and women in long-term relationships do differ in the *types* of rewards and costs they incur in their sexual relationships (Lawrance & Byers, 1995). Although many rewards and costs were equally likely to be endorsed by women and men, the women in our study were more likely than were the men to report emotional and relational qualities of the sexual relationship as rewards for themselves. That is, relational aspects of the sexual interaction (e.g., how their partner treats them when they're having sex) are particularly important to women's sexual satisfaction. These results again suggest that women's sexual satisfaction may depend not only on the physical, intrapersonal aspects of sexual interactions, but also on the affective, interpersonal relationship aspects. Yet these types of rewards are precisely the aspects of sexual functioning that have been excluded from traditional classifications of women's sexual concerns. In contrast, the New View rejects traditional models of sexual functioning that have tended to emphasize the physical and behavioral aspects of sexual interactions (Byers, 1999; Tiefer, 1988) and emphasizes the relational context in which they occur.

In sum, our research on sexual satisfaction lends strong empirical support for including the relational context in any definition of women's sexual problems. Parenthetically, it also suggests that the relational context also needs to be included in definitions of men's sexual problems.

NOTE

1. We are currently investigating the applicability of the IEMSS to women in same gender relationships.

REFERENCES

Byers, E. S. (1999). The interpersonal exchange model of sexual satisfaction: Implications for sex therapy with couples. *Canadian Journal of Counselling, 33*, 95-111.

Byers, E. S. & Demmons, S. (1999). Sexual satisfaction and sexual self-disclosure within dating relationships. *The Journal of Sex Research, 36*, 180-189.

Byers, E. S., Demmons, S. & Lawrance, K. (1998). Sexual satisfaction within dating relationships: A test of the interpersonal exchange model of sexual satisfaction. *Journal of Social and Personal Relationships, 15*, 257-267.

Lawrance, K. & Byers, E. S. (1995). Sexual satisfaction in long-term heterosexual relationships: The Interpersonal Exchange Model of Sexual Satisfaction. *Personal Relationships, 2*, 267-285.

MacNeil, S. & Byers, E. S. (1997). The relationships between sexual problems, communication, and sexual satisfaction. *The Canadian Journal of Human Sexuality, 6*, 277-283.

MacNeil, S. & Byers, E. S. (1999, September). Sexual self-disclosure and understanding among dating couples. Paper presented at the meeting of the Canadian Sex Research Forum, Montreal.

Renaud, C., Byers, E. S., & Pan, S. (1997). Sexual and relationship satisfaction in Mainland China. *The Journal of Sex Research, 34*, 399-410.

Tiefer, L. (1988). A feminist critique of the sexual dysfunction nomenclature. *Women & Therapy, 7*, 5-21.

Beyond STD Prevention:
Implications of the New View
of Women's Sexual Problems

Beth A. Firestein

SUMMARY. The new view of women's sexual problems proposed by this working group provides educators and clinicians with a multi-dimensional, context-sensitive framework for understanding sexually transmitted diseases and STD prevention. Sexually transmitted diseases function as both direct and indirect causes of women's sexual suffering. This article discusses both common and less frequently recognized issues concerning STDs and their impact on women's sexual functioning and psychological well-being. The summary focuses on implications for educators and clinicians committed to increasing women's sexual pleasure and self-empowerment. *[Article copies available for a fee from The Haworth Document Delivery Service: 1-800-HAWORTH. E-mail address: <getinfo@haworthpressinc.com> Website: <http://www.HaworthPress.com> © 2001 by The Haworth Press, Inc. All rights reserved.]*

KEYWORDS. STD prevention, women, sexuality, sexual problems, sexually transmitted disease, HIV/AIDS

Beth A. Firestein is a licensed psychologist in private practice in Loveland, Colorado. She is also a founding partner of Gender Solutions, a company that works with corporations on issues of transgendered employees.

Address correspondence to: Beth Firestein, PhD, 1104 Grant Avenue, Loveland, CO 80537 (E-mail: firewom@webaccess.net).

[Haworth co-indexing entry note]: "Beyond STD Prevention: Implications of the New View of Women's Sexual Problems." Firestein, Beth A. Co-published simultaneously in *Women & Therapy* (The Haworth Press, Inc.) Vol. 24, No. 1/2, 2001, pp. 27-31; and: *A New View of Women's Sexual Problems* (ed: Ellyn Kaschak, and Leonore Tiefer) The Haworth Press, Inc., 2001, pp. 27-31. Single or multiple copies of this article are available for a fee from The Haworth Document Delivery Service [1-800-HAWORTH, 9:00 a.m. - 5:00 p.m. (EST). E-mail address: getinfo@haworthpressinc.com].

The Working Group on *A New View of Women's Sexual Problems* offers clinicians a compelling alternative to physiologically based, performance driven models of women's sexuality derived largely from ahistorical, decontextualized views of women's sexuality. The Working Group points out that the existing system of categorization of women's sexual difficulties, canonized in the American Psychiatric Association's Diagnostic and Statistical Manual of Mental Disorders, erases the relational context of sexuality and fails to acknowledge important differences among women that affect women's sexual functioning. In contrast, the model proposed by this working group of feminist theorists is multi-dimensional, complex, and clearly contextual. This model functions as a springboard for clinicians and educators seeking a new conceptual platform for expanding their interventions to women seeking to understand their own sexual functioning better. I wish to focus on the implications of this model for opening more comprehensive discussions addressing sexually transmitted diseases and the impact these diseases have on women's sexual attitudes, behavior, functioning and relational choices.

Sexually transmitted diseases (STDs) and their impact on women's sexual functioning have generated minimal empirical interest or investigation beyond the large number of studies examining AIDS-related risk and prevention behaviors. AIDS is a critical health issue affecting women's sexuality; however, it is only one of numerous sexually transmitted diseases that cause physical, emotional, and psychological problems for girls and women. Millions of women are affected in acute and chronic ways by the vast array of curable and medically manageable, but incurable, STDs prevalent in the United States and other countries. Although most of these diseases are not life-threatening, many women are directly affected by these STDs in physically and emotionally devastating ways.

The American Psychiatric Association's Diagnostic and Statistical Manual (DSM-IV) acknowledges that sexual disorders may be due to a general medical condition, substance abuse, or psychological factors, or to a combination of these, but gives virtually no recognition to the role STDs may play in disorders of desire, vaginismus, or sexual aversion disorders. The DSM-IV does not address the issue of STDs directly, but an acknowledgement of the existence of sexually transmitted diseases affecting women's functioning can be inferred from the text describing the "sexual pain disorders," such as dyspareunia (pain with intercourse), in which physiological causes for sexual pain are to be "ruled out" before assigning a diagnosis. The classification "Sexual dysfunction due to a general medical condition" refers to vaginal infections as one category of general medical conditions that can cause disorders of arousal, orgasm, or pain syndromes, but does not acknowledge the psychological impact that STDs or the fear of contracting STDs might have on an individual.

In contrast, the Working Group's paper acknowledges sexually transmitted diseases as both direct and indirect causes of women's sexual suffering. Under the category "Sexual problems due to socio-cultural, political, or economic factors," STDs are named as one of several reasons for some women's anxiety about sex. These authors posit that inadequate access to information and services for STD prevention and treatment, as well as the absence or inadequacy of information and services about contraception, abortion and other matters pertaining to sexuality, can have a direct negative impact on women's sexual functioning. The second category, "Sexual problems relating to partner and relationship," mentions "inhibitions in arousal or spontaneity due to partner's health status or sexual problems," which could include a partner's sexual health problems, such as having frequently recurring herpes outbreaks, a positive HIV status, hepatitis, or other STD-related health difficulties. The third category of women's sexual problems, "Sexual problems due to psychological factors," clearly mentions the potential for "sexual inhibition due to fear of sexual acts or of their possible consequences," including pain during intercourse and the risk of contracting a sexually transmitted disease. Finally, the fourth category, "Sexual problems due to medical factors," refers to the presence of pain or lack of physical response during sexual activity that can occur despite the presence of a supportive and safe interpersonal situation when medical conditions, including STDs or the side effects of medical treatments, interfere with sexual pleasure and functioning.

This explicit acknowledgment of the multiple roles that sexually transmitted diseases play in the development and continuation of women's sexual difficulties is extremely important and has implications for educators and clinicians committed to increasing women's sexual pleasure and self-empowerment. This working document develops a conceptual framework that permits us to expand our understanding of the role STDs play in inhibiting women's sexual self-esteem and self-expression. This "new view" of women's sexual problems can become a springboard for the work of educators and practitioners working with female clients on their sexual difficulties.

EFFECTS OF STDS ON WOMEN'S SEXUAL FUNCTIONING: BEYOND PREVENTION

Prevention has been the primary focus of most sex education regarding sexually transmitted diseases. A second aim of STD-related education, particularly that directed at high school age girls, appears to be to use the fear of STDs to discourage girls and young women from engaging in sexual behavior and to encourage the practice of sexual abstinence. Some educational material, particularly information presented in the brochures on specific STDs available in health clinics and physician offices, focuses on how medically to prevent transmission of recurring and chronic STDs, such as HIV, venereal warts, herpes, or hepatitis, to one's sexual partner and encourages communication with partners about STD status before engaging in sexual activity.

What, then, do we offer to women who are already actively dealing with the emotional and physical challenges of having one or more STDs and to women who are dealing with partners who have STDs? Education about prevention is very important, but is not adequate to address these women's needs. The issues involved are numerous and include the following:

1. We need to assist women to develop comfort with asking a new or potential male or female partner specific questions about his or her prior exposure to STDs and teach women strategies for assessing their relative level of risk from exposure to chronic, viral STDs or STDs that may be asymptomatic in a partner. A primary concern for women who may be carriers of a viral STD is the fear of acquiring another, different STD through exposure to a partner.

2. We need to provide education and effective intervention to women whose levels of sexual self-esteem and relational trust have been damaged due to having contracted a curable or chronic sexually transmitted disease, to assist them in integrating this new element into their sexual identity in a way that does not lead to either denial (and associated risk behavior with a new partner) or to self-rejection and resignation to a life without sexual involvement and pleasure.

3. Women who have partners that suffer from recurring outbreaks of a viral STD, such as venereal warts and herpes, or neurological pain disorders, such as vulvodynia, that cause pain with sexual activity or penetration, need to be helped to separate fear from fact and to determine a personal range of safe and pleasurable sexual behaviors–behaviors that allow for sexual satisfaction of both partners while decreasing the risk of exposure to their partner's disease. Such women could also benefit from coaching in ways to deal with a partner's STD that protects the woman without eroding their partner's sexual self-esteem or healthy sense of sexual self-expression.

4. Many women suffering from STDs lack access to adequate information about allopathic and complementary treatments that might as-

sist them in reducing the physical or psychological burden on or interference level with their sexual lives. Although we certainly hope that most women have access to well-trained, sensitive medical providers who are up-to-date in their medical knowledge about STD treatment, in actuality, many women need to be encouraged to be proactive, participatory consumers of health care services. We can encourage women to be assertive with their providers about their questions, needs, and concerns related to having an STD, and train them in the skills they need to communicate their concerns effectively to their health care provider. Women also need to be taught that it is acceptable to seek a second opinion, even a third opinion, if their condition fails to improve or if their practitioner seems disrespectful, disinterested, or unknowledgeable.

5. Educators and counselors need to have a keen awareness of the role that fear of contracting another STD might have on a woman's sense of sexual well-being and be alert to relationship and intimacy avoidance patterns that might have their root in the feelings of discomfort and dis-ease that many women experience once they have acquired an STD, particularly if the circumstances of acquiring the STD involved a dishonest or unscrupulous partner.

6. Finally, these issues also affect the thinking and decision-making of women who may be considering, or be asked by a partner to consider having more than one lover simultaneously. The choice to be polyamorous, either as a single person or through involvement in a negotiated, ethical, responsible, non-monogamous relationship, has significant implications for managing the risks associated with STDs.

EXTENDING OUR VISION

As indicated earlier, prevention has been the primary focus of most sex education regarding sexually transmitted diseases. "The New View of Women's Sexual Problems" extends our thinking about the ways in which either the threat or the actuality of having an STD can affect women's sexual functioning, satisfaction, and decision-making. Educators and clinicians can effectively utilize the ideas contained in the "New View" document to become more conscious and effective in helping women retain and nurture positive sexual self-esteem and a sense of sexual safety in the face of the challenges that sexually transmitted diseases pose to our sexual health and happiness.

The New View and Latina Sexualities: *Pero no soy una máquina!*

Lisa Aronson Fontes

SUMMARY. This article compares the DSM-IV and the New View of Women's Sexualities for their fit with women's sexual concerns–and particularly those of Latina women in psychotherapy. It argues that the New View allows for a more contextualized, complex, nuanced, and humane way to discuss and understand women's sexuality. *[Article copies available for a fee from The Haworth Document Delivery Service: 1-800-HAWORTH. E-mail address: <getinfo@haworthpressinc.com> Website: <http://www.HaworthPress.com> © 2001 by The Haworth Press, Inc. All rights reserved.]*

KEYWORDS. Women, sexuality, Latina, diagnosis, dysfunction, violence

I have dedicated my professional life to exploring issues of culture and sexuality for diverse people, particularly Latinas who have been victimized by sexual assault. Traditional views of women's sexuality,

Lisa Aronson Fontes, PhD, is a psychologist, trainer, and consultant on cultural issues in violence, research, interviewing, and intervention. She conducts therapy and trainings in English, Spanish, and Portuguese.

Address correspondence to: Lisa Aronson Fontes, PhD, 359 Montague Road, Shutesbury, MA 01072.

[Haworth co-indexing entry note]: "The New View and Latina Sexualities: *Pero no soy una máquina!*" Fontes, Lisa Aronson. Co-published simultaneously in *Women & Therapy* (The Haworth Press, Inc.) Vol. 24, No. 1/2, 2001, pp. 33-37 and: *A New View of Women's Sexual Problems* (ed: Ellyn Kaschak, and Leonore Tiefer) The Haworth Press, Inc., 2001, pp. 33-37. Single or multiple copies of this article are available for a fee from The Haworth Document Delivery Service [1-800-HAWORTH, 9:00 a.m. - 5:00 p.m. (EST). E-mail address: getinfo@haworthpressinc.com].

including that implied in the DSM-IV, support a dishwasher view of sexuality (Teifer, 2000, private communication). That is, when you push the "start" button the woman should cycle painlessly through desire, arousal, and orgasm. If there is any variation in the cycle, we–the therapist/repair technicians–say she's broken or dysfunctional, and try to fix her.

This view is so far from my experience and the experience of the people I have worked with and interviewed for research, that it is almost comical. Anyone beyond adolescence should know that sex is *not* primarily about what happens with our organs. And yet mental health and medical professionals proceed as if we were speaking about plumbing.

In this commentary, I will be including examples from clinical work and research with Latinas in the United States to show why I believe the New View of Women's Sexual Problems fits better with the complex reality of women's lives. Details of the stories have been altered to protect confidentiality.

Sarita and Bobby, originally from Cuba, said they had made an appointment to see me as a "desperate" attempt to save their family. Looking at the floor, they told me that the night before their daughter had overheard an argument that ended with Bobby yelling, "What do you want me to do? Go find a *putita* (whore)?" as he walked out and slammed the door. They were concerned that their fighting was going to hurt their children.

Bobby presented as a gentle man who was sorry for his statements, but felt caught in a bind. He explained that he and his wife had not had sexual relations of any kind for more than three years, that he loved her very much and had never had an "outside relationship," but that he was "not made of stone." Sarita confirmed that it had become increasingly difficult for her to have sexual contact with her husband. She said the problems began when their daughter's physical maturation triggered her memories of her own childhood sexual abuse by two cousins. She described picturing her cousins when her husband touched her, and these thoughts were so disturbing that she had become unable to have orgasms with her husband. When she finally told him the origin of her distress, she said he replied in a sympathetic and supportive way. However, Sarita is convinced that her husband is "turned on" by her history of abuse, an idea that repulses her. He is somewhat cagey in his denials of this, saying that he likes to picture her young and sexually excited, but not in pain. Sarita says she desires her husband and is aroused by him, but cannot bring herself to resume sexual activity, which makes her feel like an inadequate wife (Santos-Ortiz & Vázquez, 1989). Sarita had discussed the broad outlines of the problem with her priest and her physician, who had told her just to keep trying with her husband. She dismissed their advice, saying, *"Pero no soy una máquina!"* (But I am not a machine!).

Sarita does not meet the diagnostic criteria for Post-Traumatic Stress Disorder nor does she suffer from a simple dysfunction of desire, arousal, orgasm or sexual pain. All of these possible diagnoses isolate her distress from her marital relationship. The New View diagnostic categories offer new options for considering the psychological, relational, and sociocultural concerns that affect Sarita and Bobby. (Unfortunately, even this New View requires an individual–rather than a couple or relational–diagnosis, perhaps due to insurance billing constraints.) Using the New View, we are able to consider and treat Sarita's discontent in its historical and current relational contexts, without reducing her to a body with a dysfunction, as if she were a broken machine.

Our cultural and social class backgrounds affect our sexuality (Fontes, 1995; Santos-Ortiz & Vázquez, 1989). What we consider normal and desirable, the acts that we find repugnant and enticing, our idea of the "proper" sexual roles for men and women (Fontes, 1993)–these are all shaped by our ethnic cultures, as well as other forces. These all have an impact on men's and women's sexual behaviors, values, and attitudes. The New View encourages these cultural factors to rise from the background for consideration in psychotherapy.

Yolanda had been incestuously assaulted by her father from the age of 9 to 15. Below, she describes how the importance placed on virginity in traditional Puerto Rican culture shaped her marriage:

> Often I think that as a man he–unconsciously–couldn't accept me, and that's why he did the things he did to me: the physical abuse, the sexual abuse, the emotional abuse–that is, the constant abuse. He, as a Puerto Rican man, could have a lot of little girlfriends and go to bed with a whole bunch of women, but when the time comes to get married, he wants a pure woman. And since I wasn't pure in his view, because–as is said in Puerto Rico, *No me rompió la chapita* (he didn't pop my cherry) that probably bothered him. Often he would tell me that he wanted to get divorced because he wanted to marry a woman he had dishonored the year before.

At the time I spoke with her, Yolanda was struggling to reclaim her sexuality in the context of a new and supportive relationship. However, to recover from her history of childhood sexual abuse and abuse in her marriage, Yolanda needed a therapist with a framework that could take into account the influence of her culture, and the inter-relationships among past and present experiences and relationships. Again, the plumbing notions implied in the DSM-IV cannot begin to address Yolanda's reality. The "dysfunction" categories of the DSM-IV imply pathology as a variation from a theoretical normal pattern. It is more helpful to use an injury model–that connects suffering with the environment in which it occurred and the person who caused it–than an illness model, which locates the source in the sufferer (Lamberg, 2000). An injury model implies recovery for victims of abuse. Yolanda is on the mend–being labeled as "dysfunctional" at this time cannot help her recovery.

At the age of 16, Elena, a Puerto Rican from New York City, had an intense relationship with her best friend and co-captain of the basketball team that included kissing and mutual fondling. Neither defined herself as a lesbian, and each went on to have boyfriends. At 22, while in college in California, Elena had another relationship with a woman, Marcia, and this time "came out" as a lesbian, informing her friends and in general settling comfortably into her life as part of an "out" lesbian couple. This climate changed, however, when Elena's family visited her, met Marcia, and learned of their relationship. They angrily told Elena that she'd be better off dead than a lesbian since if she were dead, at least she could go to heaven. Her father also said to her, "*Mejor puta que pata*" (better a whore than a dyke) as he left for the airport. Elena was crushed, divided between feelings of loyalty to her family and culture, and feelings of loyalty to Marcia and her own newfound sense of self. She began to experience periods of intense shame, with complete disinterest in sexual contact, alternating with periods of what she called "ravenous" sexual desire for Marcia.

In this case, Elena's cultural background and family pressures impacted on her sexuality in ways that needed sorting out in therapy. The diagnosis of "sexual problems due to socio-cultural, political, or economic factors" places the nexus of the problem *outside* Elena herself, onto the wider context where it belongs. A compassionate therapist can use this framework to help Elena understand the multiple influences on her sexuality and relationships, and help her develop a strategy for maintaining complex multiple loyalties to her family, culture, and sense of self, if she so desires. All this can be accomplished without needing to label Elena's sexuality–and thereby Elena–as dysfunctional.

In conclusion, I believe that the New View offers psychotherapists a non-pathologizing frame for their client's concerns, acknowledging inter-related types of complexity, and refuting the DSM-IV notion that women run like machines.

REFERENCES

Fontes, L. (1995). *Sexual abuse in nine North American cultures: Treatment and prevention.* Newbury Park, CA: Sage.

Fontes, L. (1993). Disclosures of sexual abuse and Puerto Rican children: Oppression and cultural barriers. *Journal of Child Sexual Abuse, 2*, 21-35.

Lamberg, L. (2000). Domestic violence: What it is, what to do. *Journal of the American Medical Association, 284*(5).

Santos-Ortiz M. C. & Vázquez, M. M. (1989). An exploratory study of the expression of female sexuality: The experience of two groups of Puerto Rican women from different social backgrounds. In García Coll, C. T. & Mattei, M. L. (Eds.), *The psychosocial development of Puerto Rican women.* (pp. 141-165). New York: Praeger.

Reaching the Hard to Reach:
Implications of the New View
of Women's Sexual Problems

Samantha P. Williams

SUMMARY. Much of the research regarding women's sexual issues has focused on accessible groups of women. Women who are marginalized are often harder to reach. Thus, their needs and challenges are not as visible, nor as well addressed as those who have access to resources. This commentary describes the contribution the document "A New View of Women's Sexual Problems" can make in addressing the sexual problems of women who are hard to reach. *[Article copies available for a fee from The Haworth Document Delivery Service: 1-800-HAWORTH. E-mail address: <getinfo@haworthpressinc.com> Website: <http://www.HaworthPress.com> © 2001 by The Haworth Press, Inc. All rights reserved.]*

KEYWORDS. Hard to reach, marginalized, women, sexual problems

I just don't know what to do. He doesn't touch me and we only have sex when he wants to, which isn't that often. When we have it

Samantha P. Williams, PhD, is affiliated with the Centers for Disease Control.

Address correspondence to: Dr. Samantha P. Williams, Mail Stop E-44, Centers for Disease Control and Prevention, Division of STD Prevention, Behavioral Interventions and Research Branch, 1600 Clifton Road, NE, Atlanta, GA 30333 (E-mail: stw8@cdc.gov).

[Haworth co-indexing entry note]: "Reaching the Hard to Reach: Implications of the New View of Women's Sexual Problems." Williams, Samantha P. Co-published simultaneously in *Women & Therapy* (The Haworth Press, Inc.) Vol. 24, No. 1/2, 2001, pp. 39-42; and: *A New View of Women's Sexual Problems* (ed: Ellyn Kaschak, and Leonore Tiefer) The Haworth Press, Inc., 2001, pp. 39-42. Single or multiple copies of this article are available for a fee from The Haworth Document Delivery Service [1-800-HAWORTH, 9:00 a.m. - 5:00 p.m. (EST). E-mail address: getinfo@haworthpressinc.com].

[sex] he tries to finish as fast as he can and he doesn't care if I get anything out of it or not. If I try to talk about it, that's an argument. If I try to do something different, I'm a ho. I just don't know what to do anymore. Maybe Viagra will help.

—42-year-old African-American woman living in the rural south, discussing her relationship of seven years.

Much of the research regarding women's sexual issues has focused on accessible groups of women. Although the women's sociodemographic characteristics may have been diverse, one common thread has been educators', clinicians', and interested investigators' accessibility to the populations. Another common thread has been the women's visibility within the larger social system. The role of women in our society may not be one that is perceived, by some, to be particularly empowering. However, women who are visible and accessible have value. If one can be reached, one can be utilized and thus, can be valued. If one cannot be reached, one cannot be utilized and thus, one's value is questionable.

To be marginalized is to be pushed to or maintained at the edge of a social system or to be invisible to those within the social system. Although factors such as economic barriers or disempowering life circumstances contribute to the continual marginalization of diverse subgroups of women (e.g., substance users or incarcerated women), areas of research such as HIV/STD prevention have highlighted the importance of reaching those subgroups of women. Thus, their needs and challenges have become more visible. Women who are marginalized by such factors as geographical location or controlling cultural norms (e.g., women living in rural areas or developing countries) are often harder to reach. Thus their needs and challenges are not as visible, nor as well addressed.

Several investigators have identified effective strategies for working with hard to reach populations (i.e., Pulley, McAlister, Kay, and O'Reilly, 1996; Turner and Solomon, 1996; Rowdan, Dorsey, Bullman, Lestina, Han, and Herrell, 1999). Frequently utilized strategies include outreach, use of peer workers, and diverse community involvement. However, most of the sexuality-specific work with the hard to reach has focused on the prevention of negative consequences such as HIV/STD risk reduction or the promotion of safer behaviors such as the use of condoms. Little work has been done on how to address the sexual problems of hard to reach and/or marginalized women, and it is with these specific populations that significant contributions can be made with the New View perspective of women's sexual problems.

The medicalization of sexuality, in general, and of women's sexuality, in particular, has created an environment where, instead of addressing the environmental, sociocultural or psychological contributors of sexual problems, more effort and money are invested in finding a convenient and immediate "cure." What is potentially problematic is that, with the aid of global advertising, marginalized women and men are likely to be convinced that the medical options are the best and only options.

The opening quote is borrowed from the oral narrative of an African-American woman presently living in the rural south. It is an example of how the medicalization of sexuality can impact the life of a woman who is geographically marginalized. The woman lives in an area where most of the people are employed and many of the homes are owned by one of two companies. The community does not have a physician, clinician, health educator, health care facility, or community-based organization that serves them. The local highway and the commercial railroad allow for access to the area, but they can also function as barriers that inhibit or prevent communication, assistance and collaboration between the communities and/or external systems. The community is fairly isolated, yet filled with families trying to make a good life and with women who are most often at the head of that effort.

Most women who live in challenging settings do not necessarily have the opportunity to attend to their own needs, sexual or otherwise. If and when women who live in such circumstances do become more informed of their sexual rights, they are likely to experience barriers to expressing those rights due to living in environments that do not reinforce messages of self agency, positive sexuality or personal health, or that do not establish and sustain appropriate services for women.

What is timely and important about the New View document is the much needed attention the authors have given to the plethora of causes and contributors to sexual problems that impact women across cultures, relationships and life circumstances. The proposed classification provides researchers, clinicians, and educators alike with a framework to investigate adequately and understand women's sexual problems and other related issues by integrating the woman, her mind and body with her relationships, environments and culture. It is this focus on women's integrated self that makes the New View a needed vision. The New View focuses on sexual problems, but it has much broader implications for the lives of women. If a woman's sexual problem is due to partner coercion, addressing the coercion will not only have an impact on her relationship with the partner and their sexual dynamics, it may also impact the woman's relationship with other potential partners, friends and family members, as well as her own physical, psychological and sexual well-being. The perspective can also be generalized to other areas such as women's health, and can benefit others in women's lives.

The challenge for the New View will be in reaching women who are marginalized, yet accessible, as well as those women who cannot be reached via traditional methods. For this reason, the document should also be shared with outreach workers, community organizations, activists and others who have gained the trust and respect of the members of marginalized and hard to reach populations, as well as those in isolated communities. The New View document can be made available to formal and grass roots professions via multiple venues such as community forums, popular media, profession articles or the Internet. Health (physical, psychological, sexual) professions and educators (professors, instructors, trainers, service providers) can incorporate the approach into their own services or activities. By making the New View document available to those who are able to reach the hard-to-reach, women (and their partners) can gain access to information that will educate them on how to identify sexual problems and seek help with such problems.

Finally, the New View perspective can empower women to develop a perception of their sexuality that focuses less on the sexual act and more on the factors that can contribute to the development of a healthier self.

REFERENCES

Pulley, L., McAlister, A. L., Kay, L. S., & O'Reilly, K. (1996). Prevention campaigns for hard to reach populations at risk for HIV infection: Theory and implementations. *Health Education Quarterly, 23(4)*, 488-496.

Rowdan, D. W., Dorsey, P. E., Bullman, S., Lestina, R. P., Han, C., & Herrell, J. M. (1999). HIV outreach for hard to reach populations: A cross-site perspective. *Evaluation and Program Planning, 22(3)*, 251-258.

Turner, N. H., & Solomon, D. J. (1996). HIV risk and risk reduction readiness in hard to reach drug-using African-American and Mexican women: An exploratory study. *AIDS Education and Prevention, 8(3)*, 236-246.

Sex Therapy with "A New View"

Suzanne Iasenza

SUMMARY. Sex therapy that incorporates a "new view" will question any sexual theories that essentialize women's and men's experiences and will refrain from overuse of gender socialization theories that level differences among women. Clinical examples are offered to illustrate how sex therapy with this "new view" would be conducted. *[Article copies available for a fee from The Haworth Document Delivery Service: 1-800-HAWORTH. E-mail address: <getinfo@haworthpressinc.com> Website: <http://www.HaworthPress.com> © 2001 by The Haworth Press, Inc. All rights reserved.]*

KEYWORDS. Sex therapy, essentialism, multi-variable model, gender socialization, lesbian sexuality, women's subjectivity

Even well-intentioned, feminist sex therapists face many challenges in conducting a woman-friendly sex therapy. Many of these challenges originate in limitations set by male-defined constructs and models that obscure the complexities of women's sexual relating. A New View offers us a springboard to begin articulating the varieties of sexual relating in women (and men), something urgently needed given recent media coverage about female sexual dysfunction that mostly focuses on medical interventions. As I read "A New View," I envision a time when fem-

---

Suzanne Iasenza, PhD, is affiliated with the Department of Counseling, John Jay College-City University of New York, 445 West 59th Street, New York, NY 10019.

[Haworth co-indexing entry note]: "Sex Therapy with 'A New View.'" Iasenza, Suzanne. Co-published simultaneously in *Women & Therapy* (The Haworth Press, Inc.) Vol. 24, No. 1/2, 2001, pp. 43-46; and: *A New View of Women's Sexual Problems* (ed: Ellyn Kaschak, and Leonore Tiefer) The Haworth Press, Inc., 2001, pp. 43-46. Single or multiple copies of this article are available for a fee from The Haworth Document Delivery Service [1-800-HAWORTH, 9:00 a.m. - 5:00 p.m. (EST). E-mail address: getinfo@haworthpressinc.com].

ex therapists, having incorporated its principles, refer to our work
curring with a "new view." Here are some possible applications.

Not only would we fully appreciate the falsity of viewing male and
female sexuality as equivalent, but we would question any sexual theorizing that essentializes women's and men's experiences. We would
create models of gender-sexuality that relinquish binary identity categories (male/female, heterosexual/homosexual, masculine/feminine,
sexual subject/sexual object) in favor of models that allow for a fluid,
multi-variable process. Such a model could accommodate one of my
patient's experiences, a married woman we'll call Mary, who describes
her best sexual experiences as ones that involve her being a sexual subject, the one who lusts rather than is lusted after and who most enjoys
experiencing herself as entering her husband during sexual intercourse.
While articulating such desires, Mary, who had been in relationships
with women and men in the past, expressed a fear that these "masculine" preferences, to lust after and to enter someone, meant that she really belongs in a relationship with a woman. Mary needed a "new view"
 of the complexities of sexual relating, not only as Klein et al. (1985)
taught us, that sexual orientation is multi-variable regarding sexual attraction, sexual behavior, emotional preferences and so on, but as it re-
lates to sexual agency and activity, both internal and external. Mary was
eventually able to combine her own mixture of sexual variables without
having to enforce a degree of congruity that didn't exist for her. Concurrently, her husband needed help in feeling more comfortable being a receptive object of desire, part of which involved a reconceptualization of what
it means to be manly.

Another old conceptual frame had to be relinquished for Mary to experience sexual satisfaction. Entering treatment with a "sexual desire
disorder" in the "old view" (both she and her husband had little interest
in sex), she was at a loss as to how to feel more sexually alive. Waiting
for "desire to happen," as she put it, was a frustrating and demoralizing
experience. She failed to fit the Masters and Johnson-type model where
desire leads to arousal which leads to orgasm. When I introduced
Loulan's (1984) willingness model of sexual response, which replaces
desire with willingness as a starting point, Mary felt hopeful for the first
time in many years that she and her husband may be sexual again. And,
in fact, they were.

Mary discovered, as many women do, that her sexual response process had changed over her lifespan. Now she begins with willingness,
usually becomes aroused, and then feels desire either during arousal or
after orgasm. "So, I *do* experience sexual desire after all," she pro-

claimed after reporting a particularly passionate time with her husband. "I'm so glad we found it. I guess we weren't looking for it in the right place." She smiled. We, therapists and patients, need a "new view" of the sexual response process where we allow individuals to create their own unique content and ordering of its components (pleasure, arousal, desire, orgasm, etc.), and where we appreciate changes in the existence, order, and salience of the components over the lifespan.

In our efforts not to essentialize what is "male" or "female," we hopefully also will refrain from relying too much on gender socialization theories that level differences among women. This propensity is particularly present in discussions about lesbian sexuality in which lesbian sex is desexualized when compared to heterosexual sex, as if all lesbian women experience and live out sexual scripts in the same way (Iasenza, 2000). What gets lost in these discussions, most of which rely on male-defined norms of sexual behavior, are the interesting within-group variations. In my practice, there are many different "types" of lesbian sexual problems that one sees when one takes a "new view" beyond sexual frequency as the hallmark of sexual health. Often one sees the insidious effects of homophobia, as well the effects of political, social, and historical contexts on the development of sexual norms.

When Dorothy and Sue came in for treatment, they complained of sexual infrequency. The "old view" would likely label Sue as suffering from "sexual desire disorder" since she could "take sex or leave it." And Dorothy would be characterized as being a "nice girl," too accommodating of Sue's needs to pressure her for sex, since Dorothy long ago stopped initiating because Sue would reject her advances. What emerged in therapy was a long history for both of them of secrecy regarding their lesbianism that served to disconnect each of them from their own sexual desires. What increased tension lately was Dorothy's desire, with the help of individual therapy, to come out more at work and at home which created an imbalance in their coming out processes. Dorothy, instead of feeling protected by Sue's secrecy, was now feeling rejected by it.

In addition, Sue, fifteen years Dorothy's senior and a self-identified lesbian feminist activist, expressed a struggle accepting some forms of sexual expression that she felt perpetuated unhealthy power inequities, SM being one. This was a struggle with which Dorothy, being part of a younger lesbian community, could not identify. Their mutual fears of failure in being able to negotiate sexual differences kept them from pursuing much sexual activity at all.

Dorothy and Sue were helped in therapy by nonjudgmentally identifying and accepting their differences, appreciating and healing the effects of homophobia on the individual and couple level, and by learning how to find common ground regarding their needs. This required a "new view" of women's sexuality that looks beyond the mechanics of sex and that acknowledges differences among women, including among lesbian women. This is a tall order conceptually and clinically since most of us, even well-intentioned feminist sex therapists, like to have maps to guide us.

The challenge for us as we incorporate a "new view" is to conduct qualitiative research that articulates women's subjectivities, and to build flexible multi-variable models of gender-sexuality that can provide the frames within which women (and men) may experience an integration of the physical, emotional, spiritual, intellectual and social components of sexual relating. "A New View" is a great place to start.

REFERENCES

Iasenza, S. (2000). Lesbian sexuality post-Stonewall to post-modernism: Putting the "Lesbian Bed Death" concept to bed. *Journal of Sex Education and Therapy, 25*(1), 59-69.

Klein, F., Sepekoff, B., & Wolf, T. J. (1985). Sexual orientation: A multi-variable dynamic process. In F. Klein & T. Wolf (Eds.), *Two lives to live: Bisexuality in men and women.* New York: Harrington Park Press.

Loulan, J. (1984). *Lesbian sex.* Duluth, MN: Spinsters Ink.

An Israeli Sex Therapist Considers
a New View of Women's Sexual Problems

Marilyn P. Safir

SUMMARY. By focusing on the inequalities that exist between men and women as a result of culture, ethnicity, religion, legislation, etc., the New View of Women's Sexual Problems brings to the forefront the social inequalities that may produce sexual dysfunction in women in Israel. In addition, the rights to sexual information, comprehensive sexual education and appropriate sexual health care have not been recognized in Israel. The field of sexology in Israel is also relatively young and underdeveloped. Therefore, the New View of Women's Sexual Problems' focus is extremely relevant for sexologists and sex therapists working in Israel. *[Article copies available for a fee from The Haworth Document Delivery Service: 1-800-HAWORTH. E-mail address: <getinfo@haworthpressinc.com> Website: <http://www.HaworthPress.com> © 2001 by The Haworth Press, Inc. All rights reserved.]*

KEYWORDS. Israel, women's sexual problems, sexology, sex therapy

While Israel is viewed as one of the most socially advanced countries of the world, it is a Jewish State, a part of the Middle East. Its various subcultures are extremely family oriented and, as a result, many subcul-

Marilyn P. Safir, PhD, is affiliated with the University of Haifa, Haifa, Israel.

Address correspondence to: Marilyn Safir, PhD, Department of Psychology, Haifa University, Haifa 31905, Israel (Email: msafir@psy.haifa.ac.il).

[Haworth co-indexing entry note]: "An Israeli Sex Therapist Considers a New View of Women's Sexual Problems." Safir, Marilyn P. Co-published simultaneously in *Women & Therapy* (The Haworth Press, Inc.) Vol. 24, No. 1/2, 2001, pp. 47-52; and: *A New View of Women's Sexual Problems* (ed: Ellyn Kaschak, and Leonore Tiefer) The Haworth Press, Inc., 2001, pp. 47-52. Single or multiple copies of this article are available for a fee from The Haworth Document Delivery Service [1-800-HAWORTH, 9:00 a.m. - 5:00 p.m. (EST). E-mail address: getinfo@haworthpressinc.com].

47

tures are more traditional and more patriarchal than those in the United States. A goal of the new feminist movement in the '70s was to give women control over their bodies. Feminists were successful in achieving women's freedom of choice, but the realities of Israeli politics were such that this right was maintained for less than a year.

In order for a woman to obtain a legal abortion, she must appear before a hospital committee to obtain permission. This compromise, which is still in effect 24 years later, is the result of the power and pressure of the religious parties and the compromises that the secular political parties traditionally agree to at women's expense.

The feminists' focus was on women's right to decide about abortions. The question of women's right to enjoy their bodies/sexuality was never a major focus of the feminist movement. The right to enjoy their sexuality never was and still is not a relevant issue for women of many subcultures in Israeli society. Therefore, by its focus on the inequalities that exist between men and women as a result of culture, ethnicity, religion, legislation, etc., the New View of Women's Sexual Problems brings to the forefront the social inequalities that may produce sexual dysfunction in women in Israel. The field of sexology is relatively young and underdeveloped and this focus is extremely relevant for sexologists and sex therapists working in Israel.

Several aspects of Israeli society make women candidates for problems of sexual dysfunction. While Israelis are inundated by sexual topics on radio, TV, in magazines and newspapers (focusing on the "how to"), students in public schools may never have had courses on sex education upon completion of a high school education. Offering such a course is based solely on the discretion of the school principal. While excellent films are shown on educational TV about pregnancy and public service announcements encourage the use of condoms to prevent the spread of HIV, TV programs filmed for high school students, dealing directly with sexuality and sexual orientation, were prevented from being aired by the religious members of the Israeli Knesset and only were shown when the courts intervened. The right to sexual information, comprehensive sexual education and appropriate sexual health care has not been recognized in Israel.

The centrality of religion and traditions, the centrality of the Israeli Armed Forces and the macho ideal results in men's higher status in general. It is not surprising, therefore, that young, hip Tel Aviv women have established internet sites for very clinical, mechanical discussions of how to bring about bigger and better orgasms. This is the epitome of the male stereotype that "He could perform at any time and with any available sex object–any woman." This approach makes young women who buy into it candidates for sexual disorders because it perpetuates the myth of function without the context of relationship.

In contrast with the New View of Women's Sexual Problems, these young women are not focused on improving relationships, but on changing partners to achieve better results (Livneh, 2000.) These discussions are reminiscent of conversations that used to be quite common among men. Television and radio talk shows are devoted to discussions about orgasms, the vagina, etc. Interpersonal relationships that the New View is trying to return to women's sexuality are absent from this current female picture.

A nationwide clinic (run by urologists with little training in sexology) offers technical treatment of male impotence through hundreds of commercials on the radio and in newspapers and magazines. It began its work by offering men "miracle" injections which would provide them with erections beyond their wildest dreams. Today Viagra is the treatment of choice and in either treatment the practice is to restore the function and to ignore the interpersonal aspects of sexual function/ dysfunction. The male is the patient; wives are usually not encouraged to come to these clinics.

There exist in Israel, within the Jewish sector, extreme ultra orthodox sects, in whose communities owning and viewing televisions and reading newspapers and magazines produced outside of these communities are forbidden. For women, the legal age for marriage is 17 and marriages are arranged as early as possible to assure the woman's purity. Women receive no sex education, while men receive some education days before the marriage ceremony. Should the woman prove not to have a hymen (whether she was born without one, as a result of an accident or even worse because she is not a virgin), the marriage must be annulled and she faces excommunication.

A major scandal occurred as a result of a male member of this community visiting new brides and claiming that he was sent by the rabbi to examine how well the newlyweds' sexual relations were going. He went to the homes of five women whom he raped, as if on the rabbi's orders. The women were married about six months and two were still virgins. These women had not received any instructions about sexuality and were so sheltered that letting him come into their homes (as a representative of the rabbi) seemed acceptable. He was apprehended when he attempted his story on the daughter of a rabbi, who had more knowledge and knew this practice did not exist (Cygielman, 2001).

In very traditional Muslim communities, following the marriage ceremony, the guests wait while the newlyweds retire to a bedroom to consummate the marriage. A bloodied sheet is then presented to prove that the bride was a virgin and that the marriage is consummated. A woman who appears to be a non-virgin might become the victim of a family honor killing. So might a woman about whom rumors questioning her purity circulate. A member of her own family, usually a young brother, is assigned to kill her to maintain the family honor. This can even occur if a woman is raped. In order to prevent murder, if she is unmarried, she may be forced to marry her rapist or an elderly man who would consent to marry damaged goods. As a result of the emphasis on being a virgin within the ultra orthodox or ultra traditional Jewish and Muslim communities, a gynecological subspecialty exists–the reconstruction of the hymen. It is easy to imagine that these attitudes and extreme practices result in sexual problems and without the existence of treatment settings.

Many couples with sexual problems end up at fertility clinics because of the couple's and the families' concerns with lack of pregnancy, rather than with the sexual dysfunctions that produced the infertility. This problem takes prevalence over treatment for sexual problems. Being childlessness in Israel is considered a tragedy. Israel has the highest proportion of fertility clinics for its population in the world (Iftach, 1999.) All treatment, including in vitro fertilization, is unlimited and paid for by the HMOs.

What is even more disturbing is that many physicians at fertility clinics appear not to collect information about the couple's sexual life. For example, a couple was referred to me after being married for 11 years and having had two children by artificial insemination. On their return to the clinic for additional treatment for a third pregnancy, their new physician discovered that they were not having intercourse. Fertility treatment for unconsummated marriages is unfortunately not a rare occurrence. In many instances, when couples from these communities apply for sex therapy, it is not unusual for the husband to make the request and to seek treatment without bringing his wife in as an active participant in the treatment.

Female circumcision is still performed in a few Bedouin tribes in the south of Israel, and some new female immigrants from Ethiopia were circumcised as children before their immigration. This problem has only recently been discussed openly and not many physicians or sex therapists have any training to help women who have been circumcised, in the treatment of resulting sexual problems.

Sex therapists often refer to the couple's relationship as "the patient," but go no further in examining the issues that may be affecting that patient. Tiefer (1995) has pointed out existing diagnostic classifications prove to be random lists of dysfunctions. As such, they are unrelated to the dyad as a couple. Each partner is classified independently and out of context of the dyad based on lists of male/female dysfunctions. However, as early as 1980, Safir and Hoch attempted to create a behavioral psycho-sexological, holistic classification of sexual dysfunctions based on a ranking of disorders according to the seriousness of the disruption to the dyad's functioning as a couple and according to the degree of stress activated within the couple's relationship. This approach fits with the New View suggestions of a focus on relationship issues and greater incorporation of difficulties in sexual functioning as a result of faulty learning, limited social experiences, or restrictive and negative ideas existing in very traditional and/or ultra religious backgrounds (Hoch, Safir, Shepher & Peres, 1980; Safir, Peres, Lichtenstein, Hoch & Shepher, 1982)

Traditional therapeutic approaches employed in Israel tend to ignore cultural and gender experiences. Much of sex therapy should deal with gender issues and the balance of power between the couple. In contrast to traditional psychotherapists who have helped their patients cultivate or strengthen traditional masculine or feminine behavior patterns, my approach supports the necessity of reinforcing androgynous tendencies in clients. Reeducation or education about sexual functions and techniques is also an important element. A focus on interpersonal aspects, such as open communication and trust, are also important, especially for those couples who focus almost entirely on the technical aspects of sexual functioning. This focus seems to me as important for men as it is for women. To ignore the importance of the interpersonal aspect of sexuality for both genders reinforces the existence of the very stereotypes that help to produce sexual dysfunction. The placement of relationship issues at the center of treatment for female sexual dysfunction is a major contribution of the New View.

Pfizer sponsored a workshop/meeting of the Israeli Association for Sex Therapy (IAST)–"After Viagra" on February 16, 2001. The Israeli Association for Sex Therapy was founded in 1980. There are currently only 60 members. Thirty-four are social workers, 21 are physicians, and 15 are clinical psychologists. Thirty-six of the 60 members are women. Of this group, 31 participated in the discussion. They were representative of the general membership.

According to members' reports, most Israeli hospitals have clinics to treat impotency. These clinics were set up to be money makers and there is not much interest in including sexologists on the staff. Urologists staff them. The wife is almost never included in the treatment offered by these clinics or the private clinics described earlier. It is easy to understand how a therapist who focuses on function and physiology could view Viagra as a replacement for sex therapy, especially when a Viagra-like drug for women can be provided. Several workshop participants expressed this view.

The New View includes the relational, emotional, human aspects of sexuality as an integral part of interpersonal relationships. Starting from this point, research should be generated to fill in the gaps of our knowledge as to how repressive frameworks affect women's sexual function. It should be clear that a therapist working within the New View framework could make a major contribution to sex therapy with clients from varying backgrounds. This is surely an asset to the education of sexologists and can only improve their practice and research in the new millennium. However, I am less optimistic about our ability to overcome the coercion of the religious parties in Israel in regard to improving sex education for Israeli citizens in general.

The New View suggests a return to and greater incorporation of approaching difficulties in sexual functioning as a result of faulty learning, limited social experiences, or restrictive and negative ideas existing in very traditional and/or ultra religious background (see Hoch et al., 1980; Safir and Hoch, 1980 and Safir et al., 1982). Much of the New View sex therapy should deal with gender issues and the balance of power between the couple.

REFERENCES

Cygielman, A. (1/10/2001). Caught in a modesty trap. Ha 'Aretz.

Hoch, Z., Safir, M.P., Shepher, J. & Peres, J. (1980). An interdisciplinary approach to the study of sexually dysfunctional couples preliminary findings. In Forleo, R. & Pasini, W. (Eds.), Medical Sexology. Lillenton, Mass., P.S.G. Publishing.

Iftach, A. Ed. (1999). "Women's Health in Israel." Haddasah Women's Zionist Organization of America; Israel Women's Network; Israel Center for Disease Control.

Livneh, N., (4/21/2000). Let's Talk about Sex Baby. Ha 'Aretz.

Safir, M. P. & Hoch, Z. (1980). Couple Interactional Classification of Sexual Dysfunction–A New Theoretical Conceptualization. Journal of Sex & Marital Therapy, 6, pp. 129-133.

Safir, M.P., Peres, Y., Lichtenstein, M., Hoch, Z. & Shepher, J., (1982). Psychological androgyny and sexual adequacy. Journal of Sex & Marital Therapy, 8, pp. 228-240.

Tiefer, L. (1995). Sex is not a natural act and other essays. Boulder, CO: Westview Press.

New View of Women's Sexuality: The Case of Costa Rica

Anna Arroba

SUMMARY. Certain aspects of female sexuality in Costa Rica are examined from the perspective of the New View by a Costa Rican theorist and practitioner. *[Article copies available for a fee from The Haworth Document Delivery Service: 1-800-HAWORTH. E-mail address: <getinfo@haworthpressinc.com> Website: <http://www.HaworthPress.com> © 2001 by The Haworth Press, Inc. All rights reserved.]*

KEYWORDS. Women's sexuality, Latin America, Costa Rica, appearance, the body

The situation of women's sexualities in this small, Central American country, with 4 million inhabitants, reflects some unique and particular traits in the national gender social arrangements, and it also reflects larger, universal trends which affect women individually and collectively.

Unlike the rest of the Central American countries that have suffered revolutions, invasions, genocide, civil war and natural disasters, this country has had the freedom and time to develop, if not a women's movement, definitely many women on the move, with its accompany-

Anna Arroba is Director of AMES (Association de Mujeres en Salud), a women's service agency and NGO in Costa Rica. She also teaches at the University of Costa Rica.

Address correspondence to: Anna Arroba, Apt. 583-2050, San Pedro Montes de Oca, Costa Rica (E-mail: aarroba@cariari.ucr.ac.cr).

[Haworth co-indexing entry note]: "New View of Women's Sexuality: The Case of Costa Rica." Arroba, Anna. Co-published simultaneously in *Women & Therapy* (The Haworth Press, Inc.) Vol. 24, No. 1/2, 2001, pp. 53-57; and: *A New View of Women's Sexual Problems* (ed: Ellyn Kaschak, and Leonore Tiefer) The Haworth Press, Inc., 2001, pp. 53-57. Single or multiple copies of this article are available for a fee from The Haworth Document Delivery Service [1-800-HAWORTH, 9:00 a.m. - 5:00 p.m. (EST). E-mail address: getinfo@haworthpressinc.com].

ing gender studies and theories, which in varied ways have been put into practice in different areas of the law, such as women's rights, women's studies at a graduate level, etc. This concerted effort has had positive results. Domestic and sexual violence in all its multifaceted aspects not only has been made visible, but is being fought through a national program of prevention of violence. Likewise, women's sexual and reproductive health and rights, post Cairo and Beijing, are on the agendas of some women's organizations and some state institutions, with projects mainly directed at young adolescent women, with the creation of a National Committee on Reproductive and Sexual Health and Rights, with changes in the attention women receive in health centers, to name just a few.

These significant steps must be understood in the larger context. This small country, with a "democratic" and non-military tradition, during the 1980's and early 90's served, on the one hand, as a springboard for U.S. activities (cultural and political) throughout Central America and, on the other, as an exemplary exception, which had to be kept free of the region's endemic contamination: political upheaval. The Americanization or as I prefer, the Miamification, of this culture has seen the proliferation of U.S. education, products of all types, movies, cable television, magazines, as well as U.S.-style gyms and diet or aesthetic centers, shopping malls, pornography, sex shops, and cosmetic surgery.

The body culture of this society has undergone drastic changes. The increasing secularization, where the control of women by fathers and husbands, as well as by social institutions like the church, has slackened. The control of women's virginity, marriageability and reproduction, has been supplanted by an emphasis on women's control of their bodies–meaning appearance and shape. Anorexia and bulimia are problems particularly among middle class adolescents.

The globalization process has deepened the differences between the rich and the poor. Six hundred thousand Nicaraguans, 70% female, have made Costa Rica their home. The thriving tourist industry has stimulated the prostitution and pornography industries; children are for sale to older men. Costa Rica is now an international center for cosmetic surgery. White and slim are the models that surround us in the ads, medical pamphlets and television.

As for sex, it would be erroneous to talk about a sexual culture in terms of "Costa Ricans do this or that . . ." as a national characteristic, or even to say that some women are liberated, others not. What becomes clear after working with hundreds of women from different social backgrounds are the common elements such as ignorance, silence and helplessness that color their experience, regardless of social class or religion. It is sad to hear women admit to faking orgasms, or worse, not even knowing what an orgasm is. Or to hear peasant women say, "My husband uses me twice/three times a week."

We could attribute this to poverty and third worldness, but this is a too narrow perspective. Most women are ignorant about sex and their sexuality, and very particularly, about their bodies, in all cultures that I know. An element that contributes to the separation of women are the myths and stereotypes about "others" that are perpetuated not just in the popular culture but by government institutions.

There are new discourses about sexuality that appear to be liberating for women in the sense that they are no longer tied to the old mandate of virginity. However, just to give an example, analyzing the magazine called *Sex and Beauty* (1995), which deals with sex and sexuality between heterosexual couples, with fairly explicit photos of young men and women simulating varied sexual positions and with emphasis on pleasure, it did not escape my attention that in one of the issues, the word "penetration" was mentioned 13 times, vagina twice, penis eight times, clitoris twice and the G-spot once, although it did not say where it could be found. One could well ask, sex for whom? This magazine frequently publishes articles on how to look your best, how to lose weight, and how to get a man.

On the other hand, the government projects directed at poor young women center their discourses on the sexuality of young adolescent women and on the prevention of unwanted pregnancies. These two different approaches share certain elements. They both silence women when they concentrate on male coital pleasure and ignore information which could make women be the protagonists of their own sexuality. Sexual pleasure as a right is not the objective. In the case of poor women, the problem of unwanted pregnancy is seen as the woman's problem only, and the men responsible disappear and are invisibilized. The women's sexuality is represented as being the cause of the problem.

In one comparative study of sexual behavior and expectations in relation to prevention and family planning (Schifter and Madrigal, 1996), in spite of the harsh reality of poverty and single motherhood, the young women in a poor and marginal community clearly expressed themselves in terms of getting a man, of marrying and having a "normal" family. Young women from a middle class community were much more informed about prevention and about AIDS and very clear about the importance of having a career. However, working in workshops with women from this background, I have found that despite the clarity about their economic situation, these women live out a body culture marked by self rejection and obsession with their size and form. These are the women who diet and have cosmetic surgery from a very early age and who ask to have caesarean births in order not to lose their shape. The sexuality of these two groups of women is influenced by distinct body cultures, in the sense that there are different attitudes and experiences. Nonetheless, the inability to negotiate safe and/or pleasurable sex marks both groups.

In another study of adolescent women in a marginal urban community with a high incidence of early pregnancy, illiteracy and under employment (Preinfalk Fernández, 1988), it became clear that the youngsters are pressured into having relations by men and also by their girlfriends. At the same time, these young women are aware that their value resides in being virgins, but also in having a man and in keeping him. The young men's preoccupation is in "scoring" the highest number of females, and sex is practiced with no protection of any kind. Unwanted pregnancies are the result, and sometimes the man stays for a while in a stable union. Once women have lost their virginity, they develop many different strategies to negotiate their "desirability," for an experienced woman is seen as a slut. This is also an element that exists among the middle class. We could attribute these ideas about the "good" and "bad" women to the Catholic culture, and in many ways it has a profound influence on the collective mentality, but there are many other influences that persistently devalue and debase women and their bodies. Women are depicted as objects in pornography, advertisements, television and every medium imaginable. And this is accompanied by the increase in violence against women and in what is now termed as "femicide," the assassination of women.

At another level, articles about female sexual problems and therapy, and about the female Viagra or the clitoral pump to stimulate women's arousal appear in magazines and newspapers (*La Nación*, 2000). We could say that at last the truth is coming out about the sexual misery lived by so many people. However, the problem that I detect is that centuries of silence and ignorance cannot be breached merely by the high production of new information or by the new discourses about the right to pleasure. What is not named does not exist, and for many women, the very process of naming is the very first step of appropriating their bodies and their genitals. On the positive side then I conclude by saying that the state of women's sexuality in this country is not that different from others, but that the subject of sexuality is the one that women most want to talk about. This is the beginning of breaking silence and of naming.

REFERENCES

La Nación (2000). EFE News Agency, San José, Costa Rica.

Preinfalk Fernández, M.L. (1988) *Vivencias y Prácticas Sexuales de las Mujeres Jóvenes Residentes en Rincón Grande de Pavas*, M.A. Thesis in Women's Studies, Universidad de Costa Rica and Universidad Nacional, Costa Rica.

Schifter, J. and Madrigal, J. (1996). *Las Gavetas Sexuales del Costarricense*, Imediex, San José, Costa Rica.

Sex and Beauty Magazine. Sexo y Belleza, supplement of *Perfil Magazine*, October 1995, San José, Costa Rica.

New View of Women's Sexuality: The Case of India

Sadhana Vohra

SUMMARY. Some of the implications of the New View among middle class, urban and well-educated women and men in New Delhi, India are examined through the use of a case history. *[Article copies available for a fee from The Haworth Document Delivery Service: 1-800-HAWORTH. E-mail address: <getinfo@haworthpressinc.com> Website: <http://www.HaworthPress. com> © 2001 by The Haworth Press, Inc. All rights reserved.]*

KEYWORDS. India, sexuality, marriage, women

As women and men, in our efforts to understand ourselves and our sexual behavior, we have not yet accounted for all the myriad elements that inform, enrich or detract from our sexual engagement. The new view of women's sexual problems is a well-thought-out concerted effort to understand meaningfully and to identify the pivotal aspects of women's sexuality.

Societies have practiced many kinds of cruelty toward their members. Using incorrect assessment procedures that skim over significantly impacting elements in order to facilitate a social adherence stands out in our history as a specific example of this cruelty. Unfortu-

Sadhana Vohra is in private practice in New Delhi, India.

Address correspondence to: Sadhana Vohra, PsyD, 144 Mandakini Enclave, Alaknanda, New Delhi 110 019 India (E-mail: sadhanavohra@vsnl.com).

[Haworth co-indexing entry note]: "New View of Women's Sexuality: The Case of India." Vohra, Sadhana. Co-published simultaneously in *Women & Therapy* (The Haworth Press, Inc.) Vol. 24, No. 1/2, 2001, pp. 59-62; and: *A New View of Women's Sexual Problems* (ed: Ellyn Kaschak, and Leonore Tiefer) The Haworth Press, Inc., 2001, pp. 59-62. Single or multiple copies of this article are available for a fee from The Haworth Document Delivery Service [1-800-HAWORTH, 9:00 a.m. - 5:00 p.m. (EST). E-mail address: getinfo@haworthpressinc.com].

nately, we have all suffered greatly from having our behaviors assessed simplistically or incorrectly and have had to "chop off" parts of ourselves not taken into account by authorities determining the "right" way to be. We do improve over time, however, and the New View is a significant step in that direction.

The urgency of incorporating this more comprehensive understanding of our sexuality palpably came home to me, yet again, because of a woman I am going to call Nisha. Nisha is a 28-year-old woman who has been married for over a year. She was referred to me by a feminist help line and although we have had a number of conversations over the phone, she has come to see me only twice, with a six-month gap in between. I am a clinical psychologist practicing on the south side of New Delhi, the capital of India. The south side is cosmopolitan and New Delhi's more favored area. The clients in my rather successful practice are by and large educated, well-informed and financially favored. The female to male ratio in my nine-year-old practice has roughly been 60 to 40. I primarily work with issues of mental health but obviously have had to deal with issues of sexuality, although they are not pivotal to my work.

Nisha had not wanted to marry, but she comes from a conservative middle class background and for many years she had to bear the brunt of her family's active attempts to persuade her to do so. They told her that she was selfish, that her parents needed her to "settle down" or else they would "lose face" in their community. Although Nisha was employed, her social system did not allow her the option of living independently.

Nisha does not want to have children. This is her stated reason for not wanting to marry. However, when she spoke to her parents about this, they felt that she was young, immature and naïve and expected her to change her mind eventually because she did own up to feeling normal sexual arousal. When the family demands became difficult for her to handle, Nisha did something unusual for a young woman from her background. She went to see a counselor. Unfortunately for Nisha, after determining that there were no physiological problems, the counselor advised her to marry and please her parents. She could later always refuse to have a child, the counselor added. Nisha, who is not really a rebellious type and, wishing to please her parents, said yes to the young man to whom her parents had introduced her and they soon got married.

Not surprisingly, the problems started after that. Nisha's husband refused to let her use birth control pills. He complained to her parents when he found that she was using them anyway. Her parents scolded her, tried to "reason" with her and finally brought Nisha to me, not because they believed in counseling or other such new ways of dealing with conflict, but because they do love their daughter and she had insisted. They are caught in a terrible bind where they feel that if they don't try and persuade their daughter to go the traditional way, they will have erred in some remarkable way.

Nisha, who has an admirable tenacity of spirit, was by this time quite depressed and despairing. She seemed to have used up her last resources in dragging her parents to see me and was only able to sit in front of me, despairing and suicidal, because everyone wanted her to do things she did not want to do. And she resented that her family expected that eventually, through blandishments, she would change. Nisha's younger brother, a successful professional, also came with his parents. He was a more modern, liberal young man. He clearly cared for his sister and did not wish her to be unhappy, but he felt that she did not have the strength to stand up to society all by herself and perhaps it would be better for her to give in.

I was truly worried about the suicidal potential, but the family was more concerned about how to get her to see "reason." Women have to marry and of course they have to have children because how would any society continue if a woman refused to have babies, Nisha's father reiterated. Brought up within that same system, intimidated by the pervasive view of women's sexual and reproductive life, while also wishing to help Nisha escape this abusive system, I had to reassure myself rather fast. Yes, Nisha could have gone to a battered women's shelter, and yes, I offered that option, but she did not even wish to consider it. A woman who had married against her wishes to please her parents, she felt that by going to a shelter, she would bring unbearable shame to her family. What other options were there?

When I ended up pointing out to the family that Nisha had the right to decide against having a baby, they stared at me aghast. I would have given a great deal to have a DSM available to me that supported my statement in the way that it now supports the rights of people to choose their sexual orientation. I find it significant that in my practice I am able to easily validate sexual orientation choices when they go against established social customs, but have difficulty in openly supporting the inalienable rights of women, as in this case.

The family never came back to see me. Nisha, however, maintained sporadic contact over the phone from her husband's home. The family had decided that they would wait another six months before they would push her to have a baby.

Recently, after the six months were up, Nisha came to see me with her husband. Her complaint now was that she could not enjoy sex with him at all, although she did like him and love him and wished to sit close to him and cuddle, etc. They had already been to a gynecologist and a sexologist and nothing had come of it. The differences in their positions on having a baby also came up in the session and the husband, a sincere, genial and traditional man, expressed his anger that he had after all married to have children and it was unfair to him that his wife did not want them.

The distress that this couple and their families are experiencing is entirely unnecessary. If only we had a clearer articulation of the social, political and economic issues that impact upon our sexual behavior and if only there were a wider statement of our sexual rights, Nisha would have been saved a great deal of grief. I also do not think that this situation is particular to a developing country like India. The pressures to conform to an older established way of being and to compromise one's rights are strengthened by inadequate and incomplete classification systems in all social systems. The attempt to understand sexuality within a physiological context alone is like trying to understand that the delicious meal before us has appeared because the cook is physically fit! For now, I am grateful for the New View articulation because it places on record the areas that do create difficulties in women's lives and obstruct their engagement with their world.

PART III:
NEW DEVELOPMENTS
IN THEORY AND RESEARCH
ON WOMEN'S SEXUALITIES

Arriving at a "New View"
of Women's Sexual Problems:
Background, Theory, and Activism

Leonore Tiefer

SUMMARY. This essay offers an all-embracing narrative of the "new view" project to explain how and why a feminist critique of current sex problem nomenclature, an alternative vision, and an activist campaign have emerged since 1999. The story begins with 15 years of urology-promoted medicalization of men's sexuality and the building of a female market near the end of the 1990s. The Food and Drug Administration role is illuminated by the author's advisory panel experience and the FDA's proposed guidelines for testing sex drugs for women. The pre-

Leonore Tiefer, PhD, is in private practice in New York City and is Clinical Associate Professor of Psychiatry, New York University School of Medicine.

Address correspondence to: Leonore Tiefer, PhD, 163 Third Avenue #183, New York, NY 10003 (E-mail: LTiefer@mindspring.com).

[Haworth co-indexing entry note]: "Arriving at a 'New View' of Women's Sexual Problems: Background, Theory, and Activism." Tiefer, Leonore. Co-published simultaneously in *Women & Therapy* (The Haworth Press, Inc.) Vol. 24, No. 1/2, 2001, pp. 63-98; and: *A New View of Women's Sexual Problems* (ed: Ellyn Kaschak, and Leonore Tiefer) The Haworth Press, Inc., 2001, pp. 63-98. Single or multiple copies of this article are available for a fee from The Haworth Document Delivery Service [1-800-HAWORTH, 9:00 a.m. - 5:00 p.m. (EST). E-mail address: getinfo@haworthpressinc.com].

vailing theory of women's sexual problems is traced to Masters and Johnson's biased research and continuing debates about orgasm. Finally, the origins of the "new view" campaign are described: a growing discomfort with the aggressive roles of urology and the drug industry in women's sexual medicine, the decision to take public as well as professional positions, the creation of a working group, and ongoing activism.

[Article copies available for a fee from The Haworth Document Delivery Service: 1-800-HAWORTH. E-mail address: <getinfo@haworthpressinc.com> Website: <http://www.HaworthPress.com> © 2001 by The Haworth Press, Inc. All rights reserved.]

KEYWORDS. Medicalization, women's health activism, sexual dysfunction, feminist activism, orgasm

INTRODUCTION

We live in times of momentous global, cultural, political, institutional, and personal change in women's sexual lives and experiences (e.g., Giddens, 1992; McLaren, 1999; Travis and White, 2000; Lancaster and di Leonardo, 1997; Jackson and Scott, 1996). Women's sexual emancipation has unquestionably increased almost everywhere, though there is far to go and many probable setbacks. With steps forward, however, come new challenges, and this essay will critically examine the problematic current wave of medicalization emerging to "manage" women's sexual problems.

Many factors contribute to the current medicalization of women's sexual lives, not least of which are the new deregulated, global pharmaceutical industry, the media's attraction to "magic bullet" news, the passive position of sexology, and the role of a sexually eager, but anxious and uneducated, public (Tiefer, 2000). Our story begins by examining fifteen years of medicalization of *men's* sexuality, insofar as the current aggressive approach to women emerged directly out of that successful campaign.

MEDICALIZING SEXUALITY

The Medicalization of Men's Sexuality

The Federal Drug Administration's (FDA) approval of sildenafil citrate,[1] an oral drug for "erectile dysfunction," in March, 1998, capped a fifteen year process of creating a classification system, market, and scientific literature promoting a medical view of men's sexual problems.[2] Only within social sciences such as sociology, history, cultural studies, and science and technology studies has the triumph of a medical view been seen as a cultural-political victory over other viable conceptual frameworks for sexual experience, research, and knowledge (e.g., political, humanistic, social constructionist; Boyle, 1994; Jackson and Scott, 1997; Parker, Barbosa, and Aggleton, 2000; Plummer, 1995; Parker and Gagnon, 1995).

Medicalization is construed by sociologists as a process of social control whereby diverse areas of human behavior are brought within a medical frame of discourse both conceptually and institutionally (Conrad, 1992; Riessman, 1983). The medicalization of sexuality prescribes and demarcates sexual interests and activities, defining normality and deviance in the language of sexual health and illness (Rubin, 1984; Tiefer, 1996; Giami, 2000). The process of medicalization, promoted by industry, media, health experts, and conservative political actors, produces sexual values, language, classification systems, and authorities, and profoundly shapes the popular view of sexuality, despite a culture full of diverse sexual voices.

A new medical area of "male sexual dysfunction" grew within the surgical subspecialty of urology throughout the 1980s and 1990s, greatly aided by the media's fascination with medical language and new technologies of erection (Tiefer, 1986, 1994). Urologists, previously known for stone and cancer surgeries of the kidney, bladder, and penis, became "andrologists," definers and healers of masculinity (Hellstrom, 1999).[3] The crucial evangelizing period occured in 1982-4, as conferences and textbooks trumpeted "the emergence of the urologist as the primary coordinator of care for the patient with sexual dysfunction, whether the cause of that dysfunction is an organic, a psychogenic, or as sometimes [sic] occurs, a combined one" (Krane, Siroky, and Goldstein, 1983, p. xiii).

The claims were based on the promotion of a few impotence treatments, such as penile injections and permanent penile implants (Virag, Bouilly, Daniel, and Virag, 1984; Wagner and Kaplan, 1993), although later studies showed high drop-out rates with penile injections and relatively few patients choosing surgical implants. There were few long-term follow-up studies, however, and, anyway, the media paid attention only to developments when they were exciting and new. By the time sildenafil citrate appeared in 1998 as the first bestseller treatment for erection problems, urologists had consolidated their role as authorities on men's sexual function (Porst, 1996; Tiefer, 1994).

Building the Female Market in 1997-98

Even before sildenafil/Viagra was approved, some urologists were looking for ways to expand their sexual dysfunction research and clinical practice to women. In 1997, Irwin Goldstein, a Boston University School of Medicine urologist prominent in both basic and clinical research on erectile dysfunction, said in the newsletter of the American Urological Association [AUA], "I view female sexual dysfunction as a potential explosion for the field of female urology. . . . We think [diminished blood flow to the vagina] is equivalent to vasculogenic impotence in men" (Bankhead, 1997, p. 1). That same year, based on studies of abnormal genital tissues from treated rabbits, Goldstein and colleagues named new pathological conditions of "vaginal engorgement insufficiency" and "clitoral erectile insufficiency" which they said were probably responsible for sexual response and satisfaction problems in women (Park, Goldstein, Andry, Siroky, Krane, Azadzoi, 1997).

> It is likely that future epidemiological studies will identify these organic vasculogenic female sexual dysfunction syndromes to exist in millions of aging American women whose present day symptoms of vaginal discomfort with coitus, dryness, diminished vaginal size and diminished sexual arousal are not well-appreciated. (Park et al., p. 34)

Generalizing from small and preliminary studies of animal genital tissues to broad areas of human sexual experience is a rhetorical move to establish a foothold for the framework of medicalization. Sweeping predictions that medicogenital tests and treatments can eradicate little understood and shameful personal problems are, not surprisingly, welcomed by the media and a poorly informed and embarrassed public already biased towards biological thinking about sexuality (Tiefer, 1995).

In May, 1997, an invitation-only sex research meeting was held at a hotel on Cape Cod. One of the organizers described the meeting plans to me:

> The meeting is completely supported by pharmaceutical companies, and approximately half of the audience will be pharmaceutical representatives. The goal is to foster active and positive collaboration between the two groups. Only investigators who have experience with, or special interest in working collaboratively with, the drug industry have been invited. (Rosen, 1997)

Proceedings of this meeting, which disclosed none of these parameters, were published as a 140-page supplement on "Sexual function assessment in clinical trials" to volume 10 of the *International Journal of Impotence Research* (May, 1998). The Cape Cod meeting emphasized the traditional medicalization lineup: physical mechanisms, physical assessments, physical treatments, and physical outcome measures. However, a new theme began to be heard; although experts and the public allegedly agreed that women's sexual problems were legion, the introduction to the meeting proceedings complained, "there is widespread lack of agreement about the definition of [female] sexual dysfunction [FSD], its pathophysiology or clinical manifestations, and the optimal approach for research or clinical assessment" (Rosen and O'Leary, 1998, p. S1). It is now known that some sildenafil trials on women were already completed at the time of the Cape Cod meeting, although the results were embargoed by the company until June, 2000 (Laan, van Lunsen, Everaerd, Heiman, and Hackbert, 2000). Early negative results were apparently leading industry and its academic consultants not to abandon drug development plans, but rather to look for ways to conceptualize women's sexual problems that would be more amenable to drug research and intervention.

I received several e-mail messages from women sex researchers who attended Cape Cod, celebrating how they had challenged various remarks about women's sexuality and sexual problems that belied mechanical and oversimplified understanding. They exulted that an exclusively pharmaco-medical focus for women had reached a dead end, a conclusion that, in retrospect, seems naive.

Sildenafil was approved by the FDA in March, 1998, and stories speculating about its use by women immediately appeared in major newspapers. The *New York Times* headlined its page one story, "Impotence drug prompting talk of female use" (Kolata, 1998a), while the *Wall Street Journal* observed, "Now, drug companies turn to women's sex problems" (Johannes, 1998). A meeting of representatives from industry, FDA, and academic sexology focusing on women's sexual problems was hastily set up within a month of sildenafil's approval, but as happened in Cape Cod, there was no agreement on diagnoses, assessments, or outcome measures. As the *New York Times* reporter noted, the question seemed to be "What is the female problem that Viagra or some drug like it would solve?" (Kolata, 1998b, p. A9).

The "FSD Consensus Conference"

An effort to end this quandary (or preempt its discussion) occurred in October, 1998, when Irwin Goldstein, sponsored by urology organizations and drug companies, convened a closed meeting to break the definitional and methodological bottleneck (Basson et al., 2000). The "consensus statement" produced by that group, which disclosed in a footnote that eighteen of its nineteen authors currently had financial or other consultancy relations with pharmaceutical companies, defined "FSD"[4] in language almost identical to the sexual dysfunction nomenclature in the current, fourth edition of the *Diagnostic and Statistical Manual* (*DSM-IV*) of the American Psychiatric Association [APA] (APA, 1994).

However, the new "FSD" document quietly made a major political point by insisting that sexual dysfunctions are medical, not psychiatric, disorders, a tactical coup which could strongly affect FDA clinical trials and other research. It reminded me of the AUA Executive Committee "policy statement" of 1990, "Sexual dysfunction in the male is a disease entity, the diagnoses and treatments of which deserve equal attention to that given other diseases" (AUA Executive Committee, 1993). This influential statement gave official medical permission and encouragement to study and treat men's sexual problems in ways that bypassed psychology and psychiatry.

Although the authors of the "FSD" consensus statement were all hand-picked and industry-reimbursed, the obvious conflicts of interest raised fewer ethical challenges than they would have in the past (Cho, Shohara, Schissel and Rennie, 2000). "Consensus conference" language, once the province of carefully conducted government activities, is now frequently used by industry-sponsored meetings (Sheldon and Smith, 1993). The small-circulation *Journal of Sex & Marital Therapy* recently published a special issue of thirty-six commentaries on the "FSD" consensus document (Segraves, 2001), several of which take a sharply critical perspective (e.g., Bancroft, Graham, and McCord, 2001; Maurice, 2001; Shaw, 2001; Hall, 2001; Tiefer, 2001a). The consensus classification document is likely to have wide visibility; I wonder whether these commentaries will ever be cited.

FEMINIST ACTIVISM I: RESISTING "FSD"

The Boston Conference of 1999

In late 1998, following the closed "consensus" meeting, the tireless Irwin Goldstein began advertising a multidisciplinary scientific conference on "Female Sexual Dysfunction" to be held in Boston in October, 1999. It would provide the first extended open discussion of the new medical subject, and attendees would vote on a new "FSD" professional/scientific organization and journal. Invitations were extended to "health care professionals" to submit brief papers and posters to supplement an impressive roster of paid sexological and medical speakers. The conference was expensive–registration cost $495 for physicians and $395 for "residents, nurses, and others," and rooms at the conference hotel cost $255/night. Such prices are substantially higher than social science, sexology, or psychology conferences, and signalled that the new "FSD" was not being birthed by midwives.

When I heard about Dr. Goldstein's planned "FSD" conference in early 1999, I thought it could safely be ignored. At that time, the consensus document had not been published or publicized; research on women and sildenafil was still being kept secret; and the informal reactions from the Cape Cod conference were dismissive. I knew that drug companies would surely be interested in such a conference, and some prominent sexologists were giving paid lectures, but I doubted that many others would attend such an expensive venture. I was wrong! By July, 1999, it became apparent that the Boston meeting could represent a watershed moment in the construction of a new medical era for women's sexuality. Excited by the prominent roster of speakers, many sex therapists and physicians planned to attend, and a new medical organization looked probable. It seemed important for feminists to take this conference seriously, even if challenging it might add publicity that might paradoxically contribute to its success.

Planning a Feminist Presence

I planned actions modeled on the mid-1980s, feminist "Coalition against Misdiagnosis" campaign that had opposed a slate of new mental disorders proposed by the APA, e.g., "Premenstrual dysphoric disorder," "Paraphilic rapism," and "Self-defeating personality disorder" (Caplan, 1995). Analyzing the stigmatizing effects of an "FSD" label, the neglect of sociogenic perspectives in favor of biological reductionism, and the insubstantial scientific basis for "FSD" directly paralleled Coalition positions in the earlier debate.

I asked colleagues to submit abstracts to the 1999 "FSD" conference and prepared a strong one myself: "The selling of female sexual dysfunction." Stepping outside the academic cocoon, I wrote an article for the Boston women's newspaper, *Sojourner* (Tiefer, 1999), and co-wrote an op-ed column for the *Los Angeles Times* (Tiefer and Tavris, 1999). I organized an informal seminar in Boston the day before Goldstein's conference that focused on the meanings of "FSD" and, to our delight, it received prominent and favorable coverage in the *Boston Globe* (Kong, 1999). Several of us distributed hundreds of copies of these three press pieces to "FSD" conference participants. Suddenly, we were activists.

The "FSD" conference was tightly controlled. No questions were permitted at the lectures. The CME director wouldn't reveal drug companies' contributions or speaker fees. My brief presentation called upon researchers to reject a standardized vision of women's sexuality, to study the harms as well as the benefits of all treatments, to be alert to commercial pressures on research design, and to make future meetings truly interdisciplinary (Tiefer, 2001b). It received a chilly response. Marny Hall's (2001b) feminist presentation challenged the medical model approach to low desire in lesbian couples. Everything else was bio, bio, bio.

At the business meeting, the creation of a new "FSD" organization was defeated, probably because several prominent speakers complained that many new and old organizations would now be competing for attendance and speakers. However, Goldstein received strong encouragement to host another "FSD" conference in 2000. The conference ended with well-attended sessions on how to conduct clinical trials. When an FDA speaker asked how many in the audience were connected to the drug industry, at least half the people raised their hands. The many sildenafil presentations and those on other sprays, pills, gels, creams, and patches made it clear how enthusiastically the pharmaceutical industry was involved in women's sexuality.

Throughout early 2000, media continued to promote the medicalization of women's sexuality. A cover story in *The New York Times Magazine,* for example, celebrated "The search for the female Viagra and other tales from the second sexual revolution" (Hitt, 2000), while on the cover of *Newsweek,* the words "Searching for a female Viagra: Is it a mind or body problem?" appeared above a photo of a naked woman with open lips and closed eyes and a man nuzzling her neck (Leland, 2000).

INSIDE THE FDA

Serving as a Consultant

In early 2000 I had an opportunity to serve on an FDA Advisory Committee evaluating the clinical trials of apomorphine, an old drug newly named Uprima. Although Uprima was a treatment for erectile dysfunction, not "FSD," the evaluation offered insight into the processes of sex drug approval.[5] The FDA has many non-government expert advisory committees, although not all drugs are thought to need external review. For example, Pfizer's Viagra swiftly went through the approval process without any input from external experts.

After agreeing to serve on the Uprima panel, I was sent quantities of literature about government ethics, including several forms on conflicts of interest. Three weeks before the committee meeting, I received hefty binders prepared by the FDA and Uprima's manufacturer, TAP Pharmaceuticals, containing complex research studies with either physiological (blood levels), or behavioral (erection and intercourse) endpoints. Apomorphine had been well known as an emetic (a drug to provoke vomiting) for over a hundred years, and is currently used to treat alcoholism and Parkinsonism. Recently, however, when it was noticed that apomorphine caused erections (and yawning) in rats, a new sexuality drug was born.

The advisory committee meeting was a fishbowl experience. Several hundred TAP company employees, FDA employees, press, and members of the public surrounded the committee in a hotel ballroom. The day consisted of rapid-fire presentations by TAP and the FDA accompanied by endless complicated slides. The thirteen committee members asked questions during brief allotted periods.

Almost the first slide TAP presented read, "Erectile dysfunction is the inability to attain and/or maintain penile erection sufficient for satisfactory sexual performance," the definition of erectile dysfunction since the official 1992 NIH consensus development conference. I felt everyone in the room supported this "objective and scientific" definition which identified "the erection" as the patient, ignored gender and culture, ignored the sexual partner, identified "performance" as the important endpoint, and contained nothing psychological or subjective.

I would have liked to comment on the research as psychologist, sex therapist, and sex researcher, and to raise questions from a feminist rather than medical perspective. Not only was there not enough time; it was clear that such questions would not have been understood. Thus, I couldn't ask whether the research measured whether drug side effects were psychologically burdensome, what sexual technique and sexuality knowledge study participants had, what problems emerged in completing the outcome questionnaires, or how women's interests were included in the study design.

The FDA team presented many medical concerns. Because the Uprima studies excluded patients with severe erectile dysfunction, doctors and the public wouldn't know if the drug worked or was safe in such populations. The efficacy of the drug as compared to placebo was unimpressive. Several study participants had fainted and injured themselves after taking the drug. Physiological data suggested that the lowest drug dose could act in some people like the highest dose.

In the afternoon, the committee asked questions of both TAP and the FDA, jumping dizzily from physiology to safety to prescribing patterns to alcohol interactions to label warnings. Everything focused on "the erection," practically nothing was said about sex, and nothing at all was said about pleasure or intimacy, gender or meaning, politics or public impact. At one point, I said that approving a drug with many drug side effects meant that women would worry about the impact of sexual activity on their already-compromised husbands. I argued that two people, in somewhat different ways, were patients here, and that the wives' burdens, as well as the husbands' bodies, required evaluation. Rushing to get too many points into one comment, I added that sildenafil was available in nightclubs and was reportedly being used for sexual enhancement, and suggested that a sex drug which could not be used together with alcohol posed unacceptable danger to the public. The committee chairperson said that the committee could not take illegal uses of a drug into consideration and ignored the rest of my comment.

The advisory committee voted 10 to 2 to approve the 2 mg. Uprima dose, and 9 to 3 to approve the 4 mg. dose. However, it was clear that if the FDA ultimately approved the drug, warnings about side-effects and prohibitions on use with alcohol would be included on the label. Thus it was no surprise, perhaps, that TAP withdrew its FDA application a few months after the hearing, before any official decision was made. I later heard that the company is now seeking approval in the European Union, where the criteria are somewhat less stringent.

The reason for describing this committee meeting in some detail is to illuminate how the current process of drug approval precludes any meaningful discussion of sexuality or sexual problems as they occur in intimate relationships and social context. Assumptions of "natural sex" prevail which presuppose a biologically dictated universal sexual script centering on heterosexual intercourse with intravaginal male orgasm (Boyle, 1994). Issues of power and meaning are completely invisible. One take-away message is that feminist efforts to influence popular and professional discourse about women's sexual desires and satisfactions in the new sexuopharmacology era will have to occur long before matters enter FDA committee hearings.

FDA Guidance Document on "FSD" Trials

Here's another piece of the developing story of new drugs for women's sexual problems. In May, 2000, the FDA published a draft document "intended to provide recommendations for sponsors [companies interested in developing drugs] on the design of clinical trials in support of new drug applications for the treatment of female sexual dysfunction" (Division of Reproductive and Urologic Drug Products, 2000, p. 3). The FDA wanted to offer advice to companies on how to design drug research on women's sexual problems. Individuals and groups were invited to comment on the draft document (which, interestingly, has still not been finalized as of April, 2001). This draft document offered feminists insight into the FDA's thinking about women's sexual problems and perhaps an opportunity to influence the coming steamroller of clinical trials.

In the draft document, "FSD" was defined using the familiar nomenclature of the *DSM-IV* and the urology "consensus" document (APA, 1994; Basson et al., 2000). "FSD" consisted of "four recognized components: decreased sexual desire, decreased sexual arousal, dyspareunia, and persistent difficulty in achieving or inability to achieve orgasm" (Division of Reproductive and Urologic Drug Products, 2000, p. 3). Somewhat oddly from a naturalistic perspective, though appropriate from the feminist and social constructionist perspectives, the document acknowledged that "the definition of FSD continues to evolve" (*ibid.*). The draft document also advised the drug industry on appropriate research populations, measurement instruments, and "endpoints," that is, aspects of sexual experience that would be used to assess research outcome. The endpoints would have to be very specific and quantitative–but what is an appropriate measure of "improvement"? The FDA suggested this measure:

> . . . endpoints should be based on the number of successful and satisfactory sexual events or encounters over time [as determined] by the woman participating in the trial, as opposed to her partner. Such events or encounters include: satisfactory sexual intercourse, sexual intercourse resulting in orgasm, oral sex resulting in orgasm, and partner-initiated or self masturbation resulting in orgasm. . . . If physical genital changes are measured, they should be

linked to clinically significant changes in the number of successful and satisfying sexual events experienced by the woman during the trial. (Division of Reproductive and Urologic Drug Products, 2000, pp. 5-6)

That is, count the sexual "events" and rate their "success" by presence of orgasm. While feminists can sympathize with the FDA regulators' need to provide guidelines for the looming commercial stampede, we must challenge the orgasmocentric construction of sexual satisfaction. A lengthy letter co-signed by 21 feminist colleagues took exception to the document's attempt to universalize women's sexualities:

In the real world, women's sexual problems do not exist separate from human relationships and social context. Clinical experience and research demonstrate that women often come to adult sexual life with limited sexual knowledge, negative body image, the residue of negative past experiences, and confusion as to their sexual entitlements. Remedying sexual problems is impeded by embarrassment and fear of rejection. Women frequently evaluate the desire for and the pleasure and intimacy of physical sexual experience in relation to emotional issues such as safety and satisfying their partner. Subjective sexual arousal is linked as much to socially influenced emotions and meanings as to genital stimulation. Research suggests that orgasm, while valued, does not necessarily define sexual satisfaction for women. Because of gendered social reality, women's sexual development and experience cannot be reduced to biological function.

One cannot simply assert [as the guidance document did] that "the determination of successful and satisfactory sexual events should be made by the woman participating in the [clinical] trial, as opposed to her partner" if that conflicts with women's sexual experience in the real world. The FDA or the pharmaceutical industry may feel that women "should" create their own definitions of sexual success, but this flies in the face of research on female socialization and relationship dynamics. Even if sexual partners are not included in the research (a problematic decision, as it was in erectile dysfunction trials), the determination of what constitutes a "successful" sexual encounter is hardly a decision which can be made out of social context.

Excluding women's real-life complications [e.g., excluding women with relationship difficulties or those who are using medications which could affect sexual function] is additionally problematic because of the current climate of *direct-to-consumer advertising*. Advertising budgets for sexuality drug products are growing exponentially, and current sexuality drug product advertisements appeal to romance, with images of dancing and embracing. Because of this climate, drug products for women's sexual problems must be tested on a broad range of women, using clinical endpoints which women themselves endorse. Simply importing a model of sexuality used in men's research is highly inappropriate. (Tiefer et al., 2000, pp. 3-4)

Our impassioned letter concluded with a recommendation that any product which would be advertised to help women's sexual lives be tested on a "*broad and diverse study population* using clinical endpoints appropriate to women's lives" (Tiefer et al., 2000, pp. 3-4).

FEMINIST ACTIVISM II:
OPPOSING THE CURRENT NOMENCLATURE

As the new century loomed, the steamroller of commercial and medical developments regarding "FSD" seemed unstoppable. Another Boston conference was scheduled for October, 2000, and there seemed no end to the media stories on great new medical breakthroughs. While continuing to critique the errors of omission and commission made by the advocates of medicalization, I began to think about additional lines of resistance. Most people seemed to interpret the 1999 feminist "FSD" critique as attacking *over*medicalization–the untoward influence of pharmaceutical interests on sex research and clinical practice and the exaggeration of physical as compared to relationship causes of women's sexual problems. One way to expand the "FSD" critique would be to criticize not just *over*medicalization, but the whole kit and caboodle–all the defined dysfunctions, the universal claims about normal sexual function, the biological reductionism, and the focus on sexuality as an individualistic enterprise (Tiefer, 1996). Although this, again, would offer only a critique, it could legitimize a feminist alternative to the medical model.

Refuting the DSM View of Human Sexuality

The urology/pharmaceutical industry "FSD" consensus conference of 1998 rested foursquare on the popularity of the current "sexual dysfunctions" nomenclature. This list, first appearing in the 1980 edition of the *DSM*, and persisting with minor changes through a 1987 revision to the current 1994 edition, represents Helen Singer Kaplan's addition of disorders of sexual desire to the arousal and orgasm disorders William Masters and Virginia Johnson based on their physiological research (see Table 1) (Kaplan, 1977; Masters and Johnson, 1966, 1970).

Any effort to dislodge this classification system must challenge its assumptions and underlying research (Tiefer, 1991a, 1992). This is a project I have worked on for some time. *DSM-III* and *DSM-III-R* use identical language in introducing sexual dysfunctions: "The *essential feature* is inhibition in the appetitive or psychophysiological changes that characterize *the complete sexual response cycle*" (APA, 1980, p. 275; APA, 1987, p. 290, italics added). *DSM-IV* also begins by referring to the response cycle, "A sexual dysfunction is characterized by a *disturbance* in the processes that characterize *the sexual response cycle*

TABLE 1. Sexual dysfunction (in 1980 called "psychosexual dysfunction") nomenclature found in three sequential editions of the American Psychiatric Association's Diagnostic and Statistical Manual of Mental Disorders

DSM-III (1980) (pp. 275-281)	DSM-III-R (1987) (pp. 290-296)	DSM-IV (1994) (pp. 493- 522)
Inhibited sexual desire	Hypoactive sexual desire disorder	Hypoactive sexual desire disorder
	Sexual aversion disorder	Sexual aversion disorder
Inhibited sexual excitement	Female sexual arousal disorder	Female sexual arousal disorder
	Male erectile disorder	Male erectile disorder
Inhibited female orgasm	Inhibited female orgasm	Female orgasmic disorder
Inhibited male orgasm	Inhibited male orgasm	Male orgasmic disorder
Premature ejaculation	Premature ejaculation	Premature ejaculation
Functional dyspareunia	Dyspareunia	Dyspareunia
Functional vaginismus	Vaginismus	Vaginismus
Atypical psychosexual dysfunction	Sexual dysfunction not otherwise specified	Sexual dysfunctions due to a medical condition (female/male hypoactive desire disorder, male erectile disorder, female/male dyspareunia, other)
		Substance-induced sexual dysfunction (alcohol, amphetamine, cocaine, opioid, sedative/hypnotic/anxiolytic, other)
		Sexual dysfunction not otherwise specified

or by pain associated with sexual intercourse" (APA, 1994, p. 493, italics added). All editions continue:

> The complete[6] sexual response cycle can be divided into the following phases: (1) Appetitive.[7] This consists of fantasies about sexual activity and a desire to have sexual activity. (2) Excitement. This consists of a subjective sense of sexual pleasure and accompanying physiological changes. . . . (3) Orgasm. This consists of a peaking of sexual pleasure, with release of sexual tension and rhythmic contraction of the perineal muscles and pelvic reproductive organs. . . . (4) Resolution. This consists of a sense of muscular relaxation and general well-being. . . . (APA, 1980, pp. 275-276; APA, 1987, p. 291; APA, 1994, pp. 493-494)

The idea of a staged sexual response cycle was initially introduced by Masters and Johnson (1966) to describe the sequence of physiological changes they observed and measured during sexual activities such as masturbation and coitus. The four stages, like the four movements of a romantic symphony, were initially called excitement, plateau, orgasm, and resolution:

> The division of the human male's or female's cycle of sexual response into four specific phases admittedly is inadequate for evaluation of finite psychogenic aspects of elevated sexual tensions. However, the establishment of this purely arbitrary design provides anatomic structuring and assures inclusion and correct placement of specifics of physiological response within the sequential continuum of human response to effective sexual stimulation. (Masters and Johnson, 1966, p. 7)

In their book on sexual dysfunction and therapy, Masters and Johnson (1970) generalized their original response cycle description of physical changes in a volunteer research population into a normative model for classifying health and dysfunction in the general population. Although the term "cycle" appears infrequently in that second volume, the authors rely on their earlier work:

> the greatest handicap to successful treatment of sexual inadequacy was a lack of reliable physiological information in the area of human sexual response. It was presumed that definitive laboratory effort would develop material of clinical consequence. (Masters and Johnson, 1970, p. 1)

Psychiatrist Helen Singer Kaplan collapsed the Masters and Johnson four-stage response cycle to "two distinct and relatively independent components: a genital vasocongestive reaction [arousal] and orgasm" (Kaplan, 1974, p. 13). Three years later, however, Kaplan added a third component, sexual desire, although she recognized that "we do not know exactly what normal sexual desire is . . . [and] it is not possible to formulate a precise definition of inhibition of sexual desire" (Kaplan, 1977, p. 4). By 1979, Kaplan was arguing that "the triphasic model which encompasses all three phases–desire, excitement, and orgasm–makes sense out of and organizes the data about the sexual response and its disorders" (Kaplan, 1979, p. xviii). This triphasic model was intended to be universal, biologically based, and gender-neutral, and the APA eagerly incorporated it into the new objective and behavioral focus of its 1980 manual of mental disorders, *DSM-III*.

The new category of "sexual dysfunctions" descended from the psychophysiologic/psychosomatic category in the first two *DSM* editions (1952 and 1968). In fact, psychiatrist Kaplan viewed "sexual dysfunctions as psychosomatic symptoms" (Kaplan, 1974, p. xv). By 1987, however, the *DSM-III-R* added a new category as a result of clinical observation, Sexual Aversion Disorder, even though Kaplan had explicitly asserted, "Sexual phobias are not psychophysiologic, nor are these disorders related to a specific phase" (Kaplan, 1979, p. 21). By 1987 and *DSM-III-R,* then, the sexual dysfunction nosology was a smooth-looking, but conceptually confusing combination of psychosomatic and non-psychosomatic disorders somehow tied to a universal "complete sexual response cycle."

Unfortunately, the human sexual response cycle model (HSRCM) is based on original research which, because of various methodological biases, cannot be universally generalized. Asserting universality is different than demonstrating it, and although we are so familiar by now with the HSRCM of sexual experience we take it as a biological given, it is crucial to go back to the original research and see how it was originally constructed. Exposing the research biases allows us to dismantle the foundation for the *DSM*'s sexual dysfunctions and pave the way for a feminist alternative.

Flaws in the HSRCM: Subject Selection Biases

Masters and Johnson had for their original physiological research "a requirement that there be a positive history of masturbatory and coital orgasmic experience before any study subject is accepted into the program," although this requirement is disclosed only four pages from the end of their text (Masters and Johnson, 1966, p. 311). Thus their physiological research was narrower than usually claimed. No effort was made to study sexual physiology and subjectivity in a representative sample, only in an easily orgasmic sample. The "discovery" of the human sexual response cycle turns out to be a self-fulfilling prophecy. The selection criteria for the research population compressed sexual diversity and cannot provide norms for the general population.

Identical performance requirements for male and female research subjects masked real-world gender differences in masturbatory experience. Masters and Johnson began their physiological research in 1954. In 1953, Kinsey's survey research had reported that [only] "58% of the females in our sample were masturbating to orgasm at some time in their lives" (Kinsey, Pomeroy, Martin, and Gebhard, p. 143). Married women, the predominant subjects in Masters' and Johnson's physiological research, had even lower masturbatory frequencies than divorced or single women. This contrasts with the 92% incidence of masturbatory experience for men that Kinsey had reported earlier. Masters and Johnson had to find men and women with similar sexual patterns despite having been raised in dissimilar sociosexual worlds.

Similarly, Masters and Johnson deliberately chose subjects for their physiological research who did not represent a socioeconomic cross-section.

> . . . the sample was weighted purposely toward higher than average intelligence levels and socioeconomic backgrounds. Further selectivity was established . . . to determine willingness to participate, facility of sexual responsiveness, and ability to communicate finite details of sexual reaction. (Masters and Johnson, 1966, p. 12)

Why might social class be a relevant factor to the generalizability of physiological observations? Kinsey and his colleagues had previously shown that socioeconomic class related to experience with masturbation, premarital sexual activities, petting, sex with prostitutes, and even nocturnal emissions. The use of the HSRCM becomes less and less appropriate as a universal norm for clinical purposes when we suspect that the HSRCM and the many physiological details described in Masters' and Johnson's research differ among subjects with different sexual habits and values.

Another selection bias regards how the research subjects viewed sexual life.

> Through the years of research exposure, the one factor in sexuality that consistently has been present among members of the study-subject population has been a basic interest in and desire for effectiveness of sexual performance. This one factor may represent the major area of difference between the research study subjects and the general population. (Masters and Johnson, 1966, p. 315)

At first one might think that everyone has "a basic interest in and desire for effectiveness of sexual performance," but, looking more closely, the phrase "*effectiveness* of sexual *performance*" seems to identify devotees of a particular, goal-oriented sexual style. If clinical norms based on the HSRCM are meant to apply to the general population, a "difference between research study subjects and the general population" suddenly becomes very important. Choosing enthusiasts' values as the norm gives the general population two choices–become enthusiasts, or be labeled medically inadequate.

Flaws in the HSRCM: Experimenter Biases

Masters and Johnson made no secret of the fact that subjects volunteering for their research underwent a period of adjustment, or a "controlled orientation program" as they called it (Masters and Johnson, 1966, p. 22). This "period of training" helped the subjects "gain confidence in their ability to respond successfully [sic] while subjected to a variety of recording devices" (p. 23). The fact that Masters and Johnson repeatedly refer to episodes of sexual activity with orgasm as "successes" and those without orgasm or rigid erection or with rapid ejaculation as "failures" (e.g., p. 313), makes it likely that orgasm-oriented performance standards were communicated to their subjects. Moreover, they are candid about their role as sex therapists for their subjects:

> When female orgasmic or male ejaculatory failures develop in the laboratory, the situation is discussed immediately. Once the individual has been reassured, suggestions are made for improvement of future performance. (p. 314)

We can safely speculate, I think, that sex research volunteers charac-terized by a "desire for effective sexual performance" were attentive to experimenter cues and coaching.

"Effective Sexual Stimulation": The Trojan Horse of the HSRCM

At the outset of their book, Masters and Johnson indicate that they set out to answer the question, "What physical reactions develop as the hu-man male and female respond to effective sexual stimulation?" (Mas-ters and Johnson, 1966, p. 4). What is "effective" sexual stimulation? I think this is *the key question* in deconstructing the HSRCM.

> It constantly should be borne in mind that the primary research in-terest has been concentrated quite literally upon what men and women do in response to effective sexual stimulation. (Masters and Johnson, 1966, p. 20)

The authors' intended emphasis in this sentence, I believe, is to commu-nicate that their "primary" interest is neither in euphemism nor vague generality, but in the "literal" physical reactions during sexual activity. However, another way to read this sentence focuses on the word "effec-tive," and reveals the authors' interest in only one type of sexual re-sponse, that which people experience in reaction to a particular type of stimulation. But what *exactly* is "effective stimulation"?

In each of the book's chapters, devoted to physical reactions of par-ticular organs or groups of organs (e.g., clitoris, penis, uterus, respira-tory system), the authors restate their intention to look at the responses to "effective sexual stimulation." Although the phrase appears dozens of times in the text, it is not in the glossary or the index, and no defini-tion or description can be found. The reader must deduce for him or her-self that *"effective sexual stimulation" is orgasm-oriented stimulation that facilitates the human sexual response cycle.* This can be inferred from observations such as the following, taken from the section on labia minora response in the "female external genitalia" chapter:

> Many women have progressed well into plateau-phase levels of sexual response, had the effective stimulative techniques with-drawn, and been unable to achieve orgasmic-phase tension re-lease. . . . When an obviously effective means of sexual stimulation is withdrawn and orgasmic-phase release is not

achieved, the minor-labial coloration will fade rapidly. (Masters and Johnson, 1966, p. 41)

Effective stimulation is that stimulation which facilitates "progress" from one stage of the response cycle to the next, particularly that which facilitates orgasm. Any stimulation that results in responses other than greater physiological excitation and orgasm is defined as "ineffective" and is literally not of interest to these authors. It's akin to researchers of vision being interested only in optic system response to stimuli of particular wavelengths, say red and yellow. There's nothing wrong with red and yellow, but they are not the whole spectrum, and we would challenge a study of visual physiology that called only red and yellow stimuli "effective."

This sets up a tautology. "Normal" sexual response is whatever results from effective sexual stimulation, and effective sexual stimulation is whatever produces "normal" response. Another way to put this is that Masters and Johnson (and the APA after them) defined sex as what occurs during the response cycle and produces orgasm. They were not interested in subjects whose primary sexual goals were sexual pleasure or intimacy or anything else, or who favored sexual techniques that were not necessarily orgasm oriented. Once Masters and Johnson (1966) themselves decided that orgasm represented "the ultimate point in progression" (p. 127), their model became self-fulfilling and cannot provide general clinical norms for sexual experience or satisfaction.

ORGASM: FROM MYTH TO TYRANNY?

Much of the problem of defining sexual normality for women revolves around orgasm and sexual scripting that produces orgasm, a problem which remains unsettled to this day. Is orgasm essential to sexual pleasure? Obviously not. Can it contribute to pleasure and satisfaction? Obviously, for many people, the answer is yes. We might say the same thing for kisses, feelings of love, arousing verbal exchanges, or any other script element. Can orgasm, like kissing or words of love, be learned and then elevated to a central role in sexual scripting? Of course. But where does that put orgasm in terms of sexual *normality?*

Since the influential work of Masters and Johnson, and enshrined in the various editions of the *DSM,* the contemporary medical model has made orgasm a mandatory part of normal experience, although experienced clinicians recognize that "the simple fact that we recognize and treat orgasmic problems in women, is, in part, a cultural accident" (Heiman, 2000, p. 121). The fuzzy nature of the situation is revealed by looking more closely at how "female orgasmic disorder" is handled in the *DSM*. Here's the definition offered in 1987 (almost identical to 1980), and then the one from 1994:

> Persistent or recurrent delay in, or absence of, orgasm in a female following a normal sexual excitement phase during sexual activity that the clinician judges to be adequate in focus, intensity and duration. Some females are able to experience orgasm during noncoital clitoral stimulation, but are unable to experience it during coitus in the absence of manual clitoral stimulation. In most of these females, this represents a normal variation of the female sexual response and does not justify the diagnosis of Inhibited Female Orgasm. However, in some of these females, this does represent psychological inhibition that justifies the diagnosis. This difficult judgement is assisted by a thorough sexual evaluation, which may even require a trial of treatment. (APA, 1987, p. 294)

> The essential feature of female orgasmic disorder is a persistent or recurrent delay in, or absence of, orgasm following a normal sexual excitement phase. Women exhibit wide variability in the type or intensity of stimulation that triggers orgasm. The diagnosis of Female Orgasmic Disorder should be based on the clinician's judgement that the woman's orgasmic capacity is less than would be reasonable for her age, sexual experience, and the adequacy of sexual stimulation she receives. The disturbance must cause marked distress or interpersonal difficulty. (APA, 1994, p. 505)

Note that in 1980 and 1987, probably influenced by Shere Hite's (1976) research, the APA was specifically concerned to avoid pathologizing women whose orgasm was primarily clitoral and noncoital; by 1994 an even more inclusive notion prevailed, that any "reasonable" orgasmic pattern was considered normal.

It's also worth noting that, in 1994, absence or difficulty of orgasm had to cause "marked distress or interpersonal difficulty" to qualify as a disorder. This subjectivity criterion was added for all the sexual dysfunctions in 1994 and appears, somewhat reduced in strength, in the urological-pharmaceutical "consensus conference" document as well:

> Orgasmic disorder is the persistent or recurrent difficulty delay in or absence of attaining orgasm following sufficient sexual stimulation and arousal, *which causes personal distress.* (Basson et al., 2000, p. 890, italics added)

Endorsing women's right to sexual pleasure by recognizing and even mandating sexual orgasm is sometimes thought to reflect a great emancipatory step for women's sexual lives, and we need to be mindful of recent history. Early in the feminist second wave, Anne Koedt's classic essay, "The myth of the vaginal orgasm," applauded the Masters and Johnson physiological research as proving once and for all that the clitoris, not the vagina, is the "center of [women's] sexual sensitivity" and the source of sexual orgasm (Koedt, 1973, p. 198). While arguing that "what we must do is redefine our sexuality, . . . discard the 'normal' concepts of sex and create new guidelines," Koedt suggested that women "must begin to demand that if certain sexual positions . . . are not mutually conducive to orgasm, they no longer be defined as standard" (*ibid.*, p. 199). Thus, Koedt used assumptions about the centrality of orgasm to assert women's right to create sexual choreography.

Another early second-wave argument was offered by Dana Densmore (1973) in her classic essay, "Independence from the Sexual Revolution." Densmore complained that the "right" to orgasm had become a duty.

> Some men do the dinner dishes every night. That doesn't make their wives free. On the contrary, it's just one more thing she has to feel grateful to him for . . . It will never mean more than that until the basic power relations are changed . . . (p. 110)

Densmore argued that the new sexual revolution had created pressure to have sex and orgasm that was just another form of oppression, a new way for women not to be self-determining. Her feminism was rooted in sexual self-determination, suspicious of similarities to men's sexual styles, and left open whether orgasm would be part of any particular woman's preferred sexual choreography. Carol Ellison's (2000) recent survey suggests that many feminists are following Densmore's lead–they vary greatly in the importance placed on orgasm, but agree on the central importance of sexual self-determination.

Feminists must scrutinize all sexual prescriptions offered for women, especially those that seem to suggest women's sexual experience would be better, more normal, or more fulfilling, if it more closely paralleled men's. This type of thinking has been questioned by feminists time and time again, in work and family lives, in emotional and affectional experience, in political and spiritual values, and sexual patterns cannot slip under the radar because of unquestioned biological reductionism.

Thus, for the *DSM* and urology/pharmaceutical industry consensus documents to require a woman's assertion of "distress" before she is labeled with an orgasm disorder gives only a superficial tip of the hat to women's sexual self-determination, and again models women's sexuality on men's (Tiefer, 1992, 1995; Boyle, 1994; Irvine, 1990). There is no acknowledgment of diversity in sexual goals, meaning, and choreography. The definition of normal sexual function remains committed to a linear, genital game plan. The Procrustean bed of the HSRCM, despite the recently added requirement of subjective distress, continues to constrain and contain women's sexualities.

FEMINIST ACTIVISM III:
A "NEW VIEW" OF WOMEN'S SEXUAL PROBLEMS

Beyond Medical Models into Feminist Waters

If the research underpinning the *DSM* and the urology/pharmaceutical industry consensus conference is unreliable, it then seems entirely appropriate and even urgent for feminists to offer an alternative model and nosology for women's sexual problems. Such an alternative can bypass the *DSM* and HSRCM, and be based on ideas of diversity, self-determination, and the realities of women's sexual lives as shown in women's studies and women's health research. This research, published in many different professional journals and books, has been summarized and evaluated by many, many authors (e.g., Barbach, 1975; Cline, 1993; Dallos and Dallos, 1997; Daniluk, 1998; Dodson, 1987; Ehrenreich, Hess, and Jacobs, 1986; Ellison, 2000; Federation of Feminist Women's Health Centers, 1991; Fontes, 1995; Hall, 1998; Heise, 1995; Hite, 1987; Irvine, 1990; Jackson and Scott, 1996; Lancaster and di Leonardo, 1997; Levine, 1993; Loulan, 1984; McCormick, 1994; Ogden, 1999; Oudshoorn, 1994; Snitow, Stansell, and Thompson, 1983; Travis and White, 2000; Tiefer, 1991b, 1992, 1995; Ussher and Baker, 1993; Valverde, 1985; Vance, 1984).

Early in 2000, I began internet correspondence with lesbian sex therapist Marny Hall and social psychologist Carol Tavris to draft a "new view" of women's sexual problems.[8] We felt that any alternative classification system should begin by critiquing the *DSM* nomenclature and its unwise reliance on the HSRCM biological universals of Kaplan and Masters and Johnson. Once the deck was clear, we could draft a new document using the psycho-bio-social insights of feminist clinicians and theorists who located women's sexual problems primarily in cultural and relational contexts. We adopted a social constructionist view of sexual experience that allowed us to sidestep any universal blueprint for successful sexual experience and to endorse ideas of sexual self-determination implicitly and explicitly (Tiefer, 1987). Our classification system would allow women to identify their own sexual problems, which we inclusively defined as "discontent or dissatisfaction with any emotional, physical, or relational aspect of sexual experience." This definition avoided specifying any one particular pattern of sexual experience as normal, the critical point at which we felt the medical models had gone wrong.

Following the woman-centered definition of sexual problems, our classification system embraced a familiar four-part psychobiosocial catalog of causes. The authors of the *DSM,* walking a fine line among competing theories in psychiatry, had abandoned etiology in favor of descriptions. We felt this was a wrong choice for sex and for women. We first identified sexual problems due to sociocultural, political, or economic factors, accounting probably for the largest global number of sexual complaints. In this category we included such factors as inadequate sex education or lack of access to contraception, abortion, and STD care.

We felt it was critical to affirm that the sort of large "public" issues identified by feminists were directly related to such "private" but pervasive sexual problems as embarrassment over the lack of vocabulary to describe subjective experience or lack of knowledge about human sexual biology. We wanted to make it clear that much sexual insecurity is rooted in perceived inability to meet cultural norms regarding correct or ideal sexuality. We also felt it was important to point to the sociocultural factors of fatigue and lack of personal time due to family and work obligations as a cause of women's sexual problems (Hochschild, 1989). All these matters would be amenable to social change and clinical treatment, allowing us to show explicitly how feminism offered solutions to many of women's sexual problems.

The second category locates the causes of women's sexual problems in a multitude of specific partner and relationship issues, the third in various psychological conflicts and disadvantageous elements of personal history, and the fourth in medical and physical problems. These last three factors had all received attention in the literature and research of sexology and sex therapy, but the sociocultural and political issues had been emphasized only in the writings of feminist sex therapists (e.g., Cole and Rothblum, 1988).

The Campaign for a "New View"

The new classification began to take shape over the summer of 2000 at the same time as publicity emerged for the second large "female sexual dysfunction" conference in Boston. I realized that the seven minute platform our paper would receive (assuming our "new view" abstract was accepted) would not offer enough time to counteract messages about new medical "advances," and that if a "new view" were to have any chance to influence the "FSD" zeitgeist, we needed to think and act outside the box.

I solicited colleagues with a similar feminist critique of medicalization to form a working committee to promote the "new view." As Carol Tavris and Marny Hall were both in California, I asked contacts at the National Women's Health Network (NWHN) and the Boston Women's Health Book Collective (BWHBC) to put me in touch with West Coast activists. Through e-mail, anthropologist Lisa Handwerker and sociologists Jennifer Fishman, Heather Hartley and Laura Mamo agreed to help with a campaign. I invited other Bay Area feminist psychotherapists to help finalize the classification system, and Ellyn Kaschak, Linda Alperstein, and Carol Ellison agreed to participate. Peggy Kleinplatz offered to travel from Ottawa, making our group a little bit international, and Meika Loe, who had participated in the activities of October, 1999, arranged to come from Santa Barbara. Gina Ogden in Boston put me in touch with Judy Peres, a feminist newswoman in Chicago who had been following the "FSD" story for months. Judy got her editor at the *Chicago Tribune* to support her participation.

Thus, at everyone's own expense except for the reporter, a group of thirteen feminists convened at Marny Hall's house in Oakland for the weekend of September 9-10, 2000. There was widespread support for the critique and the new classification. We spent hours polishing the language and agreed to add a sexual rights section, based on World Association of Sexology and World Health Organization language, to support a nonmedical framework for sexual norms. The second day was spent planning a campaign to get the word out: presentations at social science and sex therapy meetings, publications in social science jour-

nals and the popular press, a press conference in Boston preceding the
"FSD" meeting, and a "new view" conference in California in 2002.[9]

The Press Conference and the 2000 "FSD" Conference[10]

None of us had ever convened a press conference, and only the *Chicago Tribune* reporter had ever even been to one. However, over the next two months we used lists from the NWHN, BWHBC, and Center for Medical Consumers to fax or e-mail a press release to scores of reporters and publications. We prepared a press packet containing the final version of the "new view," lists of endorsers and resources, and four endorsing statements (from SIECUS, Planned Parenthood of New York City, psychologists Anne Peplau and Linda Garnets about a new view of women's sexual orientation, and psychologist Deborah Tolman about a new view of adolescent girls' sexual problems).[11] Gina Ogden reserved a Boston hotel room for three hours on October 25, the day before Irwin Goldstein's "FSD" conference. Ultimately, we had a roomful of students, supporters, and journalists, and were able to see articles in the next day's *Boston Herald* (Eagan, 2000), *FDA Week* (*FDA Week*, 2000), Salon.com (Raab, 2000), and CBSHealthWatch.com (Zamora, 2000).[12] Ultimately, we learned that the value of a press conference is to place activists' names in many journalists' address books for future reference.

The October, 2000, Boston University-sponsored "FSD" conference, now titled "Female Sexual Function Forum [FSFF]," was only slightly different from 1999. It lasted an additional half day, reported attendance above 600, allowed questions to be put to the paid lecturers, had 23 sponsoring medical and drug companies (up from 16 in 1999)–although the exhibit area had only two displays (the new FDA-approved clitoral stimulator, and an estrogen-testosterone combination drug)–and approved the formation of a new FSFF organization (but not [yet] a new journal) by a vote of 121 to 24. Surprisingly, I was elected to the Board of the new organization–I suppose to be a watchdog.[13] The strong attendance of gynecologists and primary care doctors (I talked with many physicians who had never been to a sex research meeting of any type before) seemed to almost everyone to indicate physicians' need for information in this highly publicized new area, and to justify a new organization with annual conferences.[14]

The program emphasized both psychological and physical causes of sexual dysfunctions. However, issues of sex education, public health, social change, access to services, sexual problem prevention, and other macro-level matters were not raised. My brief presentation of the "new view" received warm applause and two comments. A woman psychiatrist asked what was new about it, and a male psychologist asked why it was only for women.

While both these questioners raise relevant perspectives, their questions failed to acknowledge the politics of women's sexual problems, and the "new view" as a historically-situated attempt to contest medicalization. The comments thus reflected the well-meaning but narrow scientific goal of many attenders at the conference: getting at the *truth* of "FSD." Of course, the "new view" authors feel that our ideas could fruitfully be applied to men's sexual experience, and of course we recognize that the psycho-bio-social framework is hardly brand new in clinical practice or thinking. What these comments didn't acknowledge, however, was how the current model of sexual functioning is based on a male norm and a false universal physiological HSRCM. By proposing a categorization system that starts by *explicitly* putting women's experience at the center, the "new view" categories and concepts offer an understanding of human sexuality that can be used for political and educational purposes in our less-than-emancipated world. There was no time in such a forum to explain the history of "FSD," or how each contribution to the "evolving" definition of "FSD" plays a part in a political tug-of-war. There was no time to explain that it would be too late to challenge the dominant definition of "FSD" by the time the FDA met to review the clinical trials' data, and that whether something was really new or might also apply to men was not a front-burner issue for feminists who saw the Boston meeting as, in part, window-dressing for hidden interests.

The urgent matters that had drawn us into this historical moment emerged near the end of the conference when Dr. Susan Allen, Director of the FDA's Reproductive and Urologic Drug Product Division, discussed, as she had in 1999, issues of the looming "FSD" clinical trials (Allen, 2000). She had been primary author of the May, 2000, draft document for companies interested in developing drugs for "FSD" (Division of Reproductive and Urologic Drug Products, 2000). She said that she had received comments from industry, women's groups, and researchers, but that they hadn't caused her to change much in her draft document. She insisted that quantitative and genital measures, such as numbers of orgasms, were needed for outcome measure clarity in clinical trials. Even though she admitted that not everyone cared that much about orgasm, she said that relational and psychological endpoints could not be substituted. Although she admitted that the definition of "FSD" was still "evolving," she emphasized that there was no way she could stop the flood of drug trials.

This was not a happy moment for the "new view" conference participants. But, amidst the bad news, we still heard that social constructionist note, our window of opportunity, the acknowledgment that the definition of "FSD" was still "evolving." As in Cape Cod in 1997, at the birth of "FSD," there still seems to be lack of agreement about just what it is, and our campaign continues to be relevant.

USING THE "NEW VIEW"

It is clear that the medicalization of women's sexual problems represents an ongoing trend in the evolution of medicine and the social construction of women's sexuality, and that feminists must develop and promote appropriate analyses and political actions. There will be a range of political positions, however, because aspects of medicalization can bring advantages as well as disadvantages, depending on women's cultural and socio-economic locations.

For example, I recently visited TARSHI (acronym for Talking About Reproductive and Sexual Health Issues), a sex information telephone hotline service run by young feminist women in New Delhi, India (Chandiramani, 1998).[15] Most callers are men, and they often express concern about the sexual satisfaction of their wives and girlfriends, albeit largely because of the impact dissatisfaction might have on their woman's fidelity or their own status. While the TARSHI phone counselors were very interested in the critique and alternative classification offered in the "new view," they felt on balance that women's sexual well-being was best promoted by the authority of a medical model that emphasized "science": correct physiological information, women's "natural" capacities for desire, arousal and orgasm, women's proven need for longer pre-coital foreplay to become aroused, the importance of clitoral stimulation to produce orgasm, etc.

Likewise, it seemed that many of the physicians attending the October, 2000, "FSD" conference in Boston were so anxious and tongue-tied about conversing openly with patients about sexuality that focusing on physiology and other "scientific" aspects offered a place to start. As primary care physicians became the main managers of men's erectile problems, drug companies have reoriented their continuing education materials to persuade this group of time-pressed doctors of the efficacy of brief assessment and immediate sildenafil (Carson and Levine, 2001). A science-oriented discourse about women's sexual realities (abuse, body image, overwork, etc.) may be a better way than political analysis to influence this anxious group's understanding of women's sexuality.

On the other hand, the recent marketing of a new book about "FSD" targeted to American women calls out for a more direct political critique of sexuo-medicalization (Berman and Berman, 2000). The photogenic and voluble authors, promoted around the country as "pioneers" in the "neglected" area of women's sexual problems, make exaggerated diagnostic and treatment claims in their book and television appearances (Roan, 2001). This moment seems ripe for a campaign rooted in decades of women's health activism that appeals to the consumer-savvy public's distrust of pharmaceutical industry hype. The public may not be interested in technical issues of nomenclature, but it wants to know when it is being sold a pig in a poke.

The "new view" can be of immense value at a time when sex-positive messages in the media and educational materials could easily suffer biological reduction to some absurd and Procrustean fitness notion of "sexual health." Moreover, a feminist analysis seems especially called for to expose how the rhetoric of equal sexual rights conceals the subtler operations of power. The marketers insist that the new drugs offer women "choices," and what could be wrong with that? The "new view" can be used to show how apparent choices may not in fact be meaningful options when they ignore the social context of women's sexual lives.

The 1997 Cape Cod quandary, the lack of agreement on defining "FSD," essentially the familiar "what do women want?," revealed the continuing gap in generalizing from men's sexuality to women. But my brave friends at Cape Cod underestimated what it will take to promote a woman-centered view of sexuality; it will take more than simply denying that men and women are sexually the same; it will take a politics that recognizes the reasons for their differences.

These last few years have shown that attaining sexual freedom and well-being for women will require more than just a new generation of women physicians, women pharmaceutical industry employees, or women FDA administrators, whose ideas about sexuality may be unconnected to the wider social and political world (Sherwin and the Feminist Health Care Ethics Research Network, 1998). It will take more than having women invited to participate in urology/pharmaceutical industry "consensus" conferences, if such women are prohibited from raising ethical and political concerns.

The "new view" comes at a crucial moment, placing the construction of women's sexuality in historical and scholarly perspective as well as global and local contexts. Promoting our model allows our supporters to stress the need for woman-centered research on sexual satisfaction, comprehensive and community-wide sex education, and priority for sociocultural, political, and relational causes of sexual problems. The new view's critique allows us to continue revealing economic forces and other vested interests behind medicalization, and the dangers of a one-size-fits-all approach to sex.

The focus on "sexual function" at the center of medicalization represents both its greatest strength and greatest weakness. By asserting the imprimatur of universal biology, medicalization legitimizes women's sexual desire and experience, potentially sweeping all women into a great net of physical pleasure and enhanced life experience. But the discourse of sexual health and illness inexorably leads to a narrow world of medicogenital tests and treatments, and the realities of contemporary gender politics produce a sexuality too focused on performance, and too tellingly designed for men's interests (Jackson and Scott, 1997). The "new view" shows the holes in the net, and provides an alternative vision. Ironically, the emergence of a pharmacosexual marketplace offers women an opportunity and locus for feminist activism. Not surprisingly, the only magic pill for women's sexuality is broad-spectrum freedom.

NOTES

1. The first approval went to Pfizer, Inc. and its brand name "Viagra."

2. By the year 2000, most books and articles about "erectile dysfunction," the name suggested to replace "impotence" by a 1992 National Institutes of Health [NIH] conference (NIH Consensus Panel on Impotence, 1993), embraced a medical model of sexual function (e.g., Jardin, Wagner, Khoury, Giuliano, Padma-Nathan, & Rosen, 2000).

3. Outside the US, endocrinologists (medical internists who focus on hormones) remain more likely to direct "andrology" clinics. Debates about the roles and importance of hormones continue to be prominent in both men's and women's sexual medicine.

4. I will put "FSD" [female sexual dysfunction] in quotations in this paper to indicate its questionable legitimacy.

5. Any drug approved by the FDA may be legally prescribed for any condition as long as the prescribing physician can justify the prescription. Insofar as sildenafil (Viagra) is being prescribed for women despite lack of FDA approval for women, it is not so far-fetched to examine the specifics of Uprima. A recent popular book that promotes a medical view of women's sexual problems discusses Uprima without ever mentioning that it was developed for men (Berman & Berman, 2000). Perhaps tests are ongoing with women that I will soon learn about!

6. *DSM-IV* eliminates the word "complete."

7. *DSM-IV* substitutes the word "desire" for the word "appetitive."

8. This document, of course, is the heart of and justification for this book and appears elsewhere in the volume in its entirety.

9. For a complete bibliography of our "new view" publications and to be put on our conference mailing list, please contact the author.

10. An informal report of events at the October, 2000 press conference and "FSD" conference is available from the author.

11. Copies of these statements are available from the author, as is a continually updated list of endorsers. Readers so wishing can be added to the list of endorsers.

12. Other press articles and notices have appeared since then, and a list can be obtained from the author. The entire "new view" document has also been posted on many health and sexuality websites, e.g., <www.wellnessweb.com/female_sexual_dysfunction/a_new_view_of_women's_sexual_problems.htm>

13. This new organization, unfortunately, despite paying lip service to multidisciplinary intentions, has followed closely in the steps of its urology parents by hiring an expensive conference management organization that pledges to solicit pharmaceutical industry funding for its own fees ($76,000/year plus thousands for a website) and in order to underwrite future lavish conferences. Thus, even before its first birthday, FSFF has become dependent on the pharmaceutical industry for its survival. My votes carry about as much weight as they did at the FDA advisory committee on Uprima, but it is interesting to see medicalization from the inside!

14. I received email notice on March 20, 2001, of the founding of the Korean FSFF, and it appears that the movement for such organizations is about to go global.

15 See their webpage: http:\\arrive.at/tarshi

REFERENCES

Allen, S. S. (2000). Drug development and regulatory issues related to female sexual dysfunction. Presented at Female Sexual Function Forum conference, October 28, 2000, Boston, MA.

American Psychiatric Association. (1980). *Diagnostic and statistical manual of mental disorders*, 3rd ed. (*DSM-III*). Washington, D.C.: Author.

American Psychiatric Association. (1987). *Diagnostic and statistical manual of mental disorders*, 3rd ed. rev. (*DSM-III-R*). Washington, D.C.: Author.

American Psychiatric Association. (1994). *Diagnostic and statistical manual of mental disorders*, 4th ed. (*DSM-IV*). Washington, D.C.: Author.

American Urological Association Executive Committee. (1993). Policy statement of January, 1990. *AUA Today, 6*, 6.

Bancroft, J., Graham, C. A., & McCord, C. (2001). Conceptualizing women's sexual problems. *Journal of Sex & Marital Therapy, 27*, 95-103.

Bankhead, C. (February, 1997). New field could open for urologists: Female sexual dysfunction. *Urology Times, 25*, 1, 39.

Barbach, L. (1975) *For yourself: The fulfillment of female sexuality*. New York: Anchor Books.

Basson, R., Berman, J., Burnett, A., Derogatis, L., Ferguson, D., Fourcroy, J., Goldstein, I., Grazziottin, A., Heiman, J., Laan, E., Leiblum, S., Padma-Nathan, H., Rosen, R., Segraves, K., Segraves, R. T., Shabsigh, R., Sipski, M., Wagner, M., & Whipple, B. (2000). Report on the international consensus development conference on female sexual dysfunction: Definitions and classifications. *Journal of Urology, 163*, 888-893.

Berman, J. & Berman, L. (with Bumiller, E.) (2000). *For women only.* New York: Henry Holt & Co.

Boyle, M. (1994). Gender, science, and sexual dysfunction. In T. R. Sarbin & J. I. Kitsuse (Eds.), *Constructing the social.* London: Sage Publications, pp. 101-118.

Caplan, P. (1995). *They say you're crazy.* Reading, MA: Addison-Wesley Publishing Company.

Carson, C. C. & Levine, L. A. (2001). *Managing erectile dysfunction: Strategies and case studies for the primary care physician.* A continuing education monograph jointly sponsored by the School of Medicine of the University of North Carolina at Chapel Hill and the National Foundation for Sexual Health Medicine, Inc.

Chandiramani, R. (1998). Talking about sex. *Reproductive Health Matters, 6*, 76-86.

Cho, M. K., Shohara, R., Schissel A., & Rennie, D. (2000). Policies on faculty conflicts of interest at US universities. *Journal of the American Medical Association, 284*, 2203-2208.

Cline, S. (1993). *Women, passion and celibacy.* New York: Carol Southern Books.

Cole, E. & Rothblum, E. D. (1988). (Eds.) *Women and sex therapy.* New York: Haworth Press.

Conrad, P. (1992). Medicalization and social control. *Annual Review of Sociology, 18*, 209-232.

Dallos, S. & Dallos, R. (1997). *Couples, sex and power: The politics of desire.* Phila: Open Univ. Press

Daniluk, J. C. (1998). *Women's sexuality across the life span.* New York: Guilford Press.

Densmore, D. (1973). Independence from the sexual revolution. In A. Koedt, E. Levine, & A. Rapone (Eds.), *Radical Feminism.* New York: Quadrangle Books, pp. 107-118.

Division of Reproductive and Urologic Drug Products, FDA. (2000). Guidance for Industry: Female sexual dysfunction: Clinical development of drug products for treatment. Copies available at <http://www.fda.cder/guidance/index.htm> or from the Dockets Management Branch of the Food and Drug Administration, 5630 Fishers Lane, Rockville, MD 20852.

Dodson, B. (1987). *Sex for one: Joy of self-loving.* New York: Crown.

Eagan, M. (October 26, 2000). Drug firms see a goldmine in female sex woes. *Boston Herald*, P. 8.

Ehrenreich, B., Hess, E. & Jacobs, G. (1986). *Re-Making love: The feminization of sex.* New York: Anchor/Doubleday.

Ellison, C.E. (2000) *Women's sexualities: Generations of women share intimate secrets of sexual self-acceptance.* Oakland, CA: New Harbinger.

FDA Week (October 27, 2000). Researchers offer new classification of female sexual problems. *6:* 11.

Federation of Feminist Women's Health Centers (1981; 1991.) *A New View of a Woman's Body.* New York: Simon & Schuster.

Fontes, L. A. (Ed.) (1995). *Sexual abuse in nine North American cultures: Prevention and treatment.* Thousand Oaks, CA: Sage Publications.

Giami, A. (2000). Changing relations between medicine, psychology, and sexuality: The case of male impotence. *Journal of Social Medicine* (Finland), *4,* 263-272.

Giddens, A. (1992). *The transformation of intimacy: Sexuality, love and eroticism in modern societies.* Stanford, CA: Stanford University Press.

Hall, M. (1998). *The Lesbian Love Companion.* Harper San Francisco.

Hall, M. (2001a). Small print and conspicuous omissions: Commentary on the "FSD" classification report. *Journal of Sex & Marital Therapy, 27,* 149-150.

Hall, M. (2001b). Beyond forever after: Treating inhibited and discrepant desire in lesbian couples. In press, *Journal of Sex & Marital Therapy.*

Heiman, J. R. (2000). Orgasmic disorders in women. In S. R. Leiblum & R. C. Rosen (Eds.). *Principles and practice of sex therapy, 3rd edition.* New York: Guilford. pp. 118-153.

Heise, L. (1995). Violence, sexuality and women's lives. In R. G. Parker & J. H. Gagnon (Eds.) *Conceiving sexuality: Approaches to sex research in a postmodern world.* New York: Routledge. pp. 109-134.

Hellstrom, W. J. G. (Ed.) (1999). *The Handbook of Sexual Dysfunction.* San Francisco: The American Society of Andrology.

Hite, S. (1976). *The Hite report: A nationwide study on female sexuality.* New York: Macmillan.

Hite, S. (1987). *Women in love: A cultural revolution in progress.* New York: Knopf.

Hitt, J. (February 20, 2000). The second sexual revolution. *New York Times Magazine.* pp. 34-41, 50, 62, 64, 68-69.

Hochschild, A. (1989) *The second shift: Working parents and the revolution at home.* New York: Viking.

Irvine, J. (1990). *Disorders of desire: Sex and gender in modern American sexology.* Philadelphia: Temple University Press.

Jackson, S. & Scott, S. (1996). *Feminism and sexuality: A reader.* New York: Columbia University Press.

Jackson, S. & Scott, S. (1997). Gut reactions to matters of the heart: Reflections on rationality, irrationality and sexuality. *The Sociological Review,* TK, 551-575.

Jardin, A., Wagner, G., Khoury, S., Giuliano, F., Padma-Nathan, H. & Rosen, R. (2000). (Eds.) *Erectile dysfunction.* Plymouth, UK: Health Publications Ltd.

Johannes, L. (July 13, 1998). Now, drug companies turn to women's sexual problems. *Wall Street Journal.* Pp. B1, B2.

Kaplan, H. S. (1974). *The new sex therapy.* New York: Brunner/Mazel.

Kaplan, H. S. (1977). Hypoactive sexual desire. *Journal of Sex & Marital Therapy, 3,* 3-9.

Kaplan, H. S. (1979). *Disorders of sexual desire.* New York: Brunner/Mazel.

Kinsey, A.C., Pomeroy, W.B., Martin, C. E., & Gebhard, P. H. (1953). *Sexual Behavior in the Human Female*. Philadelphia: W.B. Saunders Co.

Koedt, A. (1973) The myth of the vaginal orgasm. In A. Koedt, E. Levine, & A. Rapone (Eds.) *Radical Feminism*. New York: Quadrangle Books. pp. 198-207.

Kolata, G. (April 4, 1998). Impotence drug prompting talk of female use. *New York Times*, pp. A1, A6.

Kolata, G. (April 25, 1998). Doctors debate use of drug to help women's sex lives. *New York Times*. p. A9.

Kong, D. (October 22, 1999). Doubts heard over sexual dysfunction gathering. *Boston Globe*, pp. B1, B6.

Krane, R. J., Siroky, M. B. & Goldstein, I. (Eds.) (1983). *Male Sexual Dysfunction*. Boston: Little, Brown and Co.

Laan, E., van Lunsen, R. H. W., Everaerd, W., Heiman, J. R., & Hackbert, L. (June, 2000). The effect of sildenafil on women's genital and subjective sexual response. Paper presented at the International Academy of Sex Research, Paris, France.

Lancaster, R. N. & di Leonardo, M. (Eds.) (1997). *The gender/sexuality reader*. New York: Routledge.

Leland, J. (May 29, 2000). The science of women and sex. *Newsweek*, pp. 48-54.

Levine, J. (1993). *My enemy, my love: Women, men and the dilemmas of gender*. New York: Anchor/Doubleday.

Loulan, J. (1984). *Lesbian sex*. San Francisco: Spinsters' Ink.

McCormick, N. (1994). *Sexual salvation: Affirming women's rights and pleasures*. Westport, CT: Praeger.

McLaren, A. (1999). *Twentieth-century sexuality*. Oxford: Blackwell Publishers.

Masters, W. H. & Johnson, V. E. (1966). *Human sexual response*. Boston: Little, Brown and Co.

Masters, W. H. & Johnson, V. E. (1970). *Human sexual inadequacy*. Boston: Little, Brown and Co.

Maurice, W. L. (2001). Understanding female sexual dysfunction and the consensus conference: This is progress? *Journal of Sex & Marital Therapy, 27*, 171-174.

NIH Consensus Development Panel on Impotence. (1993). Impotence. *Journal of the American Medical Association, 270*, 83-90.

Ogden, G. (1999). Rev. ed. *Women who love sex: An inquiry into the expanding spirit of women's erotic experience*. Cambridge, MA: Womanspirit Press.

Oudshoorn, N. (1994). *Beyond the natural body: An archeology of sex hormones*. New York: Routledge.

Park, K., Goldstein, I., Andry, C., Siroky, M. B., Krane, R. J., & Azadzoi, K. M. (1997). Vasculogenic female sexual dsyfunction: The hemodynamic basis for vaginal engorgement insufficiency and clitoral erectile insufficiency. *International Journal of Impotence Research, 9*, 27-37.

Parker, R., Barbosa, R. M., & Aggleton, P. (Eds.) (2000). *Framing the sexual subject: The politics of gender, sexuality, and power*. Berkeley: University of California Press.

Parker, R. G. & Gagnon, J. H. (1995). (Eds.). *Conceiving sexuality: Approaches to sex research in a postmodern world*. New York: Routledge.

Plummer, K. (1995). *Telling sexual stories: Power, change, and social worlds*. New York: Routledge.

Porst, H. (1996). Review article. The rationale for prostaglandin E1 in erectile failure: A survey of world-wide experience. *Journal of Urology, 155*, 802-815.

Raab, B. (2000). The vagina dialogues. WWW.Salon.com. (October 26).

Riessman, C. K. (1983). Women and medicalization: A new perspective. *Social Policy, 14*, 3-18.

Roan, S. (February 12, 2001). Sex and the new city. *Los Angeles Times*. pp. S1, S6.

Rosen, R. C. (May 10, 1997). Personal e-mail communication.

Rosen, R. C. & O'Leary, M. P. (1998). Introduction. *International Journal of Impotence Research, 10, Suppl 2*, S1-S2.

Rubin, G. (1984). Thinking sex: Notes for a radical theory of the politics of sexuality. In C. S. Vance (ed.), *Pleasure and danger: Exploring female sexuality*. Boston: Routledge & Kegan Paul, pp. 267-319.

Segraves, R. T. (Ed.). (2001). Historical and international connect of nosology of female sexual disorders [Special issue]. *Journal of Sex & Marital Therapy, 27* (2).

Shaw, J. (2001). Another procrustean bed for female sexual functioning. *Journal of Sex & Marital Therapy, 27*, 211-214.

Sheldon, T. A. & Smith, G. D. (1993). Consensus conferences as drug promotion. *Lancet, 341*, 100-102.

Sherwin, S., coordinator, and The Feminist Health Care Ethics Research Network (1998). *The politics of women's health: Exploring agency and autonomy*. Philadelphia: Temple University Press.

Snitow, A., Stansell, C. & Thompson, S. (1983). *Powers of desire: The politics of sexuality*. New York: Monthly Review Press.

Tiefer, L. (1986). In pursuit of the perfect penis: The medicalization of male sexuality. *American Behavioral Scientist, 29*, 579-599.

Tiefer, L. (1987). Social constructionism and the study of human sexuality. In P. Shaver and C. Hendrick (eds.), *Sex and Gender*. Newbury Park, CA: Sage Publications. (pp. 70-94).

Tiefer, L. (1991a). Historical, scientific, clinical, and feminist criticisms of "The human sexual response cycle" model. *Annual Review of Sex Research, 2*, 1-23.

Tiefer, L. (1991b). Commentary on the status of sex research: Feminism, sexuality, and sexology. *Journal of Psychology & Human Sexuality, 4*, 5-42.

Tiefer, L. (1992). Critique of the *DSM-III-R* nosology of sexual dysfunctions. *Psychiatric Medicine, 10*, 227-245.

Tiefer, L. (1994). The medicalization of impotence: Normalizing phallocentrism. *Gender & Society, 8*, 363-377.

Tiefer, L. (1995). *Sex is not a natural act, and other essays*. Boulder, CO: Westview Press.

Tiefer, L. (1996). The medicalization of sexuality: Conceptual, normative, and professional issues. *Annual Review of Sex Research, 7*, 252-282.

Tiefer, L. (1999, October). "Female sexual dysfunction" alert: A new disorder is invented for women. *Sojourner: The Women's Forum*. p. 11.

Tiefer, L. (2000). Sexology and the pharmaceutical industry: The threat of co-optation. *Journal of Sex Research, 37*, 273-283.

Tiefer, L., and 21 others (2000). Letter to FDA regarding Docket No. OOD:1278, Draft Guidance: Female sexual dysfunction: Clinical development of drug products for treatment. Mailed in two parts, June 19, 2000 (12 co-signers), and July 10, 2000 (9 co-signers).

Tiefer, L. (2001a). The "consensus" conference on female sexual dysfunction: Conflicts of interest and hidden agendas. *Journal of Sex & Marital Therapy, 27*, 227-236.

Tiefer, L. (2001b, in press). The selling of "female sexual dysfunction." *Journal of Sex & Marital Therapy, 27*, pp. 625-628.

Tiefer, L. & Tavris, C. (1999, October 20). Viagra for women is the wrong Rx. *Los Angeles Times*, B9.

Travis, C. B. & White, J. W. (Eds.) (2000). *Sexuality, society, and feminism.* Washington, D. C.: American Psychological Association.

Ussher, J. M. & Baker, C. D. (Eds) (1993). *Psychological perspectives on sexual problems: New directions in theory and practice.* New York: Routledge.

Valverde, M. (1985). *Sex, power and pleasure.* Toronto: The Women's Press.

Vance, C. S. (Ed.) (1984). *Pleasure and danger: Exploring female sexuality.* Boston: Routledge & Kegan Paul.

Virag, R., Bouilly, P. Daniel, C. & Virag, H. (1984). Intracavernous injection of papaverine and other vasoactive drugs: A new era in the diagnosis and treatment of impotence. In Virag, R. & Virag-Lappas, H. (eds.) *Proceedings of the first world meeting on impotence.* Paris: Les Editions due CERI., pp. 187-194.

Wagner, G. & Kaplan, H. S. (1993). *The new injection treatment for impotence: Medical and psychological aspects.* New York: Brunner/Mazel.

Zamora, D. (2000, October 26). Medical definition of women's sexual problems leaves a lot to be desired. WWW.CBSHealthWatch.com.

Embodying Orgasm:
Gendered Power Relations
and Sexual Pleasure

Stevi Jackson
Sue Scott

SUMMARY. In this paper we discuss the potential for developing a feminist approach to women's sexual embodiment via an exploration of heterosexual sexuality. We contest both pre-social, biological accounts of sexuality and supra-social accounts: those that fail to locate desire and pleasure in their social context. In so doing we seek to avoid more abstract forms of social constructionism by analysing gendered, sexual bodies in interaction and bodies as located in material social relations and practices. In focusing on sexual pleasure we will contest dis-embodied, asocial formulations of desire and consider how desire and pleasure may be reflexively understood in the context of everyday/everynight sexual practices. Taking orgasm as a paradigmatic case, we will consider the relationships between the ways in which women's orgasm is conventionally represented and the social construction of "faked" and "authentic" orgasms. *[Article copies available for a fee from The Haworth Document Delivery Service: 1-800-HAWORTH. E-mail address: <getinfo@haworthpressinc.com> Website: <http://www.HaworthPress.com> © 2001 by The Haworth Press, Inc. All rights reserved.]*

Stevi Jackson is Professor of Women's Studies and Director of the Centre for Women's Studies at the University of York.

Sue Scott is Professor of Sociology at the University of Durham UK.

Address correspondence to: Prof. Stevi Jackson, Centre for Women's Studies, University of York, Heslington, York YO10 5DD, UK (E-mail: sfj3@york.ac.uk).

[Haworth co-indexing entry note]: "Embodying Orgasm: Gendered Power Relations and Sexual Pleasure." Jackson, Stevi, and Sue Scott. Co-published simultaneously in *Women & Therapy* (The Haworth Press, Inc.) Vol. 24, No. 1/2, 2001, pp. 99-110; and: *A New View of Women's Sexual Problems* (ed: Ellyn Kaschak, and Leonore Tiefer) The Haworth Press, Inc., 2001, pp. 99-110. Single or multiple copies of this article are available for a fee from The Haworth Document Delivery Service [1-800-HAWORTH, 9:00 a.m. - 5:00 p.m. (EST). E-mail address: getinfo@haworthpressinc.com].

KEYWORDS. Women's sexuality, gender, power relations, orgasm, embodiment

In this paper we explore some preconditions for developing a feminist approach to gendered embodiment via an exploration of heterosexual desire and pleasure. We argue for a conceptualization of sexuality as fully social, neither biologically based nor simply a product of the psyche. We treat sexual pleasure as socially mediated, and embodied sexual selves as reflexively constructed and reconstructed through social interaction within specific social settings. Taking orgasm as a paradigmatic case, we will argue that even this most personal and physical experience is always also social and should be understood in the context of everyday/everynight sexual practices. We will begin by outlining our perspective on gender and sexuality and then move on to raise some general points about the conceptualization of gendered and sexual embodiment. In addressing the shortcomings of other influential accounts of desire and pleasure, we argue for a sociological approach to bodily pleasures before concentrating more specifically on orgasm.

GENDER AND SEXUALITY

We are treating both gender and sexuality as analytically distinct although empirically interrelated. Whereas gender refers to the social division and distinction between women and men, sexuality denotes what is socially defined as of erotic significance. We see both gender and sexuality, then, as socially constructed. The term "social construction" is sometimes used to refer only to the realm of meaning, to discursive or cultural constructions, but our conceptualization is broader, additionally encompassing social structure, social relations and everyday social practices or interaction (see Scott, Jackson and Backett-Milburn, 1998; Jackson, 1999). We also distance ourselves from any perspective that treats biological "sex differences" or bodily functions as given, as pre-social "facts." There is no biological sex, only socio-cultural gender in that the recognition of "sex differences" is always a social act (Kessler and McKenna, 1978). It is social gender that enables us to "see" biological sex: the hierarchical division of gender "transforms an anatomical difference (which is itself devoid of significance) into a relevant distinction for social practice" (Delphy, 1984, p. 144). It follows from this that we would resist any perspective reducing sexuality to reproduction or to those anatomical features defined as male or female.

We use the term gender to denote all aspects of the social division and cultural distinction between women and men, female and male, masculine and feminine. In so doing we avoid the conceptual slippage between "sex" as differences between men and women and "sex" as an erotic activity. This conflation of gender and sexuality is common in everyday thinking and has also been evident in the influence of psychoanalytic thought on feminism, since psychoanalysis explicitly ties our existence as sexed (gendered) subjects to our sexual being. Further confusion can occur when the gendered body is read as the sexual body, when a woman's body, disciplined into a sexually "attractive" appearance and demeanor, is equated with "female sexuality" (see, e.g., Coward, 1982). The performance of sexual desirability may have little or nothing to do with autonomous desires and the practice of pleasure, hence the need to differentiate between the sexualization of women's bodies and women's sexual embodiment. The sexualized body is often a passive body, looked at or acted upon; the sexual body implies more, a body capable of sensual pleasure, a body which, in experiencing desire and pleasure, cannot be *just* a body abstracted from mind, self and social context.

SEXUAL EMBODIMENT AS SOCIAL EMBODIMENT

Here we find Gesa Lindemann's (1997) distinction between objectified, experiencing and experienced bodies helpful. The "objectified body" refers to a visible, observable entity moving through physical and social space (hence the objectified body in this sense is not one reduced to a sexual object). The "experiencing body" is the sensory body, experiencing the environment through sight, hearing, taste, touch, etc. The "experienced body" is our sense of our own bodies, the body through which we feel pleasure and pain, but also the body that we sometimes experience as simply an unobtrusive part of our being. The experiencing and experienced bodies together, for Lindemann (1997), constitute the "living body." While Lindemann sees the body in all three senses as having a physical materiality–a body that bleeds when it is cut, can be seen to bleed, feels the pain of the wound and experiences that pain as its own–it is not simply a physical given, for the objectified body and living body are reflexively linked. The objectified body is not just there to be perceived; how it is perceived affects how the living body is experienced and vice versa. Gender is not, therefore, already "there" as a property of the physical body, but is a product of gendered assumptions, which enable us to "see" the objectified body and experience the living body as gendered.

In adapting Lindemann's account to our own sociological analysis, we would view the construction of gendered bodies as a product of social division and social interaction, a process that depends on socially and historically specific understandings of one's own and others' bodies. Extending this to sexuality allows us sexual bodies as gendered bodies interacting in social and physical space. How the objectified body is defined as sexual, how it is sexualized (for example, divided into erogenous zones), may well affect how the sexual living body is experienced in the progress of a sexual encounter, which parts are brought into play, which stimuli are interpreted as pleasure. Similarly our lived sexual experiences may then act back upon the way the objectified body is perceived. Thus, for instance, our first experience of the pleasure of clitoral stimulation may bring into being a zone of the objectified body that may not have previously been significant. While this reflexive interplay is crucial to understanding our own experiences of the sexual and how they become felt and embodied, we must always be wary of presupposing these links when observing others' bodies. We cannot read off properties of the living body from the objectified body; an objectified body that looks "sexy" or "seductive" is not necessarily experienced as sexual.

Our own view of the bodies in general and of gendered and sexual bodies does not deny the physical reality of bodies–but bodies are not meaningful in themselves. We are always embodied in a social context, which profoundly affects both how we see our own and others' bodies and how we experience our actual embodiment. When we engage in sex with another person, it is not two abstract bodies that meet in some extra-social space, but embodied social beings who interact in a social context, bringing with them a good deal of cultural and biographical baggage deriving from their specific social locations and histories.

SEX AS A SOCIAL ACTIVITY

Sex is not a natural act (Tiefer,1995), but persuading others that sexuality is socially constructed is never easy. We are constantly faced with new variants of the idea that human sexuality lies somehow outside the social. The crudest form of resistance to social constructionism is biological determinism, locating sexuality as an inherent property of the human organism in which bodily, sexual gratification becomes a simple need. Here we are thought of as driven by biological imperatives–to reproduce or to perpetuate our genes.[1] This version sees sexuality as *pre*-social, capable of modification by social mores but nonetheless as essentially prior to the social. Yet alongside this, there are other commonsense understandings of sexuality, investing it with magical and romantic properties, with ideas of transcendence, with the belief that it can raise us above the mundane realities of quotidian existence. Here sexuality becomes *supra*-social. In everyday terms the pre-social and supra-social frequently overlap, so that sex can paradoxically be seen both as an expression of our animal natures and a means of discovering inner "truths" about our uniquely individual selves.

In academic analysis, however, there is a large gulf between evolutionary psychologists, with their end-driven view of human sexuality, and those interested in exploring the realms of human desire as potentially subversive of the social order. In this latter view sexuality is certainly not a product of biological imperatives–desire is in excess of the functional requirements of bodily and species needs and irreducible to physiological processes. It is this version of sexuality as supra-social that appears in some feminist accounts of the sexual body, leading to a view of bodies abstracted from any social context. Elizabeth Grosz (1995), for example, sees desire as more than an interaction between lovers or an exchange of physical intimacies:

> Erotic desire . . . is a mode of surface contact with things and substances, with a world, that engenders and induces transformations, intensifications, a becoming something other. Not simply a rise and fall, a waxing and waning, but movement, processes, transformations. That is what constitutes the appeal and power of desire, its capacity to shake up, rearrange, reorganize the body's forms and substances, to make subject and body as such into something else, something other than what they are habitually . . . desire need not, indeed commonly does not, culminate in sexual intercourse but in production . . . the production of sensations never felt, alignments never thought, energies never tapped, regions never known. (1995, pp. 294-5)

Despite its quasi-orgasmic stylistic crescendo, Grosz's depiction of desire is usually read as a means of disrupting the mechanistic, end-driven model of the sexual encounter inevitably culminating in orgasm. Annie

Potts (2000) takes Grosz's ideas as suggestive of a fluid desire beyond the social that might free sex from the orgasmic imperative. These writers seem to be harking back to the old libertarian idea that sexuality itself is non-social and simply repressed by the social, that the goal of liberation is to unchain it from the shackles of civilization. We are arguing that there can be no sexuality freed from the social. If we are seeking to change current sexual practices we cannot do so by disembedding them from the social, but only by changing the social contexts and relations that currently shape them.

We too would like to question the current everyday construction of sex as a linear process culminating in orgasm, but from a more sociological perspective relating this construction to the social contexts in which it is produced. Elsewhere we have explored this in terms of the relationship between sexuality and modernity (Scott and Freeman, 1995; Jackson and Scott, 1997). We suggest that modern ideas about sexuality draw upon metaphors of labor, skill and productivity, so that heterosexual encounters are seen as a linear rationalized process–"a series of stages to be gone through before the final output: foreplay leading to coitus culminating in orgasm" (Jackson and Scott, 1997, p. 560). Feminists (and increasingly safe sex educators) have called for a less linear focus, which values non-penetrative and non-orgasmic pleasures. Yet, despite the more recent post-modern discourse of flexibility, the structure of the sexual encounter has proved resistant to disruption (Holland, Ramazanoglu, Sharpe and Thomson, 1998; Langford, 1999; Duncombe and Marsden, 1996). There has, however, been an increasing acceptance of the need for re-skilling, especially for men, and, in media representations at least, a shift from the focus on "his" orgasm to a more equal opportunities approach. However, in the main, the emphasis is still on orgasm as endpoint and highpoint. What we are arguing is that sexual change is gradual and closely linked to wider material social and cultural changes. If understandings of sexual pleasure are beginning to be re-framed though post-modern ideas of malleability and flexibility, then we need to understand this as a social process rather than as liberation from the social. These changes are illustrative of the particular ways in which sexuality is socially constructed. Our understanding of this process will be helped neither by an ahistorical focus on orgasm as a simple bodily reflex which we are hard wired to seek out, nor by a reification of sexuality as desire beyond the physical body–as a mystical, transcendental, individual experience which is immensely significant but beyond explanation. We need rather to develop analyses which enable us to understand both pre-social and supra-social accounts as themselves products of the social.

THE GENDERING OF ORGASM

We are interested then in the social meanings given to orgasm, and indeed to embodiment more generally, and take it as axiomatic that these meanings will be gendered. This stance differs from much current writing on sexuality which tends to slip and slide between seeing meaning as inherent in bodies and meaning floating free of bodies. Even those committed to an understanding of the social world as discursively constituted can sometimes see bodily events as significant in themselves. For example, in his discussion of pornography, Pasi Falk (1994) tells us that male bodies evidentially signify arousal/pleasure through erection and ejaculation. Here the "lack" of physical signs in women is represented as problematic; hence the necessity for women in pornographic movies to "act" desire and pleasure. This also reduces male sexuality to an unproblematic bodily reflex, to which some theorists of masculinity and male sexuality might object (see Reynaud, 1983).

Indeed even some feminist writers imply that the male definition of orgasm is somehow built into men's bodies. Describing models such as the Masters and Johnson sexual response cycle (arousal, plateau, orgasm, resolution), Annie Potts comments: "This tumescence and detumescence deemed to be characteristic of the 'natural' course of sex is inevitably more consistent with a male (penis)-centred version of sexual experience" (Potts, 2000: 61). But why? Certainly we should question the accepted sequence which is seen to constitute "the sex act" and which ends with (his) orgasm. But this is not the same thing as arguing that penetration is intrinsically "male" or that orgasm itself, or physiological responses preceding or following from it, is somehow given by possession of a penis. The current masculine meanings associated with the sequencing of sexual acts and orgasm itself are not given by male sexual anatomy and physiology, but are the product of culturally ordered meanings embedded in particular social practices (Scott and Freeman, 1995; Jackson and Scott, 1997). The meanings of orgasm derive from social, not biological, contexts–including the meanings conventionally given to physiological processes. That a ridiculous degree of significance is accorded to a small quantity of body fluid–with the consequent equation of coming and 'cum' with what is ejaculated from the penis–is a matter of social definition. It has nothing whatsoever to do with the intrinsic characteristics of ejaculation. Indeed it has been argued that the "myth of the phallic orgasm," the reduction of orgasm to ejaculation, is the product of a particular construction of male sexuality (Reynaud 1983).

Orgasm is not a self-evident bodily event in either men or women–it only seems more so in men because of the easy equation made between ejaculation and orgasm. Physiologically orgasm is simply a reflex, of no more social significance than any other reflex. Physical reflexes, including orgasm, happen in women's bodies, too. However, women rarely describe orgasm in purely physical terms–it has become bound up with mystical ideas of ecstasy and transcendence and associated with the romantic trappings of love and intimacy (Potts, 2000; Roberts, Kippax, Waldby and Crawford, 1995). Women may thus unwittingly collude in the social definition of their orgasms as somehow more mysterious than those of men.

THE MYSTERIOUS ORGASM

There is a strong tradition of treating women's pleasure as mysterious and unrepresentable–especially in psychoanalysis. The most infamous version of this is Lacan's (1982) notion of a female *jouissance* beyond the phallus, beyond language, beyond–even–knowledge of those experiencing it. Yet while Lacan claims that women cannot know their pleasure, his all-seeing eye can immediately discern evidence of it. Referring to a statue of the medieval mystic, Teresa of Avila he says: "You only have to go and look at Bernini's statue in Rome to understand immediately that she is coming, there is no doubt about it" (1982:147).

Lacan's deduction of an embodied event/experience from the evidence of other bodily signs is highly conventional. (His account, we're convinced, is that of a man who has never encountered a woman actually having an orgasm). He can immediately see "that she is coming" because he is interpreting a particular set of cultural insignia–manifested not by a material embodied woman, but by a statue, by another *man's* representation of a woman in a state of ecstasy: the head thrown back, the eyes closed, the lips parted, etc. What we have here are the conventions by which female ecstasy is routinely represented, which may or may not bear any relation to the embodied experience of orgasm. We would suggest that a sociological understanding of women's pleasure and the difficulty of representing it should take quite other paths. First, we must recognise that women's pleasure *is* very commonly represented in certain conventional ways. The modern version is not too distant from Bernini's except that it involves a lot of writhing and sound effects (now, after all, we have movies). Among the best-known versions is the scene from the film *When Harry Met Sally,* in which Sally demonstrates that orgasm can be convincingly faked by "performing" one in the very public setting of a diner. Many of us who live in apartments with poor soundproofing will have heard very similar, standardized performances.

These conventional representations have real effects–not least that they teach every woman how to fake an orgasm and perhaps how to have a convincingly 'authentic' one. We learn from such representations how to have an orgasm, how to signal an internal embodied event to a partner (and perhaps the whole neighborhood!), how to understand a partner's responses as an orgasm. We learn how having an orgasm is done and how to 'do' orgasm. This performance may be what makes an orgasm 'real' for ourselves and our lovers. The performance is, of course, highly gendered.

MAKING A PERFORMANCE OF IT

It is women who are expected to have audible orgasms in keeping with the idea that their orgasms are invisible and that, therefore, there is a need to provide "evidence" of it comparable to the "physical" evidence read off from men's bodily secretions. Men make a mess; women make a noise. Male orgasm is also seen as "natural" and inevitable, but that of women requires work and, in keeping with the idea of female sexual passivity and male sexual expertise, women's bodies need to be *worked on* by the male virtuoso in order to produce orgasm (Jackson and Scott, 1997; Roberts et al., 1995). Given the supposed invisibility of women's orgasm, this creates a need to show that it has happened as an affirmation of male performance. "The demand for noise . . . indicates that heterosexuality becomes an economy in which the woman's orgasm is exchanged for the man's work" (Roberts et al., 1995, p. 528).

Yet this also indicates the importance of orgasm itself, the cultural significance it has acquired as the "peak" of sexual experience, whether this is understood in mystical terms or in the clinical language of sexology (Potts, 2000). An absence of orgasm signifies a failed or incomplete sexual event, one which has not reached its proper conclusion. Its absence in a woman represents her failure, but may also reflect on her partner's "flawed" technique; its presence, given that women's orgasms are thought difficult to attain, means he can take pride in his skill. Hence she is under pressure on her to reassure him, to provide evidence for her orgasm or, if necessary to fake it: her orgasm "must not remain invisible; something must mark where it *comes* in–there must be a *show per se*" (Potts, 2000, p. 66, her emphasis).

Although deemed elusive, women's orgasm, once achieved, should properly be spectacular.

> (C)ultural representations of women's orgasm as overwhelmingly pleasurable and, therefore, loud are common in women's popular magazines and pornography . . . For indeed faking orgasm can only work because of this representation–it is far easier to make a bit of noise than, for example, to fake a vaginal spasm! (Roberts et al., 1995, p. 528)

These performances must be finely judged. Roberts and her collaborators suggest that an overly theatrical and extravagant display is likely to be read as faked, that a more subtle performance is more convincing. Their data indicate that women are expert at this deception in that most women in their sample admitted faking it on occasion, while few men thought that they had ever been with a partner who had faked. Roberts et al. argue that while faking orgasm reaffirms women as passive recipients of men's expert performances, it also requires their activity in "using their minds to perform (being) the body!" (1995, p. 530).

All this talk of faking raises the question of the 'real' or 'authentic' orgasm. What we would suggest is that similar performances might accompany both. If women feel the need to reassure their male partner of the adequacy of his performance, that felt need will persist whether or not a woman 'really' experiences orgasm. Moreover, we need also to ask what makes an orgasm a 'real' experience, what turns a simple reflex into an erotically significant event? We need to ask how "canonical orgasmic insignia . . . actually 'get into' and inform real lines of erotic conduct" (DeNora, 1997: 44), how cultural understandings of orgasm become embodied, manifested and reworked through social practice. We suggest that this should be understood as a reflexive process, accomplished in given social contexts, through which our embodied selves are continually constructed and reconstructed.[2] Experience is never given in a raw form, but always (re)constructed by us through the cultural resources available to us. As Annie Potts's (2000) data suggests, the meanings of orgasm are extremely complex for both women and men, yet rely on culturally specific interpretations of it as the ulti-mate or peak sexual experience. Hence it can become imbued with all manner of mystical and emotional connotations, creating a space for the construction of gendered understandings of what orgasm is.

NOTES

1. Do not be fooled into thinking that this is a view that no one of importance takes seriously. In its latest incarnation, as evolutionary psychology, this perspective has be-come highly influential, ensconced in respectable academic institutions and embraced by influential government advisors–at least in Britain (see Cameron, 1997/8).

2. We have explored this process in more detail elsewhere (see Jackson and Scott, 2001).

REFERENCES

Cameron, D. (1997/8) "Back to nature," *Trouble & Strife*, 36, pp. 6-15.

Coward, R. (1982) *Female Desire*. London: Paladin.

Delphy, C. (1984) *Close to Home: A Materialist Analysis of Women's Oppression*. London: Hutchinson.

DeNora, T. (1997) "Music and erotic agency–sonic resources and socio-sexual ac-tion," *Body and Society*, 3 (2), pp. 43-65.

Duncombe, J. and Marsden, D. (1996) "Whose orgasm is it anyway? 'Sex work' in long-term heterosexual couple relationships," in J. Weeks and J. Holland (eds) *Sex-ual Cultures*. London: Macmillan.

Falk, P. (1994) *The Consuming Body*. London: Sage.

Grosz, E. (1995) "Animal sex" in E. Grosz and E. Probyn (eds) *Sexy Bodies*. New York: Routledge.

Holland, J. Ramazanoglu, C. Sharpe, S. and Thomson, R. (1998) *The Male in the Head: Young People, Heterosexuality and Power*. London: The Tufnell Press.

Jackson, S. and Scott, S. (1997) "Gut reactions to matters of the heart: Reflections on rationality, irrationality and sexuality," *Sociological Review* 45 (4), pp. 551-575.

Jackson, S. and Scott, S. (2001) "Putting the body's feet on the ground: Towards a so-ciological reconception of gendered and sexual embodiment," in K. Backett-Milburn and L. McKie (eds) *Constructing Gendered Bodies*. London: Macmillan.

Kessler, S. J. and McKenna, W. (1978) *Gender: An Ethnomethodological Approach*. New York: Wiley

Lacan, J. (1982) "God and the *Jouissance* of the Woman," in J. Mitchell and J. Rose (eds) *Feminine Sexuality*. Basingstoke: Macmillan.

Langford, W. (1999) *Revolutions of the Heart: Gender, Power and the Delusions of Love*. London: Routledge.

Lindemann, G. (1997) "The body of gender difference," in K. Davis (ed.) *Embodied Practices: Feminist Perspectives on the Body*. London: Sage.

Mead, G. H. (1934) *Mind, Self and Society*. Chicago: University of Chicago Press.

Potts, A. (2000) "Coming, coming, gone: A feminist deconstruction of heterosexual orgasm," *Sexualities*, 3 (1), pp. 55-76.

Reynaud, E. (1983) *Holy Virility*. London: Pluto Press.

Roberts, C., Kippax, S., Waldby, C. and Crawford, J. (1995) "Faking it: The story of 'Ohh!,'" *Women's Studies International Forum*, 18 (5-6), pp. 523-32.

Scott, S. and Freeman, R. (1995) "Prevention as a problem of modernity: The case of AIDS," in J. Gabe (ed.) *Risk, Health and Illness*. Oxford: Blackwell.

Scott, S., Jackson, S. and Backett-Milburn, K. (1998) "Swings and roundabouts: Risk anxiety and the everyday worlds of children," *Sociology*, 32 (4): 689-705.

Tiefer, L. (1995) *Sex Is Not a Natural Act and Other Essays*. Boulder, CO: Westview Press.

A New Paradigm
for Women's Sexual Orientation:
Implications for Therapy

Linda D. Garnets
Letitia Anne Peplau

SUMMARY. This paper critiques old models of women's sexual orientation that viewed heterosexuality as the norm for mental health, characterized lesbians as masculinized sexual "inverts," and looked to biology to explain the development of homosexuality. A new paradigm for women's sexual orientation is presented. This paradigm emphasizes the importance of the social context and recognizes the multiple pathways that can lead a woman to identify as lesbian, bisexual or heterosexual. In addition, the main components of sexual orientation are considered as is the potential fluidity of women's sexuality. Throughout, implications of the new paradigm for psychotherapy with women are considered. *[Article copies available for a fee from The Haworth Document Delivery Service: 1-800-HAWORTH. E-mail address: <getinfo@haworthpressinc.com> Website: <http://www.HaworthPress.com> © 2001 by The Haworth Press, Inc. All rights reserved.]*

Linda D. Garnets and Letitia Anne Peplau are affiliated with the University of California, Los Angeles.

Address correspondence to either: Linda D. Garnets or Letitia Anne Peplau at the UCLA Psychology Department, 1285 Franz Hall, Los Angeles, CA 90095-1563 (E-mail: lgarnets@ ucla.edu or lapeplau@ucla.edu).

The authors thank Barrie Levy for her valuable comments on an earlier draft of this article.

[Haworth co-indexing entry note]: "A New Paradigm for Women's Sexual Orientation: Implications for Therapy." Garnets, Linda D., and Letitia Anne Peplau. Co-published simultaneously in *Women & Therapy* (The Haworth Press, Inc.) Vol. 24, No. 1/2, 2001, pp. 111-121; and: *A New View of Women's Sexual Problems* (ed: Ellyn Kaschak, and Leonore Tiefer) The Haworth Press, Inc., 2001, pp. 111-121. Single or multiple copies of this article are available for a fee from The Haworth Document Delivery Service [1-800-HAWORTH, 9:00 a.m. - 5:00 p.m. (EST). E-mail address: getinfo@haworthpressinc.com].

111

KEYWORDS. Homosexuality, sexual orientation, lesbian, bisexual, psychotherapy, women

In the past 50 years, scientific research has challenged many widespread beliefs about women's sexual orientation and has led therapists to reconsider their own assumptions about women's sexuality. Three important models of women's sexual orientation have failed to be supported by research. Today, therapists and their professional associations reject an "illness model" which suggested that heterosexuals are normal and mentally healthy, but homosexuals are abnormal and impaired in their psychological functioning (see review by Gonsiorek, 1991). Instead, an affirmative approach to practice has emerged that focuses on helping lesbians, gay men, and bisexuals to cope adaptively with the impact of stigma, minority status, and difference from the heterosexual mainstream (see the Guidelines for Psychotherapy with Lesbian, Gay, and Bisexual Clients that were adopted in 2000 by the American Psychological Association Council of Representatives).

Second, research has also debunked the "inversion model" which suggested that heterosexual women are feminine in their physiology, personality and attractions to men and that lesbians are sexual inverts, women who are masculine in their physiology, personality, and attraction to women (see review by Peplau, 2001; Peplau, Spalding, Conley & Veniegas, 1999). Empirical studies show that there is no intrinsic association between gender conformity and women's sexuality; masculinity and femininity are linked to sexual orientation in some social contexts but not in others.

Third, despite the popularity of speculations about "gay genes" and "gay brains," scientific research has not provided convincing evidence for biological models of women's sexual orientation (see review by Veniegas & Conley, 2000). At most, biological factors play only a minor and indirect role in the development of women's sexual orientation.

Today, scientific evidence points toward a significant paradigm shift in conceptualizing women's sexual orientation (see Peplau & Garnets, 2000a). An important starting point is evidence that the nature and development of sexual orientation are different for women and men (e.g., Garnets & Kimmel, 1991). When theorists generalize about both sexes, they tend to take male experience as the norm and may ignore unique aspects of women's sexuality. Consequently, the new paradigm puts women's experiences at center stage. In this article, we outline the key elements of the new paradigm and consider implications for therapy.

THE IMPORTANCE OF THE SOCIAL CONTEXT

Old paradigms viewed women's sexual orientation as a core attribute of the individual, largely unaffected by the social context. The new paradigm recognizes that the patterning of women's erotic and romantic attractions is profoundly influenced by the historical, cultural, and social context of women's lives (Garnets & Peplau, 2000; Peplau & Garnets, 2000b). Three examples highlight the importance of contextual influences.

First, social responses to women with same-gender attractions and relationships vary widely. In 18th century America, passionate friendships between women flourished and were socially acceptable (Faderman, 1981). Today, sexual prejudice against lesbian and bisexual women is widespread and may come not only from strangers but from friends, co-workers, neighbors and family members. Ethnic minority lesbian and bisexual women may experience prejudice from both mainstream society and from their own ethnic communities (Garnets & Kimmel, 1991).

Second, social and economic circumstances influence women's opportunities to consider same-gender relationships. It is easier for women to avoid heterosexual marriage and form relationships with women when they are financially independent and have the support of lesbian or feminist communities. As one example, in America today, education is an important predictor of whether a woman identifies as lesbian/bisexual or heterosexual. Completing college is associated with a 900 percent increase in the percentage of women identifying as lesbian/bisexual (from 0.4% of women high school graduates to 3.6% of college graduates; Laumann, Gagnon, Michael, & Michaels, 1994, p. 305).

Third, just as social customs dictate typical scripts for heterosexual dating and marriage, so too lesbian and bisexual communities shape the form of same-gender relationships. For example, among some working class communities in the 1950s, relations between women were structured around distinctions between "butch" and "femme" partners (Davis & Kennedy, 1989). For many women in the 1970s, there was a close connection between being lesbian and being feminist, and a corresponding emphasis on equality in love relationships. In the late 1980s and 1990s, a bisexual women's community emerged that defined bisexual identity not as a combination of attractions to women and men, but as an attraction to individuals regardless of their gender (Rust, 2000).

In working with clients, therapists need to understand the particular historical period and cultural context in which they have grown, developed, lived, and worked (Reid, 1995). For example, a young woman dealing with being lesbian today faces an entirely different set of social attitudes and opportunities than a woman who grew up in the 1930s or 1960s. She has grown up in an era when sexual orientation is discussed by the media, when many colleges have resource centers to assist lesbian, gay, bisexual and transgender students, and when the internet provides easy access to a wide range of information. Many cities have visible gay, lesbian, and bisexual communities and activities. At a young age, she may have learned about the legal and social advances resulting from the gay/lesbian civil rights and feminist social movements. As a result, she may feel less stigma about being lesbian and less need to hide her identity from family and friends. Indeed, she may be fairly open and assertive in revealing her sexual identity. In sharp contrast, older lesbians or bisexuals are more likely to have experienced their sexual identity formation as secretive, feared or stigmatized. Although older women can appreciate the historical changes of the past 40 years, their lives have been influenced by an earlier set of social arrangements. It is critically important that therapists consider their client's sexual identity in relation to the social and historical context in which it was formed.

Therapists must also incorporate in their work an understanding of how women's lives are shaped by social constraints and opportunities. For some women, the availability of a shared social identity is crucial. As one woman explained, "Early on I thought I was just gay, because I was not aware there was another category, bisexual. I always knew I was interested in men and women, but I did not realize there was a name for these feelings and behaviors until I took Psychology 101 and read about it, heard about it. That was in college" (Weinberg, Williams, & Pryor, 1994, p. 29). The recognition that there was a "name" for her feelings enabled this woman to identify as bisexual. In therapy, a woman might express great anxiety about the possibility that she is bisexual. In working with this woman, it is important to remember that, until very recently, bisexuality was regarded as a behavior without an identity and that bisexual people did not have an active, visible community where they could feel accepted and understood. This, in turn, has constrained many women from defining their sexual desires and behaviors as part of a bisexual sexual identity (Reynolds & Hanjorgiris, 2000).

SEXUAL ATTRACTION, BEHAVIOR AND IDENTITY CAN BE VARIED AND INCONSISTENT

It is popular belief that individuals can be readily categorized as heterosexual, homosexual, or perhaps bisexual. In fact, human experience often defies such clear-cut categories. At least three distinct components or dimensions of sexual orientation should be distinguished. Sexual attraction, the affective dimension, refers to an individual's feelings of desire and love for a same-gender or other-gender person. The behavioral dimension includes not only sexual behavior but also the formation of an intimate relationship with another person. Both attraction and behavior can be thought of as continua, ranging from exclusively same-gender to exclusively other-gender. Finally, sexual identity refers to an individual's self-categorization as lesbian, bisexual, or heterosexual. Identity can have both a private form, based on a woman's personal sexual identity, and a public form, based on how she presents herself to others.

Some women report complete consistency among these various components. For instance, a woman might identify as lesbian, be attracted exclusively to women, and have sex only with women partners. However, exceptions to this pattern of consistency are common. A woman may experience strong attractions to both men and women but identify as heterosexual rather than bisexual. A woman may identify as lesbian or bisexual, but not engage in same-gender sexual behavior. A woman who identifies as a lesbian might develop a strong attraction to a man. A heterosexual woman may employ homoerotic fantasies when having sex with her male partner.

The new paradigm rejects the view that sexual orientation is a universal attribute of individuals. Instead, sexual identity is conceptualized as "an individual's enduring sense of self as a sexual being that fits a culturally created category and accounts for one's sexual fantasies, attractions, and behavior" (Savin-Williams, 1995, p. 166). This definition acknowledges that the experiences of women are diverse rather than uniform. Further, to the extent that sexual identities are based on cultural categories, these categories may change over time. In recent years, younger generations of sexual minority women have adopted diverse and newly constructed self-identifications, including queer, lesbian-identified bisexual, bisensual, polyamorous, and bisexual lesbian (e.g., Rust, 1996). It is equally important to recognize that some women prefer to avoid labels that may not capture their unique sexuality (Diamond, 1998). What are the therapeutic implications of the diverse patterns of association among women's attractions, behavior and identity?

One implication is that therapists should not draw conclusions about a client's sexual orientation based on information about a single dimension. Rather, practitioners should strive to understand how these various dimensions interact and how the client interprets her own life experiences. The aim of therapy should be to encourage each woman to develop an identity that represents her personal sexuality at a given point in time and within the social and political context. Special sensitivity is required in working with bisexual women. Therapists should avoid thinking of a woman who describes herself as bisexual as actually in a "phase" moving toward a lesbian identity. Bisexuality is not necessarily a transitional stage. Further, some bisexual women experience enormous social pressure from peers to identify as lesbian. Therapists should be careful not to push a client into any of the existing sexual identity categories.

THE FLUIDITY OF WOMEN'S SEXUALITY AND SEXUAL ORIENTATION

There is growing evidence that women's sexuality tends to be fluid, malleable, and capable of change over time (see Baumeister, 2000; Peplau & Garnets, 2000a). This point is sometimes made in comparison to men, whose sexuality and sexual orientation are viewed as less flexible and more automatic. One sign of erotic flexibility is that some women are attracted to and have relationships with both men and women. In addition, women's sexual behavior and sexual identity can vary over their lifespan.

Old views assumed that sexual identity is established by young adulthood and is then fixed and unchanging. New empirical findings present a very different picture. Female sexual development is a potentially continuous, lifelong process in which multiple changes in sexual orientation are possible (Diamond, 1998). Women who have had exclusively heterosexual experiences may develop an attraction to other women, and vice versa. Consequently, acquiring a sexual identity has been redefined as "an ongoing process of attempting to maintain an accurate self-description of one's sexuality in a world of sexual meanings that vary over time and across context" (Rust, 1996, p. 10). It is important to emphasize that the capacity for erotic fluidity does *not* mean that most women will actually exhibit change over time. At an early age, many women adopt enduring patterns of other-sex or same-gender relating. To the extent that the social influences acting on a woman remain constant, there is little reason to expect change. Nonetheless, some women do show patterns of change over time.

Therapists must remember that women who think they have already finished acquiring their sexual identity may find changes in their sexual feelings and behaviors to be very confusing. Consider a client who reports that for the first part of her life, she was married and defined herself as heterosexual. At age 45, she has recently fallen in love with a woman and now sees herself as a lesbian. How are the therapist and the client to conceptualize these changes and what alternative interpretations might be possible? One interpretation is that the woman has finally recognized her "true" sexual identity as a lesbian. This, in fact, is how some women interpret that experience. An alternative interpretation is that the woman's sexual orientation has changed. Using this approach, the therapist could encourage a woman to think of these changes in her attractions and identity as a part of an ongoing process of sexual discovery and reassure the client that some people do change their sexual identities over the course of their lives (Rust, 1996). As Schneider reminds us, "it is misleading for the therapist to assume that any one person's sexual and affectional orientation will remain static over their lifetime, or to assume, when there are shifts in sexual orientation, that one orientation is necessarily more authentic than the other" (in press, p. 116).

MULTIPLE PATHWAYS TO THE DEVELOPMENT OF SEXUAL ORIENTATION

Although some might relish the simplicity of identifying the "gay gene" or single formative experience that leads one woman to be heterosexual and another to be lesbian, reality is far more complex. Recent research leads to a view of sexual orientation as multiply determined by many influences. No single factor reliably predicts whether a woman will embark on a path toward heterosexuality, homosexuality, bisexuality or some other pattern. For example, some youthful tomboys who like so-called masculine games and activities grow up to become lesbians, but *most* become heterosexuals. In addition, there are multiple developmental pathways leading to common outcomes (Diamond & Savin-Williams, 2000). Just as women become therapists for diverse personal reasons, so too, women may adopt the same sexual identity for distinctive reasons (Peplau & Garnets, 2000a). Women who identify as lesbian (or as bisexual or heterosexual) may have experienced quite different developmental trajectories. Indeed, knowing how a woman labels her sexual identity does not necessarily inform us about the pattern of her life experiences or the nature of her current erotic thoughts and feelings.

As therapists try to understand the antecedents of their client's sexual orientation, it is not useful to search for a single cause. Rather, clinicians should explore with their clients of all sexual orientations the multiple influences that may have affected the development of their sexual orientation.

Further, new research has challenged the adequacy of stage models of lesbian and gay sexual development. Such models have hypothesized a linear process involving a specific sequence of steps or stages moving toward the establishment of a stable identity as lesbian. In such models, all individuals who arrive at the end state of having a lesbian identity are assumed to have gone through the same sequence of events. Stage models have been useful in identifying such central developmental tasks as reorganizing one's self-concept, coping with the social stigma surrounding homosexuality, learning about and exploring lesbian and gay subcultures, and disclosing one's sexual identity to others. Nonetheless, stage models suffer from at least four limitations.

First, empirical research has clearly demonstrated that many sexual minority women do not follow the steps outlined in stage models (e.g., Diamond, 2000). Although sequential models may apply to the experiences of some women, they do not provide a general description of sexual identity development for most women. Second, stage models of homosexuality either fail to acknowledge the existence of bisexuality, or seem to suggest that women who adopt a bisexual identity or who prefer not to adopt any sexual identity label are psychologically "immature" (Rust, 1996). Third, stage models have taken the experiences of Euro-Americans as normative and have ignored the impact of race and culture on women's lives. This makes "their use with LGB people of color questionable if not inappropriate" (Reynolds & Hanjorgiris, 2000, p. 46).

A fourth problem is that stage models were derived from exclusively male samples and so tend to take male experiences as the norm (Savin-Williams, in press). A consequence is that these models may not do justice to the experiences of sexual minority women. For example, stage models tend to give prominence to sexual attraction and behavior. In contrast, for many lesbian and bisexual women, sexual orientation is not merely about sex, but more broadly about personal relationships. Increasingly, researchers have shown that love and intimacy are more important for understanding women's sexuality than men's sexuality (Peplau, 2001; Peplau & Garnets, 2000a). Regardless of their sexual orientation, women have been characterized as having a relational or partner-centered orientation to sexuality. As a result, sexual identity development and explorations of same-gender experiences may follow different developmental patterns in women and men.

In contrast to stage models, an emerging new perspective views the development of sexual identities as diverse and complex. Instead of a single step-by-step sequence, development may be nonlinear. Further, there are multiple trajectories for the development of a lesbian, gay, bisexual, or heterosexual identity (Peplau & Garnets, 2000a). The multiple pathways approach has implications for psychotherapy. First, therapists should not assume that a stage model is appropriate for all clients and should not try to fit each client's experiences of arriving at their current sexual identity into predetermined sequential stages. Practitioners should examine their own assumptions, for instance, that clients are "healthier" if they follow a specific developmental sequence and reach identity integration. Clinicians should also consider how race, ethnicity and culture may affect the experiences of sexual minority clients. For example, in some cultures, acquiring a nontraditional sexual identity may be perceived by a woman's family as a betrayal of her own people or a sign of assimilation into White mainstream culture. Moreover, when working with lesbian or bisexual clients, therapists should focus on relational aspects of their developmental process.

In conclusion, the new paradigm emphasizes the importance of recognizing the highly individualized and personal meanings of the process of arriving at a sexual identity for each person. Instead of focusing on assessing identity labels, therapists should attend to descriptive narratives of each client's actual feelings and behavior in different circumstances to understand the woman's unique developmental pathway and her personal interpretation of her sexual orientation.

REFERENCES

American Psychological Association. (2000). *Guidelines for psychotherapy with lesbian, gay, and bisexual clients*. Washington, DC: Author.

Baumeister, R. F. (2000). Gender differences in erotic plasticity: The female sex drive as socially flexible and responsive. *Psychological Bulletin, 126*, 347-374.

Davis, M., & Kennedy, E. L. (1989). Oral history and the study of sexuality in the lesbian community: Buffalo, New York, 1940-1960. In M. B. Duberman, M. Vicinus, & G. Chauncey (Eds.), *Hidden from history: Reclaiming the gay and lesbian past* (pp. 426-440). New York: New American Library.

Diamond, L. M. (1998). Development of sexual orientation among adolescent and young women. *Developmental Psychology, 34*, 1085-1095.

Diamond, L. M. (2000). Sexual identities, attractions, and behavior among young sexual-minority women over a two-year period. *Developmental Psychology, 36*, 241-250.

Diamond, L. M., & Savin-Williams, R. C. (2000). Explaining diversity in the development of same-sex sexuality among young women. *Journal of Social Issues, 56*(2), 297-313.

Faderman, L. (1981). *Surpassing the love of men*. New York: Morrow.

Garnets, L. D., & Kimmel, D. C. (1991). Lesbian and gay male dimensions in the psychological study of human diversity. In J. Goodchilds (Ed.), *Psychological perspectives on human diversity in America* (pp. 137-192). Washington, DC: American Psychological Association.

Garnets, L. D., & Peplau, L. A. (2000). Understanding women's sexualities and sexual orientations. *Journal of Social Issues, 56*(2), 181-192.

Gonsiorek, J. (1991). The empirical basis for the demise of the illness model of homosexuality. In J. Gonsiorek & J. Weinrich (Eds.), *Homosexuality: Research implications for public policy* (pp. 115-136). Newbury Park, CA: Sage.

Laumann, E. O., Gagnon, J. H., Michael, R. T., & Michaels, S. (1994). *The social organization of sexuality: Sexual practices in the United States*. Chicago, IL: University of Chicago Press.

Peplau, L. A. (2001). Rethinking women's sexual orientation: An interdisciplinary, relationship-focused approach. *Personal Relationships, 8*, in press.

Peplau, L. A., & Garnets, L. D. (2000a). A new paradigm for understanding women's sexuality and sexual orientation. *Journal of Social Issues, 56*(2), 329-350.

Peplau, L. A. & Garnets, L. D. (2000b). Women's sexualities: New perspectives on sexual orientation and gender. *Journal of Social Issues, 56*(2), whole number.

Peplau, L. A., & Spalding, L. R. (2000). The intimate relationships of lesbians, gays and bisexuals. In C. Hendrick & S. S. Hendrick (Eds.), *Close relationships: A sourcebook* (pp. 111-124). Thousand Oaks, CA: Sage.

Peplau, L. A., Spalding, L. R., Conley, T. D., & Veniegas, R. C. (1999). The development of sexual orientation in women. *Annual Review of Sex Research, 10*, 70-99.

Reid, J.R. (1995). Development in late life: Older lesbian and gay lives. In A. D'Augelli & C. Patterson (Eds.), *Lesbian, gay, and bisexual identities across the lifespan* (pp. 215-240). NY: Oxford University Press.

Reynolds, A. L., & Hanjorgiris, W. F. (2000). Coming out: Lesbian, gay, and bisexual development. In R. M. Perez, K. A. DeBord, & K. J. Bieschke (Eds), *Handbook of counseling and psychotherapy with lesbian, gay, and bisexual clients* (pp. 35-55). Washington, DC: American Psychological Association.

Rust, P. C. R. (1996). Managing multiple identities: Diversity among bisexual women and men. In B. A. Firestein (Ed.), *Bisexuality: The psychology and politics of an invisible minority* (pp. 53-83). Newbury Park, CA: Sage.

Rust, P. C. R. (2000). Bisexuality: A contemporary paradox for women. *Journal of Social Issues, 56*(2), 205-221.

Savin-Williams, R. C. (1995). Lesbian, gay male, and bisexual adolescents. In A. R. D'Augelli & C. J. Patterson (Eds.), *Lesbian, gay male, and bisexual identities over the life span*. New York: Oxford University Press.

Savin-Williams, R. C. (in press). Differential developmental trajectories. *Mom, Dad, I'm gay: How families negotiate coming out*. Washington, DC: American Psychological Association.

Schneider, M. J. (in press). Toward a reconceptualization of the coming-out process for adolescent females. In A. R. D'Augelli & C. J. Patterson (Eds.), *Lesbian, gay, and bisexual identities and youth: Psychological perspectives*. New York: Oxford University Press.

Veniegas, R. C., & Conley, T. D. (2000). Biological research on women's sexual orientations: Evaluating the evidence. *Journal of Social Issues, 56*(2), 267-282.

Weinberg, M. S., Williams, C. J., & Pryor, D. W. (1994). *Dual attraction: Understanding bisexuality*. New York: Oxford University Press.

On the Outside Looking In:
In Search of Women's Sexual Experience

Peggy J. Kleinplatz

SUMMARY. Predominant notions in our culture of sexuality per se and of female sexuality in particular obscure the discovery of alternate models. There is an absence of paradigms reflecting female sexuality and emerging out of women's experience. Women's life-cycle events, specifically pregnancy, childbirth and breastfeeding, are used as examples to illustrate how narrow definitions of sexuality prevent our society and our field from recognizing and appreciating the spectrum of female sexual experience. Such events have been sanitized and denuded of their sexual dimension, reduced to medical and reproductive events, thereby depriving us of an avenue for exploration of fully embodied, female sexuality. New models, more sensitive to phenomenological experience as well as to the contextual origins and nature of women's sexual difficulties, are required. The value of attending to women's voices in developing new models of female sexuality is emphasized. *[Article copies available for a fee from The Haworth Document Delivery Service: 1-800-HAWORTH. E-mail address: <getinfo@haworthpressinc.com> Website: <http://www.HaworthPress.com> © 2001 by The Haworth Press, Inc. All rights reserved.]*

KEYWORDS. Psychosexual behavior, feminism, pregnancy, lactation, childbirth, sexual function disturbances, female orgasm

Peggy J. Kleinplatz, PhD, is affiliated with the School of Psychology, University of Ottawa. Address correspondence to: Peggy J. Kleinplatz, PhD, 161 Frank Street, Ottawa, Ontario, K2P 0X4, Canada (E-mail: kleinpla@uottawa.ca).

[Haworth co-indexing entry note]: "On the Outside Looking In: In Search of Women's Sexual Experience." Kleinplatz, Peggy J. Co-published simultaneously in *Women & Therapy* (The Haworth Press, Inc.) Vol. 24, No. 1/2, 2001, pp. 123-132; and: *A New View of Women's Sexual Problems* (ed: Ellyn Kaschak, and Leonore Tiefer) The Haworth Press, Inc., 2001, pp. 123-132. Single or multiple copies of this article are available for a fee from The Haworth Document Delivery Service [1-800-HAWORTH, 9:00 a.m. - 5:00 p.m. (EST). E-mail address: getinfo@haworthpressinc.com].

123

How much do we know about the nature of women's sexual problems, sorrows and pain, as defined by women? What do we know about "normal" women's sexual feelings, behaviour and expression, let alone about optimal female sexuality? In trying to comprehend the entire spectrum of women's sexual phenomena, that is, sexual functioning, sexual events, relationships, issues and concerns, it is striking that the predominant vantage point is from the outside looking in. Female sexuality tends to be defined and studied in terms of male-dominated paradigms.

Women's subjective experience is conspicuously lacking from the popular and sexological discourses of female sexuality. The predominant belief systems obstruct the integration of this missing dimension into existing models as well as the discovery of new paradigms. The prevailing models and accompanying images come from three sources: The first of these is the conventional model of sexuality per se; the second is the conventional model of female sexuality in particular; the third is the infiltration of these ideas into sexology and especially into sex therapy. It is precisely this set of existing perspectives which eclipses women's sexual experience and impedes us from generating new paradigms.

THE CONVENTIONAL MODEL OF SEXUALITY

Conventional models of sexuality define sex as that which happens between the legs in bed (Christina, 1992), with an emphasis on heterosexual intercourse as the ultimate end of sex. This perspective tends to be fairly narrow, constricting, heterosexist, phallocentric and procreative. The presumptions in such a view come mostly out of (perceived) male sexual norms. It is easy to project male paradigms onto women because women are so rarely asked about their own sexual experiences.

The traditional model portrays part-objects operating mechanically, as in "insert tab A into slot B"(McCormick,1994) rather than whole beings encountering one another (Kleinplatz, 1996). Furthermore, the focus is on those parts most relevant for reproduction rather than sexual pleasure (Ash, 1982). For example, from the outset, children (at least those from homes progressive enough to name the genitals at all) are told either, "A boy has a penis and a girl doesn't," or "A boy has a penis and a girl has a vagina." They are taught about the body parts that are important for intercourse. What is missing is mention of the clitoris or even the vulva, that is, the parts of a girl's body most relevant for her pleasure (Federation of Feminist Women's Health Centres, 1991).The message communicated in the silence about the clitoris and vulva is that we need not have language to articulate our sexual experience, only words which correspond to male sexual functioning and which are necessary for reproduction. The failure to name aloud the parts of women's bodies most salient for pleasure sends a powerful injunction to girls: Don't talk about experience or desire.

THE CONVENTIONAL MODEL OF FEMALE SEXUALITY

Although it has become a cliché, images of female sexuality portraying woman as object rather than as subject remain ubiquitous. Cultural myths and stereotypes obscure our vision of female sexuality and prevent our society from discovering women's own realities. Even worse, being raised on a never-ending supply of alleged "truths" about female sexuality impedes women from exploring our inner worlds. (Similarly, myths about male sexuality may prevent men from fulfilling their own sexuality [Zilbergeld, 1992]).

Compounding the difficulty of connecting within and with one's partners in the face of overpowering myths, is the nature of these notions; double messages left over from the Victorian era still predominate (McCormick,1994). For example, the residual Madonna/whore imagery suggests that young women should be sexy but not overtly sexual; women are to be desirable but our desires are to be limited. "Sexy" women are portrayed stereotypically as simplistic Barbie dolls while "real" women are depicted as too complicated, not liking sex as much as the fantasy models do, not wanting "it" as often as men do, taking "too long" to have orgasms, "needing" to be romanced, and "needing" non-genital intimacy and touch. Each of the stereotypes is rife with the insinuation that these alleged characteristics are bad. Furthermore, it is implicit that all sexuality is to be judged by a standard which sets male sexuality (or at least our beliefs concerning men) as the norm. This perspective leaves the spectrum of women's (and perhaps men's) sexuality diminished and invisible, except as viewed through this severely limited prism.

The cultural context determines how women are freed to enjoy our own bodies as sexual or expected instead literally to mold our bodies and sexuality into the currently preferred model–to become whatever is in vogue. Women are alienated from within, distanced ironically by conventional sex scripts during precisely the events that could help to

ground us in our bodily sexuality. This effort reduces women to specta-
tors, never fully embodied.

MODELS OF WOMEN'S SEXUALITY IN SEX THERAPY

Sex therapy has its own conceptions of sexuality which parallel those of
our society. Here too, the focus is on coitus and orgasm. Problems are delineated in terms of obstacles to a biologically-based norm of intercourse
and tension release (i.e., Masters and Johnson's 1966 model of the Human
Sexual Response Cycle). The template projected onto female sexuality
comes from this male-defined norm (Ogden, 1994; Stock, 1988; Tiefer,
1991, 1996). Criteria for normal functioning emphasize objective, mechanical and physiological indices rather than subjective experience. As
such, sexual problems are identified in terms of deviations from normative,
heterosexual, performance standards with little attention to individual
uniqueness and inter- or intra-gender differences. There is no emphasis on
the intrapsychic, relational or socio-cultural contexts in which problems
are identified, diagnosed and treated. The subjective experience of self as a
sexual being has been obscured and designated irrelevant. Because of the
unexamined assumption that sexologists already know what is normal for
women, we have learned little about how women might identify what constitutes sexual experience, sexual problems, wishes, hopes, dreams or in
short, optimal sexual experience, expression or relations.

Women are often trained to view themselves from the outside instead
of being grounded in their own experience as sexual beings. This perspective may be reinforced in conventional sex therapy which often
pathologizes female sexual problems. Our perspective is at best periph-
eral to women's sexuality, given that women's subjective experience is
not featured in our paradigms. Predominant models of women's sexuality emphasize problems and perils rather than potential; regard major
life cycle changes as fraught with the possibility for trouble rather than
growth (Daniluk, 1998; Ussher, 1989); and fail to study, let alone appre-
hend and incorporate into new models, the nature of women's lived experience as sexual beings.

WOMEN'S LIFE-CYCLE EVENTS:
UNCHARTED SEXUAL TERRAIN

One surefire way of distancing women from their own sexual experience is by medicalizing women's bodies and life cycles. This promotes

disconnection within, which in turn makes women more susceptible to internalizing pronouncements from advertising, the media, the medical and mental health professions and more recently, the pharmaceutical industry.

Changes in women's bodies are seen as dangerous, volatile, evidence of instability and unpredictability, in need of control–not something to delight and revel in and to experience as an entry point to profound, erotic joy.

The medicalization and neutering of women's sexuality and bodily changes is not new (Masson, 1986). We laugh today at Victorian euphemisms like "in the family way" and "confinement" for pregnancy and labor, respectively, but how long has it been since "nymphomania," "hysteria" and "involutional melancholia" were removed from our official diagnostic nomenclature, the DSM? These classifications may have been eliminated but other terms such as "Postpartum Depression" and newer terms, such as "Premenstrual Dysphoric Disorder," "Menopausal Estrogen Deficiency" and "Self-defeating Personality Disorder" may be more modern ways of suggesting, "Why can't a woman be more like a man?" (Tavris, 1992).

The role of this reductionistic, clinical view in denying female sexuality is readily illustrated by examining our views of pregnancy, childbirth and breastfeeding. Our society in general and both medical and mental health professions tend to medicalize and simultaneously de-sexualize these events. The irony is that although reproduction is typically emphasized over sexuality when girls are taught about their future sex lives, for those women who do procreate, even this experience is sterilized of all sexual traces. Motherhood is made asexual (Weisskopf, 1980). Although a small, but steady steam of articles (cf., Newton, 1973; Rossi, 1973) has attempted to highlight and reverse the twentieth century trend to denude reproduction of its sexual components, little has changed in the last 30 years. If anything, notwithstanding the feminist discourse surrounding women's needs to re-appropriate female bodily phenomena, the trend to medicalization of female sexuality continues unabated.

Pregnancy is a time in a woman's life where her body proclaims that she has been sexually active. Yet this contrasts sharply with her invisibility as a sexual being (Kleinplatz, 1992). Pregnant women are seen as asexual instead of in a heightened state of awareness of their power as a sexual being/creator. The sexological literature tends to ignore pregnancy except insofar as it may interfere with sexual desire, expression and satisfaction (Reamy & White,1987) and swollen bellies may get in the way of missionary-style intercourse. The fact that prolonged pelvic vasocongestion may result in sexual arousal is somehow overlooked in our (but not all) cultures and literature. Thousands of years ago, the Talmud (Babylonian Talmud, Niddah, 31a) recognised the powerful sexual desires often engendered in women during pregnancy and encouraged husbands to fulfill their wives' sexual cravings during the second and third trimesters of pregnancy (after the cessation of first trimester nausea).

Similarly, childbirth is mostly seen as a medical event to be managed rather than the culmination of a sexual experience. In the sexological literature, childbirth is viewed as leading to dyspareunia, lack of desire and frequency of intercourse (Barrett, Pendry, Peacock, Victor, Thakar, & Manyonda, 1999). Girls are brought up to dread the pain of childbirth rather than regarding it as the climax of a woman's body functioning at optimal capacity. To the extent that we are indoctrinated into the prevailing belief system, we become victims of a self-fulfilling prophecy; we anticipate labour as a horrific experience, which will literally tear our flesh and from which we gladly pay to be delivered via epidurals and episiotomies.

In the American system, pregnant women who are "overdue" are routinely given a synthetic hormone, pitocin, intravenously to induce labour. The more sexual and sensual alternative, which would permit women to enjoy the culmination of their pregnancies just as they began, is denied in this culture. This entails having an orgasm, engaging in sexual intercourse and allowing semen to rest against the woman's cervix briefly thereafter (Kitzinger, 1984). (Ejaculate contains the largest natural concentration of prostaglandins, which combined with her orgasm, provide a trigger for uterine contractions.) This knowledge, however, is rarely transmitted to pregnant women. As such, childbirth happens to pelvises and uteri and vaginas rather than being experienced by fully embodied, sexual beings.

The sanitizing of childbirth is further seen in the customary usage of yet more pitocin to speed up the rate of contractions, often to painful levels, thereby necessitating additional medical intervention. The alternative involves the use of nipple stimulation which can lead gently to the release of the hormone oxytocin and to more effective contractions (Kitzinger, 1988). This knowledge is common among women in other cultures, for example, in Bolivia and among the Lepchas women of Sikkim (The Body Shop, 1991) but considerably less so in American pre-natal instruction.

That many women in other cultures experience orgasm during childbirth (Kitzinger,1984) is left out of popular or even professional knowledge/discussion of this event. In the sexology literature, too, discussion of childbirth tends to emphasise the dyspareunia that often results from episiotomy scars or perhaps post-partum lack of desire (Barrett & Pendry et al., 1999; Reamy & White,1987). However, there is little emphasis on the possibility that notwithstanding the very real pain, birth can literally be an orgasmic experience (Kitzinger, 1988). The astonishing feelings of aliveness, excitement, the surge of power and sense of sexual/erotic energy are again conspicuously absent from a discourse which defines women's sexuality so narrowly. In childbirth, too, we are viewed from the outside looking in yet are rarely asked about how this extraordinary event feels. As such, women demur from sharing with one another the erotic aspects of an event that has been so thoroughly neutered that we fear being judged as weird or perverse for expressing erotic delight therein. Unfortunately, childbirth is seen as the turning point in becoming mother instead of sexual being. The two are seen as incompatible, if not mutually exclusive.

Lactation has been similarly circumscribed. Our society regards breastfeeding women as subject to bleeding and cracked nipples; engorged, painful breasts; stretch marks and sagging breasts; as "tied" to their babies and as maternal rather than sexual. Such attitudes may influence women's choices surrounding lactation; conversely, sex-positive attitudes "may override physiological inhibitors of sexual behavior (low hormone levels)" which are found during lactation (Fisher & Gray, 1988, p. 392). It is not surprising that notwithstanding public health advisories recommending lactation for at least one year (American Academy of Pediatrics, 1997), the number of women who continue to breastfeed at six months post-partum continued to drop throughout the 1990's (Losch, Dungy, Russell, & Dusdieker, 1995; Ryan, 1997).

The sexological literature barely refers to lactation; when it is mentioned, it is discussed as a cause of poorly estrogenated vaginas, lack of lubrication and vaginal atrophy (Alder & Bancroft, 1988; Kayner & Zagar, 1983). Breastfeeding women, like post-menopausal women, are seen as all dried up. It is as though sexologists have colluded with the conventional belief that the primary function of breasts is aesthetic–to be more erotic for the male viewer than for the woman within. Whatever might reduce the allure of breasts, by either altering their preferred/ideal shape or size or paradoxically, by making them more visible as maternal rather than sexual symbols, is to be prohibited.

The knowledge that breastfeeding can be a profoundly erotic experience–not just in some rarefied (and permissible) sense of nurturing and life-affirming–but a physically pleasurable experience, right down to the uterine contractions stimulated by the sucking, has been kept from women and has prevented us from beginning breastfeeding with anticipation and joy. And what of those who do speak of it? What of women who break the taboo and acknowledge that breastfeeding can provide uniquely pleasurable stimulation and sensations? Well, they may pay for it. In 1991, Denise Perrigo found herself becoming sexually aroused while breastfeeding. Her telephone call to a Syracuse community information line with questions about this phenomenon led to her arrest on charges of child abuse (Perrigo, Personal Communication, February, 1992: Ryckman, 1992). Her daughter was taken away by social services. Perrigo was separated from her child for over a year, until La Leche League representatives testified as to the normalcy and commonality of sexual response, even to the point of orgasm, during breastfeeding. This disturbing case highlights the dilemma women face in expressing the sexual components of their embodied sexual experience. Twenty-five years ago, Adrienne Rich wrote: "Since there are strong cultural forces which desexualize women as mothers, the orgasmic sensations felt in childbirth or while suckling infants have probably until recently been denied even by the women feeling them or have evoked feelings of guilt" (1976, pp. 179-180). Unfortunately, there is no sign that this situation has changed. Until women are freed to reclaim all aspects of our sexuality, particularly those marginalized by male-dominated paradigms, our pictures of female sexuality will remain at best incomplete.

IMPLICATIONS FOR THEORY, RESEARCH AND CLINICAL PRACTICE

Alternate models of female sexuality are called for which embrace the entire range of female sexuality from the vantage point of lived experience. New paradigms must be more sensitive and attuned to phenomenology as well as to the contextual origins of women's sexual difficulties. A new epistemological stance is required which features women's subjectivity at the center of inquiry. Female sexuality is best understood by listening to women's own voices rather than attempting to peer from a safe distance and have our views filtered through the distorting lenses of conventional and sexological images of sexuality and female sexuality.

Tiefer (2001) has called for "an avalanche of qualitative research." Such studies must broaden our perspectives to encompass the full spectrum and diversity of girls' and women's sexual/erotic phenomenology. The spirit of such research must veer towards discovery of unknowns rather than hypothesis testing, replication of existing findings and further reification of conventional beliefs. Cross-cultural studies may prove valuable in this endeavour by necessitating a shift in assumptions about fundamental "truths."

Similarly, therapists have a responsibility to discard the images and notions that stand in the way of coming to know our clients and to guide them, whether women or men, in exploring new ways of being sexually. Having grown up with narrow sexual parameters and skewed images of female sexuality, women often become alienated and detached from their own eroticism. The choice is to help clients to fit repressive norms or to guide them in re-appropriating and redefining themselves as embodied sexual beings. Therapists can collude to further pathologize clients by aiming for a return to normative performance standards; alternately, we may consider supporting women as they move from disconnection to becoming congruent with their own sexual values, hopes and aspirations.

REFERENCES

Alder, E. & Bancroft, J. (1988). The relationship between breast feeding persistence, sexuality and mood in postpartum women. *Psychological Medicine, 18*, 389-396.

American Academy of Pediatrics. (1997). Breastfeeding and the use of human milk. *Pediatrics, 100*, 1035-1037.

Ash, M. (1982). The misnamed female sex organ. In M. Kirkpatrick (Ed.), *Women's sexual development*. New York: Plenum Press.

Barrett, G., Pendry, E., Peacock, J., Victor, C., Thakar, R., & Manyonda, I. (1999). Women's sexuality after childbirth: A pilot study. *Archives of Sexual Behavior, 28*(2), 179-191.

The Body Shop (1991). *Mamatoto: A celebration of birth*. London, U.K.:Virago Press.

Christina, G. (1992). Are we having sex now or what? In D. Steinberg (Ed.), *The erotic impulse: Honoring the sensual self* (pp. 24-29). Los Angeles: Putnam.

Daniluk, J.K. (1998). *Women's sexuality across the life span: Challenging myths, creating meanings*. New York: Guilford.

Federation of Feminist Women's Health Centres. (1991). *A new view of a woman's body*. West Hollywood, CA: Feminist Health Press.

Fisher, W. A. & Gray, J. (1988). Erotophobia-erotophilia and sexual behavior during pregnancy and postpartum. *Journal of Sex Research, 25*(3), 379-396.

Kayner, C. E. & Zagar, J. A. (1983). Breast-feeding and sexual response. *Journal of Family Practice, 17*(1), 69-73.

Kitzinger, S. (1984). *The experience of childbirth.* London: Penguin.

Kitzinger, S. (1988). *The complete book of pregnancy and childbirth.* New York: Alfred A. Knopf.

Kleinplatz, P.J. (1992). The pregnant clinical psychologist: Issues, impressions and observations. *Women & Therapy, 12* (1 / 2), 21-37.

Kleinplatz, P. J. (1996). The erotic encounter. *Journal of Humanistic Psychology, 36*(3), 105-123.

Losch, M., Dungy, C.I., Russell, D., & Dusdieker, L.B. (1995). Impact of attitudes on maternal decisions regarding infant feeding. *Journal of Pediatrics, 126*, 507-514.

Masson, J.M. (1986). *A dark science: Women, sexuality and psychiatry in the nineteenth century.* New York: Noonday.

Masters, W. H., & Johnson, V. E. (1966). *Human sexual response.* Boston: Little, Brown.

McCormick, N.B. (1994). *Sexual salvation: Affirming women's sexual rights and pleasures.* Connecticut: Praeger.

Newton, M. (1973). Interrelationships between sexual responsiveness, birth, and breast feeding. In J. Zubin & J. Money (Eds.), *Contemporary sexual behavior: Critical issues in the 1970s* (pp. 77-98). Baltimore: Johns Hopkins University Press.

Ogden, G. (1994). *Women who love sex.* New York: Pocket Books.

Reamy, K.J., & White, S.E. (1987). Sexuality in the puerperium: A review. *Archives of Sexual Behavior, 16*, 165-186.

Rich, A. (1976). *Of woman born.* New York: Bantam.

Rossi, A. (1974). Maternalism, sexuality, and the new feminism. In J. Zubin & J. Money (Eds.), *Contemporary sexual behavior: Critical issues in the 1970s* (pp. 145-174). Baltimore: Johns Hopkins University Press.

Ryan, A.S. (1997). The resurgence of breastfeeding in the United States. *Pediatrics, 100*, 99.

Ryckman, L.L. (1992, February 5). Mother's question cost her a child: Sexual abuse charged after query about breast-feeding. *The Montreal Gazette*, pp. A1-A2.

Stock, W. (1988). Propping up the phallocracy: A feminist critique of sex therapy and research. *Women & Therapy, 7*(2/3), 23-41.

Tavris, C. (1992). *The mismeasure of woman.* New York: Touchstone.

Tiefer, L. (1991). Historical, scientific, clinical and feminist criticism of "The Human Sexual Response Cycle" model. *Annual Review of Sex Research, 2*, 1-24.

Tiefer, L. (1996). The medicalization of sexuality: Conceptual, normative, and professional issues. *Annual Review of Sex Research, 7*, 252-282.

Tiefer, L. (2001). Feminist critique of sex therapy: Foregrounding the politics of sex. In P. J. Kleinplatz (Ed.) *New Directions in Sex Therapy: Innovations and Alternatives*, (pp. 29-49). Philadelphia: Brunner-Routledge.

Ussher, J. M. (1989). *The psychology of the female body.* New York: Routledge.

Weisskopf, S. C. (1980). Maternal sexuality and asexual motherhood. *Signs, 5*(4), 766-782.

Zilbergeld, B. (1992). *The new male sexuality.* New York: Bantam Books.

Gendered Messages in Sex Ed Films: Trends and Implications for Female Sexual Problems

Heather Hartley
Tricia Drew

SUMMARY. This article presents a content analysis of gendered messages in contemporary sex education films aimed at adolescents. The data set consists of 28 films, dated from 1990 to 2000. The authors analyzed the films for presence or absence of differential gender scripts across four categories. Additionally, the authors compiled the results of the category-level analysis so as to determine each film's composite gender-based sexuality message. Results indicate that these contemporary sex education films contain different messages about male versus female sexuality. Overall, 63% of individual scripts were gender differentiated, and 89% of films contained at least some gender-differentiated scripts. The films reinforce a sexual double standard in which male erotic desire and sexual agency is legitimized whereas female erotic desire and sexual agency is minimized, and the films convey a "sex as danger" message regarding female sexuality, thus creating a social context conducive to the suppression of female sexual desire, pleasure and initiative. *[Article copies available for a fee from The Haworth Document Delivery Service: 1-800-HAWORTH. E-mail address: <getinfo@*

Heather Hartley, PhD, and Tricia Drew, MS, are affiliated with the Department of Sociology, Portland State University.

Address correspondence to: Heather Hartley, PhD, Department of Sociology, Portland State University, P.O. Box 751, Portland, OR 97207 (E-mail: hartleyh@pdx.edu).

[Haworth co-indexing entry note]: "Gendered Messages in Sex Ed Films: Trends and Implications for Female Sexual Problems." Hartley, Heather, and Tricia Drew. Co-published simultaneously in *Women & Therapy* (The Haworth Press, Inc.) Vol. 24, No. 1/2, 2001, pp. 133-146; and: *A New View of Women's Sexual Problems* (ed: Ellyn Kaschak, and Leonore Tiefer) The Haworth Press, Inc., 2001, pp. 133-146. Single or multiple copies of this article are available for a fee from The Haworth Document Delivery Service [1-800-HAWORTH, 9:00 a.m. - 5:00 p.m. (EST). E-mail address: getinfo@haworthpressinc.com].

133

KEYWORDS. Gender, sexuality, script, sexuality education, films, sexual problems, adolescents, sexual culture

As specified in "A New View of Women's Sexual Problems," there is strong need to give appropriate priority to sexual problems that result from socio-cultural, political, or economic factors. One important cultural factor that impacts sexuality is sex education. The intent of this article is not to discuss the need for sex education or why abstinence-only education is problematic. This article instead focuses on understanding the gendered content of one aspect of sex education: contemporary sex education films aimed at adolescents.

As the Sexuality Information and Education Council of the United States (SIECUS) has noted (2000), sexuality education is often "disaster prevention" focused on preventing teen pregnancy and STDs. As a result, evaluation of sex education has drawn heavily from a public health point of view (i.e., assessing whether sex education prevents pregnancy and promotes safe sex). However, as SIECUS states (2000), "it is time to take a new view of sexuality education, one that holds as its primary goal helping adolescents develop the values, attitudes, maturity, and skills they need not only to avoid unprotected and unwanted sexual behaviors but to become sexually healthy adults." Becoming a sexually healthy adult with minimal sexual problems involves, of course, many factors. As noted in "A New View of Women's Sexual Problems," one of the factors that can create sexual problems for women is "lack of information about how gender roles influence men's and women's sexual expectations, beliefs, and behaviors." While there are many cultural sources informing adolescents' understandings of gender and sexuality (e.g., families, the media, peers, church organizations), one important source can be sex education. Accordingly, it is important that social scientists and others conduct research on sex education from every possible angle. As part of this mission, our research examines the social construction of gender and sexuality in sex education films. The intent is to unravel the hidden curriculum of gender (Sadker & Sadker, 1994) manifested in these films.

Although the films under examination target an adolescent audience, an assumption of this research is that the messages contained within these films have broader importance, are reflective of the parameters of the sexual culture. Moreover, although sex education films represent only a small part of sexuality education in general, the trends revealed in the films may have important ramifications for understanding the social basis of sexual pleasure and sexual problems. As Tolman (1994, 2000) has pointed out, adolescent girls describe feeling sexual desire but also report conflict and worry regarding that desire. Notes Tolman (2000), "It seems likely that girls who describe their own embodied sexual desire as a secret dilemma and source of distress in adolescence become women who have trouble feeling sexually secure, comfortable, spontaneous, and unworried in adulthood." The intent of our research is to shed light on the gendered *content* of early messages about sexuality. However, while the messages in sex education films might impact adolescent girls' feelings about sexuality and desire, our research is not positioned to assess the *impacts* of the gendered messages promoted in sex education films.

This article presents a content analysis of sexuality scripts in these films. Sexuality scripts are societal messages that transmit information about a culture's sexual values to individuals; they provide cultural scenarios which act as guidelines for sexual expression (Simon & Gagnon, 1986). Historically, sexuality scripts within sex education films have given differential evaluations to male and female sexuality, thus promoting a sexual double standard (Eberwein, 1999; Pernick, 1996). Sexuality education has tended to characterize females' sexual desire in terms of its possible negative or unwanted consequences, such as pregnancy, and has reinforced the notion that young men are sexual actors while young women are objects of male sexuality (Fine, 1988). A growing body of recent research has investigated how adolescent girls navigate a world in which only male sexual desire is expected and sanctioned (Martin, 1996; Tolman & Higgins, 1996; Tolman, 1994; Thompson, 1995). However, research into the gendered content of messages within *contemporary* sex education films–an important source of sexual scripts presented to adolescent girls–is lacking. While contemporary films may replicate historical patterns, it is also possible that the films (or some portion of them) contain non-gendered sexuality scripting, identically evaluating the acceptability of erotic desire and sexual activity for males and females, as would be suggested by certain recent pieces (Carpenter, 1998; Hedgepeth & Helmich, 1996; Mackler, 1999). Understanding the gender trends in contemporary sex education films will add to our collective knowledge of the social forces shaping female sexuality.

METHODS:
CONTENT ANALYSIS OF SEX EDUCATION FILMS

The Patchwork Nature of Sex Education

Sex education regulations vary by state and within states. Variation exists in regard to whether or not sex education is taught as well as in the content of curricula. In 2000 sexuality education was mandatory in only 18 states and the District of Columbia (NARAL, 2000). However, there was some form of school sponsored sex education in 48 states (SEICUS, 2000). State governments, and the school districts attached to them, direct sex education on a local level, greatly shaping the content of the curricula (Di Mauro, 1989/1990; Kenney, Guardado, & Brown, 1989). The variation in sex education regulations within the U.S. presents a methodological challenge. This research was limited to a specific segment of the total population of sex education films. Specifically, we examined the sex education films available within *one school district* in the state of Oregon. Therefore, the results of this project are not generalizable to the larger population of all pubescent sex education curricula. In the state of Oregon, HIV/AIDS education is mandated but sexuality education is not required. However, Oregon law states that when public school districts choose to teach sexuality education, the programs' content cannot be abstinence-only (ORS 336.455). The school district we examined requires that sex education be taught, but not necessarily at every grade level. The district compiles a list of sex education films suggested for use in its sex education programs. This research focused upon the sexuality scripts in films that were owned and suggested by the school district, not what films the teachers actually showed in the classroom. There were two reasons for this choice: (1) we wanted to capture the ideological message promoted by the district in general; and, (2) teachers in the school district were reluctant to participate in a research project with us (i.e., fewer than 10% of teachers returned an exploratory survey we sent to them).

Sampling the Population

A sex education film had to meet four criteria to fall into the study's population: the film is owned and recommended by the school district; the film is contemporary (published between 1990 to 2000); the film does not focus only on HIV/AIDS (has a broader sexuality education focus); and the film targets the middle and/or high school grade levels.

Fifty-five (55) films met these specifications. In order to examine each film thoroughly, the sample size was purposely limited. Twenty-eight (28) films were included in the sample, an approximately 1:2 sampling ratio. Random selection procedures were used to select the films. Both traditionally entertainment-oriented production companies (i.e., those producing programs for a television audience) and traditionally education-oriented production companies (i.e., those producing materials explicitly for use in schools) produced the films, but this research did not examine variations in scripts between these two types of films. Twenty-six (26) of the sampled films were produced in the United States, and two (2) films were of Canadian origin. The films' running times varied from 11 minutes to 60 minutes; however, the vast majority of the films were 20 to 35 minutes in length.

Content Analysis

Scripting theory (Simon & Gagnon, 1986) proposes that social role requirements can be indirectly/impersonally taught to individuals through cultural scenarios. In other words, individuals' *interactions with abstract social phenomena* (e.g., the tacit and overt messages regarding gender that are contained within commercial billboards or presented by religious doctrine) can affect their role conceptions. The indirectly acquired, role-related messages embedded within the cultural construct–the billboard, the church, or, in this case, the sex education film–are called "cultural scenario scripts." Cultural scenario scripts (also referred to simply as "scripts") are found within sex education films' dialogue, characterizations of individuals, and presentations of subject matter. Any one film can contain multiple scripts.

In order to evaluate the scripts that sexuality education films transmit to adolescents, we examined the films, and the scripts they contain, as documents. This analysis was conducted through a combination of qualitative and quantitative content analysis (Altheide, 1996). We appraised the gendered nature of the film's messages through a qualitative examination of the scripts, and we documented the relative frequency of gender differentiated or gender symmetrical scripts.

We examined the films' presentations of sexuality scripts within four thematic areas. Each of the areas, which are discussed below, is considered a *script category*. In the first stage of analysis, *individual scripts* were the unit of analysis: we analyzed the sexuality scripts in each film, and we show the results across the four categories. The number of scripts in a film varies, depending on the nature of the film. In the second stage of analysis, the *individual film* is the unit of analysis: we compiled the results of the category-level analysis so as to determine each film's composite gender-based sexuality message. Drawing from the first stage of analysis, we categorize each film as belonging to one of two categories: (1) films showing at least some scripts depicting gender differentiation, or (2) films depicting only gender symmetrical scripts.

Content analysis has several limitations. It relies upon the researcher's own understanding of subject matter definitions. To minimize the impact of researcher bias, we relied heavily upon previous researchers' work when developing a coding scheme. An additional problem associated with content analysis is that of inter-rater reliability, where multiple document reviewers may hold differing ideas regarding the coding scheme. The possibility of fluctuation was eliminated through use of a single document reviewer (Drew). However, when one individual acts as the sole reviewer of documents, the research once again is subject to an individual's interpretation because there are no other assessments verifying the observations. That only one researcher acted as a coder is thus a weakness of the study. Future studies of this topic would want to include independent assessments during the coding process.

DATA ANALYSIS

First Stage: Analysis of Four Sexuality Script Categories

We relied on a review of past research and a pre-test of six randomly selected sex education films to determine the relevant script categories. Through the pre-test, we determined that four sexuality-related themes were especially prevalent in the films. The themes, which became our script categories, included: (1) *Erotic desire*–an individual's desire to think about sexual activity, to have sexual feelings, or to wish to engage in sexual activity (Messner, 1992); (2) *Sexual activity*–an individual's engagement or intention to engage in sexual activities with another person (Fine, 1988; Tolman, 1994); (3) *Sexual decision-making*–an individual's decision to request a sexual activity or to engage in a sexual activity (Fine, 1988); and (4) *Responsibility for sexuality outcomes*–the ways in which an individual is affected by or is responsible for birth control, pregnancy, parenthood, or sexually transmitted diseases (STDs) (Nathanson, 1991; Schneider & Jenness, 1995).

An assumption of this study is that when sexuality is scripted differently for each gender, one gender's script could be more permissive. Previous researchers have shown that differential sexuality scripts privilege males' sexuality above that of females (Eberwein, 1999; Fine, 1988; Martin, 1996; Nathanson, 1991; Schneider & Jenness, 1995; Tolman, 1994; Tolman & Higgins, 1996). *Gender differentiation* was observed when a sexuality script in a film differently evaluated sexual behaviors for males and females and privileged males' sexuality above females'. *Gender symmetry* was observed when a sexuality script identically evaluated sexual behaviors for males and females. As gender symmetrical scripts do not differentiate on the basis of gender, neither gender's sexuality script was privileged.[1]

In the first stage of analysis, we examined all films for the presence of sexuality scripts across these four categories. Not all of the sampled films displayed each of the four scripting categories (e.g., a film may show several depictions of erotic desire but no depictions of sexual decision-making). Additionally, in a single sexuality script category, a film could depict both gender differentiating and gender symmetrical scripts (i.e., a film can have "mixed messages"). Each of the scripts was categorized as depicting either gender differentiation or gender symmetry (see Table 1). When a film presented a script in a particular category, the characteristic shown was circled on a coding sheet. Below that notation, detailed comments were added about the script, and in many cases, portions of film dialogue were transcribed. We tabulated and compared the relative occurrence of gender differentiated and gender symmetrical messages within each of the four sexuality script categories (Table 2).

Second Stage: Analysis of Films' Composite Sexuality Scripts

In the second stage of analysis, we compiled the results of the category-level analysis for each film so as to determine each film's composite gender-based sexuality message. We categorized each film as belonging in one of two categories: (1) films showing at least some scripts depicting gender differentiation, or (2) films depicting only gender symmetrical scripts. After each single film was categorized, we tabulated the results in order to assess the overall dominant pattern in the films as a group (Table 3).

RESULTS

The Four Script Categories

We identified and coded 75 scripts from the 28 films. Analysis revealed that asymmetrical gender-based sexuality scripts were much

TABLE 1. Characteristics of Messages Observed in Sexuality Script Categories

Sexuality Script Category	Gender Differentiating Characteristics	Gender Symmetrical Characteristics
Erotic Desire	-Male erotic desire is accepted -Female erotic desire portrayed as nonexistent or unacceptable -Erotic desire is acceptable for both genders, but more so for males	-Evaluation and acceptance of erotic desire is identical for males and females
Sexual Activity	-Male sexual activity is accepted -Female sexual activity is evaluated as nonexistent or unacceptable -Sexual activity is acceptable for both genders, but more so for males	-Evaluation of engagement in sexual activity is identical for males and females
Sexual Decision-Making	-Male requests sexual activity from female -Female regulates decision to engage in sexual activity	-Both genders can request sexual activity -Both genders regulate decision to engage in sexual activity -Decision to engage in sexual activity is shown as a couple's decision
Responsibility for Sexuality Outcomes	-Female has primary or sole responsibility for sexuality outcomes	-Male and female have equal responsibility for sexuality outcomes

TABLE 2. Gender Differentiation by Category

	Gender differentiated scripts	
Category	N	Percent
Erotic desire	11	58%
Sexual activity	14	70%
Decision-making	9	69%
Outcomes	13	57%
Total scripts (n = 75)	47	63%

TABLE 3. Films' Composite Sexuality Scripts (n = 28)

Ideology	Number of Films	Percent of Films
Gender differentiating	25	89%
Gender symmetrical	3	11%

more common than symmetrical scripts. Almost two-thirds (63%) of those scripts contained sexuality messages that were qualitatively different for males and females (Table 2). Only slightly more than one third (37%) of the analyzed sexuality script category messages were gender symmetrical. Over 50% of scripts in *each of the four categories* contained gender differentiating messages. There were distinct gender differences in the films' portrayals of sexual agency, responsibility for sexuality outcomes, the dangers and pleasures of sexuality, and the legitimacy of sexual desire. The predominance of gender differentiating scripts creates a sexual environment that consistently privileges males' sexuality above females'.

Of the four categories, *sexual activity* contained the largest percentage of gender differentiating scripts (70%). Scripts that differentiated between the genders portrayed females' sexual activity as unacceptable and dangerous, while concurrently presenting males' sexual activity as normative. These scripts positively evaluated males' sexual activity by portraying sexually agentic males, and whether or not the male was successful in attaining sexual activity, the quest for sexual activity was presented as valid. Conversely, in gender differentiating scripts, sexually active or would-be sexually active females were evaluated negatively, thus reinforcing a double standard. A few gender differentiating scripts did evaluate female sexual activity as somewhat tolerable but evaluated males' sexual activity as universally acceptable.

In the 30% of sexual activity category scripts that were gender symmetrical, females' and males' sexual activity was assessed identically. When an appraisal of sexual activity was presented it was done without regard to gender. A number of symmetrical scripts evaluated sexual activity as tolerable and normative, sometimes specifically referring to teenage sexual activity and other times to sexual activity in general. Other gender symmetrical scripts displayed universal disapproval of teen-agers' engagement in sexual activities.

Over two-thirds (69%) of the *sexual decision-making* scripts featured gender differentiation, permitting only the male to make sexual overtures or propositions. In these scripts, males were depicted as sexual agents, while females were shown as sexual objects, only able to react to male sexual overtures. For males, sexual decision-making was scripted as the ability to request access to the female body. Males were seldom depicted reflecting on the decision to become sexually active, and when males did engage in reflection, it was not to the extent that females did. Rather, males were largely portrayed as ever-ready for sexual activity. Females' sexual decision-making script focused upon gatekeeping: permitting or denying access to the terrain of their bodies. Films often followed females through a lengthy decision-making process in which females would agonize, consult their friends, and acknowledge society's prohibitions.

In only 31% of the sexual decision-making scripts were the genders equally able to make sexual propositions and also regulate access to their bodies. In these scripts, males and females were seen making and reacting to sexual activity propositions in approximately even numbers. Additionally, two symmetrical scripts featured co-decision-making, where neither the male nor the female clearly initiated a proposition. These scripts presented decision-making as a couple's decision, rather than one individual's request and another's regulation.

The *erotic desire* scripts displayed a tendency to legitimize erotic desire for males but not for females. Gender differentiation was visible in the majority (58%) of erotic desire scripts; these scripts either presented erotic desire as only acceptable for males or as more acceptable for males than for females. Many of the gender differentiating scripts evaluated males' sexual desire as normal or expected but neglected to mention females' sexual desire altogether. When females' erotic desire was discussed it was frequently portrayed as qualitatively different from males' desire. Unlike males' erotic desire, females' desire was often recast into an exchange mechanism, with the female purportedly feeling erotic desire, but in actuality desiring relationships, affection, or attention. These portrayals undermine erotic desire by giving alternate accounts for why females would want to engage in sexual activity.

Forty-two percent of erotic desire scripts permitted females and males equal access to feelings of erotic desire. None of the symmetrical scripts recast an individual's erotic desire into a wish to exchange sexual activity for relationship stability or love. Rather, individuals' desires were portrayed as erotic urges sometimes backed up with emotional connections to potential partners.

The majority (57%) of scripts in the *responsibility for sexuality outcomes* category displayed gender differentiation. In these scripts sexuality outcomes were largely explored from a female vantage point: birth control, STD protection, pregnancy, and parenthood were depicted as mainly "female issues." Females were portrayed as either solely or primarily affected by negative sexuality outcomes, and they were depicted as either solely or primarily responsible for sexuality outcomes and for providing birth control and STD protection. With such assumptions, sexual activity comes to be portrayed as more dangerous (and less pleasurable) for females than for males. Some scripts did emphasize that males should be held accountable for sexuality outcomes, but conceded that males can only be expected to do so much (e.g., males were shown as having responsibility for birth control only if condoms were the chosen method).

The responsibility for sexuality outcomes category contained the most gender symmetrical messages of any scripting category–43% of the scripts. Scripts that held non-gendered assumptions about sexuality held both genders equally accountable for providing birth control and STD protection. Despite the fact that STDs affect females more than males and that pregnancies occur in females' bodies, gender symmetrical scripts divide sexual responsibility evenly between males and females.

Heterosexuality, it should be noted, was normatively assumed for both males and females in all of the sampled films. Scholars such as Rich (1980) have made the case that when heterosexuality is presented as compulsory, it bolsters a gender differentiating and patriarchal system. While Rich's work may be applied to this research, the examination of sexual orientation falls beyond the scope of this paper.

The Films' Composite Scripts

The second level of analysis assessed the composite sexuality scripts of the sampled films. While the first stage of analysis revealed that gender differentiation is the most prevalent pattern for individual scripts (shown in 63% of the scripts), an even stronger pattern of gender differentiation emerges from this second level of analysis. While 37% of the *individual scripts* were gender symmetrical, just 11% of the *films* depicted only gender symmetrical scripts (Table 3). Therefore, the vast majority of the sampled sex education films (89%) contained at least some gender differentiating sexuality scripts that privileged males' sexuality above females'. In other words, the gender differentiating sexuality scripts (which make up 63% of the total scripts) are thus distributed throughout 89% of the sampled films. The implication of this finding is that even though more than one-third (37%) of the scripts do show gender symmetry, these messages are oftentimes presented alongside gender differentiating messages within the same film.

CONCLUSIONS AND IMPLICATIONS

The results of the content analysis indicate that the sampled contemporary sex education films contain different messages about male versus female sexuality. Over half of the individual scripts in every script category displayed gender-based script differentiation. In the sexual activity and sexual decision-making categories, the pattern of gender differentiation was even more extreme (with 70% and 69% of scripts depicting gender differentiation, respectively). These sampled contemporary films are thus, by and large, replicating historical patterns. In aggregate, the films reinforce a sexual double standard in which male erotic desire and sexual agency is legitimized whereas female erotic desire and sexual agency is minimized, and the films convey a "sex as danger" message regarding female sexuality.

This construction of gender and sexuality has important implications for scholars and health care practitioners who are evaluating the various forces contributing to female sexual problems. This analysis, though limited by small sample size and lack of generalizability, suggests that messages in contemporary sex education films may create a social context conducive to the suppression of the healthy expression of female sexual desire, pleasure and initiative. It is encouraging to see that over a third (37%) of the individual sexuality scripts do portray gender symmetry and thus pose some challenge to a sexual double standard. However, that these gender symmetrical messages are oftentimes presented in films that also advocate gender differentiation (89% of the total films) may work to undercut the power of the gender symmetrical depictions.

These films as a group fail to promote an empowering view of female sexuality. Because these films reflect our broader sexual culture, it is no surprise that adolescent girls report significant distress about their sexuality. Nor is it a surprise that adult women have myriad sexual problems. We hope that the findings of this research will be used by organizations such as SIECUS in their advocacy of a new view of sexuality education and that these findings will inform ongoing evaluations of sexuality education programs, reinforcing the need to consider the importance of gendered messages about sexuality.

NOTE

1. Characteristics of gender symmetry in sexuality scripts have not been as overtly defined by academic researchers as have gender-asymmetrical scripts. Academic discussion of gender symmetry was found in the responsibility for sexuality outcomes category (Campbell, 1995; Pleck, Sonenstein, & Swain, 1988). With the other categories, we inverted previous researchers' definitions of gender asymmetry and drew from non-academic publications to deduce the character of gender symmetry (Eberwein, 1999; Hedgepeth & Helmich, 1996; Mackler, 1999).

REFERENCES

Altheide, D.L. (1996). *Qualitative media analysis.* (Vol. 38). Thousand Oaks, CA: Sage.

Campbell, C. (1995). Male gender roles and sexuality: Implications for women's AIDS risk and prevention. *Social Science and Medicine, 41*(2), 197-210.

Carpenter, L. (1998). From girls into women: Scripts for sexuality and romance in *Seventeen* magazine, 1974-1994. *The Journal of Sex Research, 35,* 158-168.

Di Mauro, D. (December1989/January 1990). Sexuality education 1990: A review of state sexuality and AIDS education curricula. *SEICUS Report, 18,* 16-20.

Eberwein, R. (1999). *Sex ed: Film, video, and the framework of desire.* New Jersey: Rutgers University Press.

Fine, M. (1988). Sexuality, schooling, and adolescent females: The missing discourse of desire. *Harvard Educational Review, 58,* 29-53.

Hedgepeth, E. and Helmich, J. (1996). *Teaching about sexuality and HIV: Principles and methods for effective education.* New York: New York University Press.

Kenney, A. Guardado, S. and Brown, L. (1989). Sex education and AIDS education in the schools: What states and large school districts are doing. *Family Planning Perspectives, 21,* 56-64.

Mackler, C. (1999). Sex ed: How do we score? *MS. Magazine.* August/September.

Martin, K. (1996). *Puberty, sexuality, and the self: Girls and boys at adolescence.* New York: Routledge.

Messner, M. (1992). *Power at play: Sports and the problem of masculinity.* Boston: Beacon Press.

Nathanson, C. (1991). *Dangerous passage: The social control of sexuality in women's adolescence.* Philadelphia: Temple University Press.

National Abortion Rights Action League (1995). Sexuality in America: A state by state review. USA: The NARAL Foundation.

Oregon State Law, ORS 336.455. Human sexuality education courses: Criteria.

Pernick, M.S. (1996). The Black stork: Eugenics and the death of defective babies in American medicine and motion pictures since 1915. New York: Oxford University Press.

Pleck, J., Sonenstein, F., and Swain, S. (1988). Adolescent males' sexual behavior and contraceptive use: Implications for male responsibility. *Journal of Adolescent Research, 3*(3-4), 275-284.

Rich, A. (1980). Compulsory heterosexuality and lesbian existence. *Signs*, *5*(4), 647-650.

Sadker, M. and Sadker, D. (1994). *Failing at fairness*. New York: C. Scribner's Sons.

Schneider, B. and Jenness, V. (1995) *Women resisting AIDS: Feminist strategies of empowerment*. USA: Temple University Press.

Sexuality Information and Education Council of the United States (SIECUS). (2000). School health education clearinghouse. USA: SEICUS.

Sexuality Information and Education Council of the United States (SIECUS). (2000). Unpublished paper. A new view of sexuality education.

Simon, W. and Gagnon, J. (1986). Sexual scripts: Permanence and change. *Archives of Sexual Behavior*, *15*, 97-119.

Thompson, S. (1995). *Going all the way: Teenage girls' tales of sex, romance, and pregnancy*. New York: Hill and Wang.

Tolman, D. (2000). Unpublished paper. A new view of adolescent girls' sexual problems.

Tolman, D. (1994). Doing desire: Adolescent girls struggle for/with sexuality. *Gender and Society*, *8*(3), 324-342.

Tolman, D. and Higgins, T. (1996). How being a good girl can be bad for girls. In Maglin and Perry (Eds.), *Bad girls, good girls: Women, sex, and power in the nineties* (pp. 205-225). New Brunswick, NJ: Rutgers University Press.

Working group on a new view of women's sexual problems. (2001). A new view of women's sexual problems. *Women & Therapy 24*(1/2), 1-8.

A Research Inquiry into Some American Women's Sexual Concerns and Problems

Carol Rinkleib Ellison

SUMMARY. The New View of Women's Sexual Problems is supported by findings of the 1993-94 Ellison/Zilbergeld sexuality survey of 2,632 mostly white, college-educated women born 1905-1977 (Ellison, 2000; see questionnaire at www.womenssexualities.com). Sexual experiences of women with previous year sexual partners are reported. The most important sexual concerns or problems in the previous year of 1,637 women are categorized: 34% desire/frequency (low sexual desire, desire discrepancy); 28.5% physical responsiveness (female arousal, orgasm; male partners' erectile difficulties, ejaculatory control); 16% lovemaking (sexual technique); 7.5% finding a partner; < 5% sexual relationship, fertility, pregnancy, STDs/safe sex, the woman's body/health, non-monogamy, orientation; 547 others reported none. Exemplary quotes from respondents are included. Sex therapy for low sexual desire is addressed. Recommended solutions emphasize individual differences and the multidimensionality of sexuality. *[Article copies available for a fee from The Haworth Document Delivery Service: 1-800-HAWORTH. E-mail address: <getinfo@haworthpressinc.com> Website: <http://www.HaworthPress. com> © 2001 by The Haworth Press, Inc. All rights reserved.]*

KEYWORDS. Sexual problems, sexual desire, sexual dysfunctions, Ellison/Zilbergeld Survey, sex survey, New View

Carol Rinkleib Ellison is in private practice in Oakland, CA.

Address correspondence to: Carol Rinkleib Ellison, 6114 LaSalle Avenue, PMB 476, Oakland, CA 94611-2802 (E-mail: DrCarol@womenssexualities.com).

[Haworth co-indexing entry note]: "A Research Inquiry into Some American Women's Sexual Concerns and Problems." Ellison, Carol Rinkleib. Co-published simultaneously in *Women & Therapy* (The Haworth Press, Inc.) Vol. 24, No. 1/2, 2001, pp. 147-159; and: *A New View of Women's Sexual Problems* (ed: Ellyn Kaschak, and Leonore Tiefer) The Haworth Press, Inc., 2001, pp. 147-159. Single or multiple copies of this article are available for a fee from The Haworth Document Delivery Service [1-800-HAWORTH, 9:00 a.m. - 5:00 p.m. (EST). E-mail address: getinfo@haworthpressinc.com].

147

The Working Group on Women's Sexual Problems defines sexual problems as "discontent or dissatisfaction with any emotional, physical, or relational aspect of sexual experience," which "may arise in one or more . . . interrelated aspects of women's lives." These aspects include socio-cultural, political or economic factors, partner and relationship factors, psychological factors, and medical factors.

What is typical in the sex lives of contemporary college-educated American women? Which of these factors are mentioned most frequently when these women are asked about their sexual problems and concerns? In 1993-94, Dr. Bernie Zilbergeld and I surveyed a nationwide sample of convenience, asking women how they experienced and expressed their sexualities. The 2,632 women who responded to our 16-page questionnaire were born between 1905 and 1977; 556 were age 50 or older. Thirty-two percent had some college or a two-year degree; 21% had a four-year degree; and 40% had done some graduate work or had a graduate degree. Although we had planned for and attempted to have greater ethnic diversity, 83% were Caucasian. With respect to sexual orientation, 7% described themselves as lesbian, 5% as bisexual, the remainder as heterosexual. The survey was preceded by in depth interviews of about 100 women, 72 done by me, the rest by others. For additional details of this research, see Ellison (2000) or www.womenssexualities.com. The survey questionnaire can be seen on the website.

ASPECTS OF SEXUAL EXPRESSION EXPERIENCED IN THE PREVIOUS YEAR

Seeking to understand women's sexual problems and concerns more fully, we asked those of the 2,632 respondents who'd had a sexual partner in the previous year to respond to a series of questions on "some aspects of sexual expression you may have experienced." We presented the following list of 23 sexual circumstances and asked the respondents to indicate if they had experienced each in the previous year *not at all, rarely, sometimes, often,* or *all the time.*

Under the heading "I have experienced the following in the last year" were (1) difficulty finding a partner I wanted to be sexual with; (2) lower sexual desire than I wanted to have; (3) being too tired to have sex; (4) being too busy to have sex; (5) not feeling sexually satisfied; (6) my partner not as interested in sex as I was; (7) my partner less interested in closeness after sex than I; (8) my partner choosing inconvenient times for sex.

Under the heading "During sex in the last year I have experienced" were (9) difficulty getting excited/aroused; (10) feeling distracted; (11) inability to relax; (12) involuntary vaginal spasm so that vaginal entry and/or intercourse was impossible or difficult; (13) inadequate vaginal lubrication; (14) pain during intercourse or other internal stimulation; (15) fantasizing that I am having sex with someone other than my partner; (16) difficulty in reaching orgasm; (17) inability to have an orgasm; (18) reaching orgasm too quickly; (19) my partner seeming distracted; (20) my partner wanting shorter foreplay than I wanted; (21) my partner having difficulty getting aroused; and two that were specifically for women with male partners: (22) my partner ejaculating too quickly; and (23) my partner having difficulty getting and/or maintaining an erection. There also was a blank where the respondent could specify "other." Henceforth, I will refer to these above 23 items as the *overview list.*

The Experiences

The experiences on this overview list are clearly a part of women's lives. Of the 2,295 Survey respondents with a previous year sex partner, 98.6% checked at least one as experienced *sometimes, often,* or *all the time.* When *sometimes* was omitted, 72% had experienced at least one *often* or *all the time.*

Problems–or "Just How It Is?"

In 1978, Ellen Frank, Carol Anderson, and Debra Rubinstein reported the results of their study of 100 predominantly white, college-educated, and happily married couples. They found that although over 80% of the couples described their marriages and sexual relationships as happy and satisfying, their sexual lives were far different from those typically portrayed in the media. "Forty percent of the men reported erectile or ejaculatory dysfunction, and 63% of the women reported arousal or orgasmic dysfunction. In addition, 50% of the men and 77% of the women reported difficulty that was not dysfunctional in nature (e.g., lack of interest or inability to relax)" (p. 111).

Influenced by this groundbreaking study, we asked respondents to our survey who had experienced any of the items on the overview list to consider which, if any, they thought of as "problems" and which they thought of as "just the way life is." Depending on the item, from 50% to virtually 90% of those who had a particular experience concluded:

"That's the way life is" rather than "This is a problem." No one item was called a problem by more than half of the women who had had it happen at all, whether sometimes or more frequently.

Our survey demonstrated that, in general, many of us accept the realities and imperfections of our sex lives. There were, however, six circumstances that were more likely than the others to be considered problems, even if experienced only *sometimes*. I call these *The Big Six*; I will say more about them later.

Most Important Sexual Problem or Concern in the Past Year

One survey question asked about the woman's most important sexual problem or concern in the past year. Respondents could indicate an item on the overview list or write in another answer. Table 1 categorizes the responses of the 1,637 women who reported a most important concern or problem. There were 547 others who reported having *no* most important sexual problem or concern in the previous year.

Certain issues, particularly those related to fertility, physical responsiveness and health, tended to vary with age. For example: of the most important problems or concerns related to women's bodies and health, 69% were reported by women age 40 or older, while only 45% of the respondents were in that age group.

Issues of Desire and Frequency: The American Way of Life

Among the factors in Category I of the New View (sexual problems due to socio-cultural, political, or economic factors) are "lack of interest, fatigue, or lack of time due to family and work obligations" (p. 6). Category II (sexual problems relating to partner and relationship) includes "discrepancies in desire for sexual activity or in preferences for various sexual activities" (p. 6).

In the Ellison/Zilbergeld Survey, the three most marked items on the overview list were being *too tired to have sex,* being *too busy,* and *lower sexual desire than I wanted to have.* There is no doubt that these are typical experiences of today's American women. The desire and frequency category–these three items plus one not included on the overview list: the woman and her partner having different levels of sexual desire and interest–also led the more specific list of most important sexual concerns and problems. One out of three of the women with a most important concern or problem reported an issue from this category.

TABLE 1. Most Important Sexual Concerns and Problems in the Past Year

Problem or concern category	N = 1637	Percent
Desire/frequency	555	34%
Physical responsiveness	469	28.5%
Lovemaking	261	16%
Finding a partner	123	7.5%
Relationship	71	4%
Fertility/reproduction	45	3%
STDs/safe sex	37	2%
Her own body/health	31	2%
Miscellaneous–abuse, non-monogamy, orientation, other	45	3%

Too tired/too busy. Although being *too tired to have sex* and being *too busy to have sex* were the items selected most often from the overview list, they were not among the experiences most likely to be considered problems when they occurred; they were among those most likely to be considered as the way life is. Being at least sometimes too tired and/or too busy for sex is a part of the American way of life that many of us take pretty much for granted. Often both a woman and her partner are affected. A woman in her forties commented: "Lack of sex is due to exhaustion on both our parts. We are coming to terms with the fact we're older, work two fulltime jobs, and are actively involved in our three young children's lives." Another woman, younger, mentioned "difficulty juggling–balancing–being a parent, a worker, time for myself, my relationship and my sexuality."

In these comments we see clear examples of *role fragmentation*: one woman filling many roles. Role fragmentation is a part of the American way of life. Where is the time, energy and attention to come from for sexual desire?

Lower sexual desire than I wanted to have. Having *lower desire than I wanted* was reported by women of all ages and was more likely to be considered a problem than being too tired or too busy. Here, too, however, some respondents specifically voiced their acceptance of their low desire for sex. One woman, close to age 50, explained, "I no longer feel my low desire is a 'problem' or 'something wrong with me' but a path to a new way of being sexual. My partner and I are experimenting with sex that is not goal (orgasm) oriented." Some women of reproductive age noted a link between diminished desire and taking birth control pills. Other respondents mentioned links to grief and loss, and to anger and resentment. Some problems and concerns seemed to be more a loss of interest than lack of desire. For example: "I haven't been wanting to be with my primary partner in a sexual way. I am bisexual."

A sexual detective considers low sexual desire. Three of the hats I wear as therapist include: (1) sexual choreographer™, in which I am a coach, facilitator, instructor for creating erotic pleasure; (2) sexual detective/problem solver, in which I try to figure out what is going on, diagnose the sexual problems my clients bring to me; and (3) sexual advisor, in which I assume the role of mentor, knowledgeable teacher, guide, counselor, consultant–and provide solutions and information about, for example, hormones, methods of birth control, or anything else that might be relevant and appropriate.

The World Health Organization (WHO, 1975) has defined "sexual health" as "the integration of the somatic, emotional, intellectual, and social aspects of sexual being" (*New View,* p. 4). In my sex therapist roles of detective and problem solver, I recognize that lower desire for sex than someone wants is not just one simple condition that is the same for all; it can be arrived at by many different paths and often reflects a complex combination of factors. If a woman is currently experiencing less sexual desire than she wants, I consider the following questions:

- When and under what circumstances did she first notice she had lower sexual desire than she wanted?
- Is there anything related to her health that might be affecting her sexual desire?
- Does she eat well and regularly? Does she get enough sleep?
- Does she experience chronic pain? If so, when is it most intense? Least bothersome?
- What birth control pills, medications, and vitamins does she take?
- Does she smoke cigarettes, drink alcohol, coffee, and/or use other recreational drugs? If so, how much? How often? Under what circumstances?
- Does she eat sweets and/or drink soft drinks? If so, how much?
- Is she depressed? If so, how often? Under what circumstances?
- Is she resentful or angry at her partner?
- Does she have sex with her partner when she is not truly consenting?
- Is she trying to get pregnant or concerned that she might become pregnant?

- Is she concerned that she might acquire a sexually transmitted disease?
- Does she get enough time for herself?
- Is she protecting her relationship in some way by not having sex?
- Is her partner a skillful and satisfying lover?
- Are she and her partner effective together at initiating sex?
- Does she have a history of sexual abuse or trauma that is affecting her now?
- What pressures and demands does she have in her life outside of her relationship?

Usually the answers to these questions will deepen our understanding of her sexual desire and suggest changes that might begin to enhance it. Desire is likely to be optimum when a woman is in harmony with her partner and is herself physically, mentally, emotionally, and spiritually in balance.

Desire discrepancy. Each of us has a personal ebb and flow of sexual desire. Each sexual relationship also has its own ebb and flow of sexual desire that is specific to that partnership. A couple's individual rhythms may more or less synchronize, or there may be a discrepancy in which one partner seems to desire noticeably more or less sex than the other. Over 100 survey respondents specifically indicated that their major problem or concern was that they wanted more sex than their partners did. Their partners were avoiding sex or were not as interested as they were. It is noteworthy that many of the comments in this section were from women older than age 40. Heterosexual women ages 40 to 60 described male partners who avoided sex, were less interested in closeness after sex, and had difficulty getting aroused; some men also had delayed ejaculation. Most of these women felt quite strongly about their partners' unavailability for as much sex as they would like. Some younger women also had similar complaints.

Problems Related to Physical Responsiveness

Of the reported most important problems and concerns, 28% had to do with the physical responsiveness of the woman or her partner. Of the 457 responses in this category, 138 involved a partner's responsiveness and 329 the survey respondent's. Of these, 186 had something to do with her orgasms, sometimes in combination with another problem or concern.

The Big Six. There are six items on the overview list that were not the experiences of the greatest number of women, but they were the ones most likely to have been called "problems," not just accepted as "the way life is," by those who experienced them. I call these *The Big Six.* All six have to do with what goes on during sexual activity, something to do with attention or with the physical responsiveness of the woman or her partner. Three have to do with her partner's involvement and three the woman's own.

Compared to the other items on the overview list, a woman was more likely to experience it as a problem if her partner, male or female, had difficulty getting aroused or seemed distracted during sex, and/or if her male partner had difficulty getting and/or maintaining an erection. She also was likely to experience it as a problem if she herself reached orgasm too quickly; experienced pain during intercourse or other internal stimulation; or experienced involuntary vaginal spasm so that vaginal entry and/or intercourse was impossible or difficult.

There were five other items that were almost as likely to be called problems and not just accepted as the way life is by the women who experienced them. These too have to do with what goes on during sexual activity. They include the woman's own difficulty getting excited/ aroused during sex; inability to relax during sex; insufficient vaginal lubrication; inability to orgasm; and one other experience, specifically with male partners, that could well be related to the woman's own difficulties with arousal and orgasm: her partner ejaculating too quickly.

It is clear that many of us can accept being too tired and too busy for sex, or even not desiring very often to do it. We're much less likely to say "That's just how it is" when we don't get relaxed and caught up in sex or don't fully enjoy doing it. When we and/or our partners regularly don't seem able physically, mentally, and emotionally to get into the dance of sex, we are likely to experience that as a problem.

A male partner's difficulties with arousal and erections. Male partners with erectile difficulties were mentioned by women of all ages. (Seven percent of the survey sample described themselves as lesbian; the rest were self-defined as heterosexual or bisexual.) An 18-year-old woman reported: "My partner has difficulty getting aroused and getting erections. He has been taking an orgasm-inhibiting medication (Zoloft)." Another in her early 20s said: "My partner had what I consider to be erectile dysfunction, and our sexual relationship went nowhere fast. I'd never before had a man I couldn't turn on in a big way." Women whose partners have erectile difficulties often convey this sense of frustration at their powerlessness to elicit a sexual response from their partners. Frequently, however, a man's erectile difficulties have underlying causes that a partner's attractiveness can't overcome.

Whenever a man has erectile difficulties I ask about medications, because these difficulties can be iatrogenic. Pharmacological treatment for one aspect of health may be negatively affecting quality of life in another. I ask women about medications, too. Medications for blood pressure, heart conditions, anxiety, depression, allergies—in fact almost any medications—can affect erections in men and vaginal engorgement and lubrication in women. When a medication is involved, I often recommend that someone having engorgement or erectile difficulties talk to her or his physician about trying out a different brand, a related drug, or other-than-pharmaceutical interventions to treat the "medical" condition.

Not every woman whose male partner has erectile difficulties finds them a problem. A woman in her seventies told me that her husband of the last four years had difficulty getting strong erections but was "very good with oral. He wasn't at first, but I taught him what I want." A woman in her mid-thirties told me, on the other hand, of her frustration with her husband's difficulty with his erections and arousal and added: "When I say I think you should see a doctor, he gets completely upset and refuses, says he just needs time."

This survey was done before the introduction of Viagra into the sexual lives of the American public. One benefit of the introduction and advertising of Viagra is that men like this woman's husband are much more willing to seek help for their erectile difficulties than previously. In my experience as a therapist, Viagra has been very helpful for some couples, such as those who desire sexual intercourse while the male partner has erectile difficulties due to diabetes. It does concern me, however, when a man is given Viagra without any discussion of the importance of his partner's consent, receptivity and pleasure. Those who prescribe Viagra often seem to ignore that producing a male's erection should be an enhancement to creating *mutual* erotic pleasure, not an end in itself. I describe my work with couples as intimacy-based sex therapy and sexual choreography. Recommending a drug like Viagra is a very specific intervention I would choose from among many other possibilities. As we are demonstrating, the majority of women's sexual problems and concerns will not be remedied with sexual arousal pills for their partners or themselves. Ironically, one group who might find such pills beneficial are those whose difficulties with sexual responsiveness are caused by other prescribed pills they are taking.

A male partner's difficulties with ejaculation. Women whose male partners ejaculated too quickly reported difficulties reaching orgasm, anger, frustration and feeling unsatisfied. Retarded and absent ejaculation were not on our overview list but also were among the problems and concerns women mentioned. Like other aspects of physical responsiveness, delayed or absent ejaculation can be medication- or drug-related as well as indicative of distraction, performance anxiety, and breathing patterns that inhibit arousal.

Aspects of women's physical responsiveness other than orgasm. We rarely can reduce a problem with physical responsiveness to only one of its aspects. Inability to relax during sex, for example, may lead to and be a part of difficulty getting aroused, which would be reflected as insufficient vaginal lubrication, which could be one of the underlying causes of pain during intercourse or other internal stimulation; pain could lead to involuntary vaginal spasming.

Difficulties with relaxation, distraction, arousal, and vaginal lubrication may be related to a woman's own health, her hormonal status, her female or male partner's difficulties (e.g., her partner's inability to relax or to sustain arousal), relationship issues, or numerous other factors. Inability to relax during sex affects women of all ages and may be situational. When a woman is experiencing pain during sex, I refer her for a medical consultation.

Involuntary vaginal spasm. While only 6 women marked *involuntary vaginal spasm so that vaginal entry and/or intercourse was impossible or difficult* as their most important problem or concern in the previous year, 59 women said they had this experience either often or all the time, and that same number considered the experience a "problem" rather than "the way life is." This experience is perhaps more common than many people realize; 10% of all respondents to the overview list of sexual circumstances had experienced this kind of vaginal spasming at least *sometimes* during the previous year.

Partner-focused problems and concerns that may inhibit arousal and orgasms. Category II of the New View addresses "sexual problems relating to partner and relationship" (*New View*, p. 7). Some partner-related factors that may inhibit a woman's arousal and orgasms involve sexual technique. In my research, women of all ages mentioned partners who wanted shorter foreplay than they wanted, didn't touch or kiss much, didn't like to perform oral sex, didn't make their needs known, weren't aggressive enough, didn't express their excitement more, and who were less interested in performing manual and oral stimulation than the women wanted. One respondent, whose partner was male, noted: "His inhibitions make me more inhibited."

Other issues involved relationship dynamics and the initiation and timing of sex. For example: "My partner chooses inconvenient times. He is a night owl, I am more alert in the morning; he helps little with evening activities of dinner, children's homework, getting kids ready for bed, but expects my sexual receptivity regardless."

Other Aspects of Lovemaking and Relationship

There were other miscellaneous aspects of lovemaking among women's sexual concerns and problems, such as: the weight put on one woman by her overweight partner; another's lack of confidence in her lovemaking ability; passing gas at the time of orgasm; feeling inhibited to express likes and dislikes; and needing pain for pleasure. A lesbian described a partner "not wanting to receive (bottom) as much as I want to give (top)."

Many of the problems and concerns already noted–differences in sexual desire and differences regarding sexual practices, for example– are relationship issues. The "other relationship issues" grouping included a miscellaneous assortment of 71 responses that did not readily fit into other categories. Among them are: issues of love and intimacy; the woman's dissatisfaction with her partner or the relationship; coercion or pressure from her partner; and the ending of her relationship.

Finding a Partner

The main problem or concern reported by 123 survey respondents was finding a partner with whom to be sexual. While difficulty finding a partner was mentioned by women of all ages, there is a reality for an older woman that the older she gets, the fewer *male* partners there will be available to her, because women tend to live longer than men.

A once-divorced respondent, whose last partnered sexual activity had been 15 years previously, wrote: "I would like to have a partner, but no one (is) (1) available, (2) interested in me, (3) attractive intellectually and physically. I have no physical impairment, I am active in several groups for non-sedentary pursuits, and I feel I could and would enjoy a fulfilling sexual life, even at age 66, if Mr. Right came along." Another woman, over 50, said of her recent good fortune: "Until I met my current partner ten months ago, I'd had no partner for two years since my divorce. I'm just realizing how fortunate I am!" A woman in her forties was interested in "finding the right woman to live with" and another in "finding a partner I want to be sexual with–but it's more about intimacy than sex. I need someone who cares for me and don't really want to be sexual just for the sake of doing it." A woman of about 30 wrote of wanting "a relationship with someone beyond sexual intercourse."

Other Categories of Problems and Concerns

Three percent of the most important problems or concerns of the previous year fit into the fertility/reproduction category. Included were fear of pregnancy (sometimes accompanied by concerns about sexually transmitted diseases), inability to get pregnant, trying or wanting to get pregnant, being pregnant, having a new baby, and birth control. Two percent were related to sexually transmitted diseases or to practicing safe sex. Several women, across the age spectrum, mentioned their fear of getting AIDS; others had contracted herpes. A male partner using his difficulties in maintaining an erection as an excuse to practice unsafe sex was also an issue.

An additional two percent were related to the women's own bodies or health. The women in this category tended to be an older group. As one put it: "My issue is degenerating health, plus my partner having major prostate problems. Hello old age!" Women in their sixties and seventies mentioned severe emphysema, slowing down due to age, and the effects of "illness, surgery, recovery." Two respondents mentioned feeling inhibited by the weight they had gained. Some between ages 47 and 53 reported changes due to menopause and pre-menopause as their most important sexual concerns and problems.

Themes representing one percent or fewer of the most important problems or concerns included issues of molestation and abuse, sexual orientation, and nonmonogamy.

CONCLUDING REMARKS

The Ellison/Zilbergeld Survey demonstrated that the sexual problems and concerns reported by a group of predominantly white, college-educated American women do reflect the interrelated aspects of women's lives described in the New View of Women's Sexual Problems. In the Survey, the top three items associated with satisfying sex in an ongoing relationship were *feeling close to my partner before sex, emotional closeness after sexual activity,* and *feeling loved.* The survey demonstrated what many of us already intuitively know; most women associate sexual satisfaction in an on-going relationship with closeness, love, acceptance and safety. For most women, sexual satisfaction is an emotional experience closely linked to feeling attuned and connected with a sensitive partner.

In the face of sexual problems or concerns, it helps to know when to say "That's how it is," and also when to ask, "How, a step at a time, can I improve this?" The New View recognizes that a medical framework by-passes the relational context of sexuality. The New View reminds us to seek solutions that acknowledge individual differences and integrate the somatic, emotional, intellectual, and social aspects of sexual being.

NOTE

1. Based on Chapter 12, Sexual Concerns and Problems of American Women in Ellison, C. R. (2000) *Women's Sexualities. Generations of Women Share Intimate Secrets of Sexual Self-Acceptance*. Oakland, CA: New Harbinger Publications.

REFERENCES

Ellison, C. R. (2000) *Women's Sexualities. Generations of Women Share Intimate Secrets of Sexual Self-Acceptance*. Oakland, CA: New Harbinger Publications.

Frank, E., Anderson, C. & Rubinstein, D. (1978) Frequency of sexual dysfunction in "normal" couples. *New England J. of Medicine*, 299:111-115.

The Working Group on A New view of Women's Sexual Problems (2001) *A New View of Women's Sexual Problems*. Binghamton, NY: Haworth Press.

WHO (World Health Organization) Technical Report, series Nr. 572 (1975). Full text available on the Robert Koch Institute sexuality website <www.rki.de/GESUND/ARCHIV/HOME.HTM>.

Not Tonight Dear,
I'm Deconstructing a Headache:
Confessions of a Lesbian Sex Therapist

Marny Hall

SUMMARY. The meanings attributed to sexual encounters are notoriously fluid. At the beginning of the twentieth century, eroticized contact between two women was widely regarded as evidence of moral and physical degeneracy–even by those women engaging in such contact. By the end of the century, a significant proportion of self-identified lesbians had come to regard same-sex erotic contact as a healthy expression of love. In fact, the meanings ascribed to same-sex erotic contact had changed so dramatically that, by 1979, the absence of such contact in lesbian relationships was considered unhealthy–a condition for which couples often sought "treatment." In this article, the author, a longtime San Francisco Bay Area lesbian sex therapist, chronicles the evolution of these treatments and reflects upon the twenty-five years she spent adapting and administering them.

KEYWORDS. Lesbian, sex therapy, social construction, female sexual disorder, women's sexuality

---

Marny Hall is in private practice in San Francisco and Oakland, CA.

Address correspondence to: Marny Hall, 4112 24th Street, San Francisco, CA 94114 (E-mail: MarnyHall@aol.com).

This article first appeared in *Lesbian Erotics*, edited by Karla Jay, NYU Press, New York, 1995 and is reprinted with permission.

[Haworth co-indexing entry note]: "Not Tonight Dear, I'm Deconstructing a Headache: Confessions of a Lesbian Sex Therapist." Hall, Marny. Co-published simultaneously in *Women & Therapy* (The Haworth Press, Inc.) Vol. 24, No. 1/2, 2001, pp. 161-172; and: *A New View of Women's Sexual Problems* (ed: Ellyn Kaschak, and Leonore Tiefer) The Haworth Press, Inc., 2001, pp. 161-172.

1979: LESBIAN BED DEATH

When I started my career as a lesbian psychotherapist in the mid-'70's, lesbian feminist culture was in high gear. The delights of lesbian love were celebrated in our bookstores and galleries, at our coffee houses and festivals. But despite the siren songs of Meg Christian and Margie Adam and Chris Williamson, not all of us were feeling liberated and lusty. No sooner had I opened my practice than lesbian couples came in complaining of sexual problems. Either one or both partners had lost their desire.

Since my graduate studies program hadn't equipped me for this particular exigency, I signed up for the Masters and Johnson sex therapy training offered by the University of California Medical school. It made no difference that my goal, in contrast to the rest of the sex therapy trainees in my class, was to work exclusively with lesbian couples. We were taught that sex was a natural function–a set of responses so universal that it obliterated differences in sexual orientation, and even gender. Our instructors assured us that if the blocks to eroticism–ignorance, prudery and performance anxiety–were removed, Mother Nature would reassert herself with vigor, whether our clients were gay or straight, men or women.

The first two libido killers, naivete and leftover Victorian attitudes, were not my clients' particular nemeses. Unlike the heterosexual clients with whom I was also working at the time, lesbians seeking treatment for sexual disinterest knew exactly where their clitorises were. Most had long ago given themselves permission to touch their genitals, and many had been stroking themselves with great gusto for years. Such genital conversancy was not necessarily connected with partner sex, however, and partners often worried if there was any variation in their usual sexual frequency. In fact, they seemed to have built-in erotic abacuses which were constantly computing the days since they had last "done it." After a sexless month or two had passed, partners often concluded that their stalled passion required jump-starting. At this point some women made trips to the local porn emporium or vibrator store. The romantically inclined scheduled special dates or exotic vacations. The politically correct stalwarts, eschewing such artifice, simply tried to white knuckle their way through disinclination, while the astral-minded traced each other's auras with crystals or had their chakras adjusted. When all home remedies failed, they ended up in my office.

By now indoctrinated in the tenets of the training program, I diagnosed these clients' presenting problem as performance anxiety. Misconstruing the normal ebb and flow of sexuality as loss of desire, the partners had become panicky, and their attempted solutions had only exacerbated the problem. According to my mentors in the training program, they had tried to ford the river when they needed to dally on the bank.

The cure for this brand of performance jitters was a goal-free regimen of sensuality. It was up to me to transform these orgasmic overachievers into sensual dawdlers. With that in mind, I gave out massage homework. Clients were told to "explore" each other in certain sequences–find out what sort of touch felt good and talk about it with each other. These exercises were not as effective as my teachers had predicted. Couples in treatment often replaced battles about whether or not to have sex with debates about whether or not to do the sensuality exercises I had prescribed.

In successive rounds of training, my instructors told me that such arguments meant that performance anxiety was not my clients' only problem. The absence of sex might also be the couple's attempt to rebalance an out-of-whack relationship. If partners' boundaries were too permeable, for example, they would feel much too threatened by the additional intimacy of sex. In other words, such couples could stay together only if they *didn't* have sex. If the boundaries of such a couple were strengthened, the need for such symptomatic behavior would wither away and their love life would flourish again.

In the parlance of psychotherapy, many of the lesbian couples I was seeing were "mind readers." They could describe their partners' feelings in as much detail as their own. Perhaps such attunement was evidence of the permeable boundaries my teachers were warning us about. Maybe such perfect rapprochement made sex redundant, a superfluous form of intimacy. If this were the case, I had to somehow reduce the rapport that for some couples seemed, indeed, to border on the telepathic. If I could fortify each partner's individuality by pointing out the ways she glossed over differences or made unfounded assumptions, perhaps I could curb anti-erotic boundary meltdown. I could also give the couple homework assignments that would continue to emphasize each partner's individuality. Under my guidance, partners would make separate friends, go to separate twelve-step meetings, sleep apart, even jog apart. If they could bear to separate from each other outside the bedroom, perhaps they might be more willing to connect those intimate parts of their anatomy once they slipped between the sheets. Some of my border patrols even seemed to work, at least temporarily.

Meanwhile, like ambitious fledgling professionals of any stripe, we lesbian sexperts were also lecturing and publishing. The first wave of articles on lesbian couples' problems by lesbian professionals tended to mix the cultural and the clinical. Lesbians, went our refrain, hadn't escaped female conditioning. The result–a relentless focus on nurturing–would increase exponentially when two women coupled. This forfeiture of individuality, compounded by our us-against-the-world outlaw stance, created a relational greenhouse effect which suffocated passion. The articles I and my colleagues were writing, e.g., "Another Perspective on Merger in Lesbian Relationships" (Burch, 1985) and "The Problem of Fusion in Lesbian Relationships" (Krestan & Bepko, 1980) reappeared, often, in popularized form, in the lesbian press. When, shortly after publication of these articles, my clients came in caricaturing themselves as "textbook lesbians" and "merger queens," I laughed ruefully and wondered if my colleagues and I, in our earnest attempts to write about lesbian bed death, were also authoring a new genre of lesbian self-doubt. In previous eras, lesbians had been sick when they were sexual. Now, compliments of lesbian affirmative therapists, they were sick when they weren't. And therapy didn't seem to be helping. In the long run, my attempts to strengthen my clients' boundaries hadn't worked any better than the massages. Even more disheartening, the ranks of uncured therapy graduates began to include second generation couples; partners I had originally seen together were now bringing in their new partners with the same old problems.

Adding to my scepticism about the effectiveness of sex therapy were the revolutionary ideas of social theorists. All our truths about sex, they maintained, were nothing more than social constructions.

In 1979 a radical historian, Robert A. Padgug, summed up sex both as a set of categories which ordered our experience and a set of relationships which were historically and culturally specific.

And in 1980, the philosopher Michel Foucault wrote that " . . . modern notions of sex made it possible to group together, in an artificial unit, anatomical elements, biological functions, conducts, sensations and pleasures, and enabled one to make use of this fictional unity as a causal principle, an omnipresent meaning" (p. 154).

If sex was such an endessly shifting, ultimately unknowable social/historical quark, were lesbian bed death and sex therapy equally chimerical? Were sexual diagnoses nothing more than the codification and dissemination of information which, by creating a feeling of deficiency in particular groups, served other groups? And were we sex therapists actually helping clients or merely benefiting from the proliferation of anxiety-producing social constructions about unhealthy sexual functioning?

1984: SEX AND OTHER SOCIAL SCIENCE FICTIONS

My focus was shifting from the bedrock "facts" of sexuality to my position as conveyer (perhaps even self-interested shaper) of these truths. And the change in my perspective was not confined to my office musings. One spring day in the early 1980's, as I sat in the undergraduate psychology library at the University of California at Berkeley catching up on some reading, I took a bathroom break. Sitting in the stall, I began to read the grafitti scrawled around me:

"I would like to make innocent love to another woman. Nice and slow love making. I am a normal person with no crazy desires. Does anyone know of someone?"

Several suggestions followed, each in different script.

"Try Hoyt Hall, the co-op on Ridge Road. There are some nice women living there or ask at the gay/lesbian/bisexual alliance on campus."

"I live at Hoyt Hall. There are only a few lesbians there."

"What's wrong with wanting to lick a woman's cunt?"

"Nothing. It's called homosexual tendencies."

Bemused, I scribbled the restroom commentary down on a scrap of paper, went back to my carrel and picked up Masters and Johnson's *Homosexuality in Perspective* (1979) again. "By showing," I read in the foreword, "that there are no physiologic norms clearly distinguishing homosexual and heterosexual function . . . , [Masters and Johnson] invite an abandonment of many of the stereotypes of normal versus abnormal function" (Engelhardt, p.vii). I looked at my john door notations again. Apparently, lesbianism had been decreed normal both in the formal sphere of sexology and in the informal, private ruminations of University of California undergraduates. The defiant query, "What's wrong with wanting to lick a woman's cunt?" seemed aimed at the very same disapproving establishment that Masters and Johnson were trying to educate. I wondered if one could always track the latest "truths" across different discourses. Would, for example, the personal musings of nineteenth century citizens mirror the scientific wisdom of the day as accurately as the bathroom stall had reflected Masters and Johnson? Foraging in the stacks, I found an excerpt from *Sexual Physiology and Hygiene,* a marriage manual written by Dr. R. T. Trail in 1866:

The frequency with which sexual intercourse can be indulged without serious damage to one or both of the parties depends, of course, on a variety of circumstances–constitutional stamina, temperament, occupation, habits of exercise, etc. Few should exceed the limits of once a week, while many cannot safely indulge oftener than once month. But as temperance is always the safe rule of conduct, if there must be any deviation from the strictest law of physiology, let the error be on that side. (Gordon, 1971, p. 37)

Rummaging around in Jonathan Katz's *Gay/Lesbian Almanac* (1983), I found an interesting passage from Mary Casal's 1905 diary.

Our lives were on a much higher plane than those of the real inverts. While we did indulge in our sexual intercourse, that was never the thought uppermost in our minds. We had seen over-indulgence on the part of some of those with whom we came in contact, in loss of vitality and weakened health, ending in consumption. (p. 305)

The mirroring was unmistakable. Were lesbians continually refurbishing their identities according to scientific trends? Perhaps the stentorian declamations of experts simply lent authority to popular opinions. Like characters in a cartoon, I imagined us all–scientists and lay people, therapists and clients, students and faculty, even dogs and cats–simultaneously babbling the identical nonsense in different jargon. But something wasn't quite accurate about the cartoon. After all, if the same information was merely reiterated in different registers, how did our truths evolve? When I considered the course of my own career, I realized a system of not-so-subtle rewards existed for those of us positioned to reconfigure information–to tell slightly altered "truths." I remembered, for example, that before I handed them to my clients, I edited the guides to proper massage sequences. I infused them with what I considered to be the necessary esprit de clit by whiting out all references to penises:

Nipple . . . [white space] erections should not get extra attention, although patterns of goosebumps may be given further attention since, if the room isn't cold, this is a sign of successful stroking. (Apfelbaum, Williams, & Greene, 1979, p. 86)

The newly de-dicked sentences earned me special cachet. After all, I had been able to import cutting-edge sexpertise from the mainstream and tailor it in such a way that the marginal status of my lesbian clients was whited out along with the penis references.

But the gelling of certain perspectives into accepted wisdom did not always proceed in such a straightforward way. Imaginative flourishes, misconstruals and compression of ideas probably accounted for most new truths. For example, when they were first published in journals and anthologies, the articles on fusion in lesbian relationships were complicated hybrids which grafted together notions from mainstream marriage manuals, the sociology of deviance, and gay identity politics. Summaries of the articles appeared in lesbian newsletters and gay studies syllabi, and the community grapevine, in turn, summarized these summaries. Eventually all the commentary boiled down to one new and quite unintended "fact": Lesbians were "merger queens."

But everyone knows that psychology–a soft science–is always suspect, its findings always fictional. An analysis, however, of the hard science of Masters and Johnson reveals the same process of expedient story-telling.

As couples' therapists and medical scientists, as traditional married partners and nontraditional work colleagues, William Masters and Virginia Johnson were positioned to weave together elements of the warring discourses about sex and gender. Tradition defined women as wives and mothers, and sex as the natural, inexorable conjunction of opposites. On the other hand, the sexual and women's liberation movements proclaimed the new woman to be a lusty self-determining female who, by separating procreation from recreation, heralded the triumph of science over nature.

When they set out to write *Human Sexual Response* (1966), the two researchers looked for a bit of neutral ground, an Archimedean Point outside the debate, upon which to build their theories. They found it in the post-Kinsey consensus about orgasms. Whatever their sexual ideology, most Americans knew that almost all men and a substantial proportion of women had experienced orgasms. Consequently, centering their research around orgasms was a safe bet. During laboratory trials–hardly a "normal" setting for sex–Masters and Johnson "discovered" the "normal sexual response cycle." It consisted of orgasms, which they elaborated into a four phase sequence consisting of excitement, plateau, orgasm and resolution stages. When women's sexual response data were not parallel to men's, however, Masters and Johnson tried to shoehorn them into a male tumescent/detumescent boilerplate:

> Only one response pattern has been diagramed for the human male
> . . . comparable to three different sexual response patterns . . . dia-
> gramed for female . . . there is a great variation in both the intensity
> and the duration of the female orgasmic experience. (p. 5)

This finding should have led to a quite opposite conclusion, i.e., that
women's orgasmic patterns are *not* parallel to men's. Nevertheless,
Masters and Johnson claimed the four part human response cycle was
universal. And in my training program, this equivalency between men
and women was extended to include sexual appetites and genital structures. We were shown color coded slides depicting penises and vulvas.
Matching colors denoted homologous structures. Thus the scrotum and
labia majora were the identical canary yellow, the glans penis and glans
clitoris both mauve, etc. The message was explicit: the difference between men and women was largely a matter of sex role stereotyping and
quirks, not innate capacity.

But were Masters and Johnson really so intent upon proving analogous male and female sexuality? Was there a hidden agenda? The data
about equivalent orgasms and the pictures of homologous genital structures can be read, depending on one's perspectives, in contrary ways.
One possible interpretation is that women are the equals of men; another is that men *are,* themselves, the norm. Women may approximate
them, but our orgasms are more diffuse, our dicks (clitorises) diminu-
tive. Thus women can be "liberated" and, simultaneously, reminded of
our subordinate position.

1989: ANTI-SEX THERAPY

The research and conclusions of Masters and Johnson were insepara-
ble from–actually shaped by–mainstream ideology. And my prescriptions for a healthy sex life, despite the lesbian-friendly window dressing
I had given it, were laced with the phallocentric values and suppositions
that I had imbibed as a trainee. Now that lesbian bed death seemed a
particularly oppressive fiction, a "condition" to be deconstructed rather
than treated, I could no longer, in good conscience, be a lesbian sex
therapist. Instead, I decided I'd become an anti-sex therapist. Instead of
trying to goose slumbering libidos, I would simply discuss the politics
of sex. Together, clients and I would explore the origins of consensus
about sexuality, the ways in which such universal beliefs affected different groups, and the benefits that accrued to the "discoverers" of these

truths. In short, I would tell them what I knew. Equally important, by assigning exercises that illuminated the fuzzy provisionality of sex, I would show them that no one, including me, knew anything for sure. Other exercises would, I hoped, isolate, scramble, and desanctify phallic patterns of tumescence and detumescence which had been enshrined as normal sex. And finally, I hoped we would collaboratively design a series of activities which, defying categorization as sexual or non-sexual, would open a new realm of intimacy for partners.

One of the first couples to experience my anti-sex approach were two white working class women I'll call Melanie and Gina. After they moved in together a few months before, they had become increasingly polarized over sex. Gina described herself as "completely shut down" while Melanie complained that her sexuality, an essential part of herself, had no outlet.

Both partners had been raised in families whose ability to nurture them had been compromised by alcoholism, divorce, and economic distress. It was hard to separate such early deprivation from their current sexual problems. From a psychodynamic point of view, their sexual impasse could be interpreted as a struggle to get the special attention that had been in short supply all their lives. I couldn't bypass Melanie's and Gina's feelings of deprivation and abandonment. Entwined with an exploration of these issues was an ongoing discussion of the precepts of anti-sex.

I described the rather torturous path I had followed to anti-sex, including my Masters and Johnson training and my own previous hit-and-miss record of treating lesbian bed death. Before they came back the next time, I asked Melanie and Gina to begin a series of experiments which I hoped would blur the line between sex and non-sex. As a beginning assignment, I proposed a massage that would scramble standard erotic/nonerotic zones. They could avoid the standard sequences of working up to the erotic zones by interspersing random touches of noses, nipples, toes, vaginas, and knees or by designating a new sacred zone. If they used the elbow, for example, they could gradually work up to it through a subordination of all the other, now less important, zones. We collaborated on the design of other similar experiments. On a day before they planned to go to the park and play catch, they decided that along with the ball which they could toss underhanded from the vicinity of their crotches, they could also hurl dirty words at each other. On another occasion, before bedtime, they tied scarves around themselves in such a way that they brushed against their genitals as they were going to sleep. At one point, when she was recounting her early sexual experiences, Gina reported some pleasant erotic encounters with boys in the back seats of cars. Since emotional abandonment continued to be a theme, I suggested that we try to combine both Gina's early memories of sexual experimentation with the forlornness they both felt in the present. Modifying Gina's teen scenario, they disrobed under a blanket in the back of their car and were simply "waifs together," simultaneously naked and woebegone.

At the end of two months of these exercises, Gina and Melanie threw in the towel. They had had enough. When I ran into them six months later, they were succinct about the ineffectiveness of anti-sex therapy.

"We wanted," Melanie said, "to have a sex life of abandon and you wanted us to abandon our sex life."

Gina added, "I just wanted to be fixed. I didn't want a revolution."

They had, they told me, found a new therapist, who, in addition to helping them with their sex problems, had recently officiated at their wedding. When I ran into Gina a year later, she told me they had thrown in the towel on their relationship as well. Her final analysis: "I fell in love. And I found out that I'm really a bottom. I've found someone who can really top me."

Anti-sex therapy was a bust. Upon reflection, I understood why my approach hadn't worked with Gina and Melanie. Sex may have been a phallocentric social construction. It was also the only way we certified our existences. When we made love, we were "performing" our essences, enacting a pivotal aspect of an embattled identity. Perhaps lesbian bed death was a way of affirming our essences as well. Even if we weren't doing it, we could at least worry about it, talk it over, or confer with an expert. Rather than give up the whole category, and our identities along with it, we would find new techniques, new roles, new therapists, new lovers, or merely new ways to lament the absence of sex in our lives.

1993: LESBIAN BED DEATH REVISITED

The passage of time from 1979 to 1993 has been marked not by a decline in lesbian bed death, but rather by my clients' reluctance to admit they still suffer from it. After years of workshops, how-to books, and butch/femme liberation, something really must be wrong if they're not having sex. Home remedies have also gone through some transformations: handcuffs have replaced crystals, strap-ons dildos now sub for plug-in vibrators.

My own brand of sex therapy has changed again. I know too much to do sex therapy. I don't know enough to do anti-sex therapy. I haven't got any formulas to offer lesbian clients as sex substitutes, and even if I could imagine such alternatives, I don't have the cultural authority to legitimize them.

Now when clients complain of lesbian bed death, I simply try to coax into consciousness the ways their experiences, cultures, and temperaments have shaped their versions of sex. I can only hope that in this process of detailing histories and reactions, partners will come to appreciate the plurality of sexual meanings and how very distinct their maps are. I hope, too, that they will collaborate on mutually inclusive maps.

One of the couples I am currently seeing stopped having sex two years ago. One grew up in El Salvador in an extended matriarchy; the other in Ohio in a series of foster homes. To the Central American woman, constantly supervised by a cadre of aunts, grandmothers, and older sisters, "private parts" meant exactly that; her body was not to be shared with anyone. And she was taught that every man she encountered would try to inveigle her into sharing it. Her first erotic encounter occurred "in her sleep" with another equally protected girl. "Sex" for her is something entirely different from what it is to her North American lover who, as a foster child, was molested many times. A dangerous male-dominated universe is apparent in both women's stories. Yet phallocentrism has affected each partner so differently that, as a template, it is almost irrelevant. Because their erotic maps are so different, misunderstandings are the norm; any synchronization of desire is rare, unpredictable, a minor miracle.

We have spent many sessions exploring every contrasting detail. Just when I feel we have finally given each difference its due, I discover another nuance which, filtering in from some unexpected source, mediates sexuality in yet another unanticipated way. During the most recent session, they reported they were feeling particularly intimate. Having moved into the bedroom, they were holding each other when one woman interrupted the embrace long enough to take a piece of lint from her partner's eyelash. The lint remover explained that the speck had broken her concentration. Her partner said the removal had interrupted hers. Both partners felt misunderstood, victimized by the other's insensitivity. They were as estranged as they were when they first came in months ago. We were back to square one. Was the misunderstanding a collaborative way of avoiding a perilous encounter? Or was it simply a clash of physiologies—one partner relying more on sensation, the other more visually oriented? I can't tell without more exploration, more information about their particular maps. I am reminded of Jorge Louis Borges' fable, *Of Exactitude in Science* (1975).

> In that Empire, the craft of Cartography attained such Perfection that the Map of a Single province covered the space of an entire City, . . . In the course of Time these Extensive maps were found somehow wanting and the . . . Cartographers evolved a Map of the Empire that was of the same Scale as the Empire and coincided with it point for point." Eventually the mapmakers finding such maps cumbersome, discarded them. . . . Now tattered fragments of the Map are still to be found, Sheltering an occasional Beast or beggar; in the whole Nation, no other relic is left of the Discipline of Geography. (p. 131)

Perhaps, someday, our sexual maps will become equally cumbersome and we will discard them. Perhaps the only relic of the days of lesbian bed death will be a quaint jumble of lab equipment and the abandoned offices of sex therapists. On one of their dusty desks, some wild sibyl will have etched the truths that liberate us, once and for all, from the discipline of sex.

REFERENCES

Apfelbaum, B., Williams, M. & Greene, S. (1979). *Couple sex therapy assignments. Expanding the boundaries of sex therapy.* Berkeley: Selected Papers of the Berkeley Sex Therapy Group. 84-91.

Borges, J.L. (1975) *Of exactitude in science. A universal history of infamy.* Middlesex: Penguin.

Burch, B. (1985) Another perspective on merger in lesbian relationships. In L.B. Rosewater and L.E.A. Walker (Eds.), *Handbook of feminist therapy.* New York: Springer. 100-109.

Casal, M. (1983). I was not a creature apart. In J. Katz (Ed.) *Gay/lesbian almanac.* New York: Harper Colophon. 303-307.

Engelhardt, H.T. (1979). Foreword. In W. Masters and V. Johnson, *Homosexuality in perspective.* Boston: Little Brown and Company, v-viii.

Foucault, M. (1980) The history of sexuality. New York: Vintage.

Gordon, M. (1971) Marital education literature. In J.M. Henslin (Ed.) *Studies in the sociology of sex.* New York: Appleton-Century-Crofts. 28-45.

Katz, J. (1983). *Gay/lesbian almanac.* New York: Harper Colophon: 305.

Krestan, J. & Bepko, C. (1980) The problem of fusion in lesbian relationships. *Family Process* 19: 277-289.

Masters, W. & Johnson, V. (1966). *Human Sexual Response.* Boston: Little Brown and Company.

Padgug, R. Sexual matters: On conceptualizing sexuality in history, *Radical History Review* 20: 16-24.

Epilogue:
The Demiurge Remaps the Semi-urge

Marny Hall

Almost ten years have passed since I produced the downcast and de-featist "Not tonight dear . . ." It is hard to pinpoint the precise day, or even year, when my perspective changed. I only know that, sometime during the decade, the wild sibyl did breeze into my office.[1] She threw open the windows, dusted off the desk, and rummaged around in the closet until she found the cumbersome sex therapy map I had been on the verge of discarding. Then she did something I could not have pre-dicted. She held it up to the office mirror. Gazing at the reflected image, I saw that each of the major features on the now reversed map was indi-cated by monogrammed pushpin. Read all together, the monogram spelled out L.E.S.B.I.A.N. I realized that the counter-map demarcated a new way of configuring the lesbian-love-sex-romance territory that I had been so busily critiquing.

L

For example, on the original map the letter L had marked the site of a particularly treasured ideal: Long-lasting lesbian love. It was in this ver-dant oasis that women met, fell in love, and, realizing the cosmic inevi-

Marny Hall is in private practice in San Francisco and Oakland, CA.
Address correspondence to: Marny Hall, 4112 24th Street, San Francisco, CA 94114 (E-mail: Marnyhall@aol.com).

[Haworth co-indexing entry note]: "Epilogue: The Demiurge Remaps the Semi-urge." Hall, Marny. Co-published simultaneously in *Women & Therapy* (The Haworth Press, Inc.) Vol. 24, No. 1/2, 2001, pp. 173-178; and: *A New View of Women's Sexual Problems* (ed: Ellyn Kaschak, and Leonore Tiefer) The Haworth Press, Inc., 2001, pp. 173-178. Single or multiple copies of this article are available for a fee from The Haworth Document Delivery Service [1-800-HAWORTH, 9:00 a.m. - 5:00 p.m. (EST). E-mail address: getinfo@haworthpressinc.com].

tability of their convergence, pledged that only death would part them. On the reverse map the backward L pointed to a variety of microclimates—some temperate, some chilly—in which fluctuated a legion of semi-permanent intimacies. Instead of being demarcated by crisp boundaries as they had previously, these alliances simply changed shape and form and spilled over into previously unexplored territory.

E

On the original map, the next letter, E, signified equity in all matters. Ideal love-making, for example, was depicted as a mutually desired and effortlessly egalitarian erotic activity. Although some of the same mutuality was depicted on the counter-map, asymmetries were far more common. For example, certain twosomes might be comprised of one partner who was consistently passive—at times, even indifferent to love-making—and another more eager, active partner. Furthermore, on the counter map, such inequities were often prized, elaborated, and dramatized by means of costumes and formal roles.

S

Capping the highest elevation of the old map, and dominating the landscape for miles around was the letter S. Marking the ascent to this almost sacred, sexual pinnacle were several distinct and clearly delineated arousal steps—brief resting places for peak performers. In contrast, the counter-map showed no signs of a staged ascent. Even the single, awesome peak was absent. Instead, the terrain, variegated, was liberally sprinkled with small, medium and large S's. These sites reflected differences in histories and hormones, in life stages and cultural conditioning, temperaments and relationships. Among the profusion of S-sites were locations for earthmoving sex, for silly sex, for mood-elevating or sorrowful sex, for placating sex, for relaxing or energizing sex, for barter sex, or for signature sex—a way of making a statement about one's culture or identity. There were sites for solo sex with and without a partner, sex for intimacy and sex for distance. There was even a sex-free zone, a place sex-aversives could congregate.[2]

Along with the L, E, and S sites, the zones indicated by the push pins B, I, A, and N had also been reversed in cunning ways.[3] I don't know how long exactly I puzzled over the contrary map. I only know that, for a long time, the implications of the topsy-turvy reflection eluded me. Finally, it occurred to me that disparaging–or even discarding–the old map was not enough. When I realized that, in order to make a difference, I had to announce the existence of the new map and the territory it represented, I got cold feet.

When it comes to challenging the status quo, I have never been particularly bold. Furthermore, my psychotherapy training had never emphasized assertiveness. Effective therapy, I learned, consisted of listening, supporting, analyzing, and occasionally confronting the client, not the framework of sex therapy itself. Difficult as it had been for me, I had screwed up the courage necessary to challenge the received wisdom. But critiquing the old map was one thing; substituting a contrary one was an entirely different matter. For me to contemplate, even in my most private moments, formulating and proposing specific and detailed alternatives to the standard approaches to lesbian sex and love struck me as a terrifying and aggressive act. Consequently, I had hoped that my clients and I could collaborate in the process of designing mutually inclusive erotic couples maps, collages which somehow braided partners' distinctive styles, desires, and bio-rhythms into satisfactory encounters. But I had found that even if couples believed, as I did, that conventional ideals and goals were spurious, they did not produce these alternative erotic composites. Adrift and anxious, they often fell back on familiar, and typically ungratifying, patterns of interaction.

Before I could pitch the reinvented counter-map to couples clients, therefore, I had to reinvent myself. I had to tolerate what was, for me, a degree of authorship, of power, that was both unfamiliar and taboo. I had to anoint myself as mapmaker, guide, even demiurge of a new erotic territory.

LESBIAN NATION BECOMES SELF ORDIN-NATION

The sibyl had first tipped me off about the new map. Now, the queer community provided me with inspiration. All around me, a sea change was underway. Many dykes with whom I had contact, as clients and friends, were reinventing themselves. Lesbians who for years had been declaring that they felt like gay boys or daddies or trannies, who had been fantasizing about being the proud possessors of giant phalluses, stepped out from behind these prepositional and adverbial hedges. Instead of feeling "like " or fantasizing "about," they *were*. They *had*. Inscribed surgically and hormonally, these new grammatical truths became the truths of the body. The ambiguity once conveyed by the discarded prepositions now began to appear as hyphens. Almost overnight, a blizzard of them settled on the newly declared identities. Pre-op and post-op, M-to-F and F-to-M, cross-dressers and third-genders, femme-tops and butch-bottoms became the lingua franca of Lesbian Nation.

Though these women were far braver than I, their creative self-ordinations were contagious. Even I, mildest-mannered of lesbian sex therapists, began to believe that I could reinvent myself as a topographer. As confident maker and purveyor of maps, I could point out previously hidden borderlands–those in-between gray areas and gradations overshadowed on the old map by sharply defined boundary markers. Inside these borderlands, I could locate and identify the features that been erased by the old map. Cobbled together into new sex lives, these features included solitary habits and occasional urgencies. Mixed messages and borderline acquiescence were also identifiable and legitimate precincts within the new erotic territory. There were mechanical sex sites and once-a-month-if-we-feel-like-it-or-not ritual zones. There were the only-if-I don't-have-to-lift-a-finger regions of resignation and maybe-I'll-feel-like-it-after-we-start patches of willingness. There was even a place on the map for aversive sex, and for the interminable why-aren't-we-having-sex-anymore processing marathons. In short, within the terra incognita depicted on the new map, contradictory impulses, semi-urges, and orgasmic habits had replaced the romantic one-size-fits-all ecstasex of the old terra (in)firma.

CIRCA 2000: THE RETURN OF THE SIBYL

By 2000, the counter map was working so well that I had almost forgotten about the old one. Then, one day, the sibyl paid me another unexpected visit. She pulled out the cumbersome old map that I had held up to the mirror so long ago, and suggested I glance over it again. Stowed away ever since the waning years of the twentieth century, I had assumed it had remained static, unchanged except for the additional dust it was collecting. I saw immediately that I was very mistaken. The S site, grown even loftier, has become both more inaccessible and more desirable. And now, its base was entirely occupied by clusters of life-sized models of doctors' offices, laboratories, computerized marketing and distribution centers, all connected and pulsating with energy. The products produced by this pharmaco-medical industrial complex, apparently designed as aids for the mountain climbers (who I noted were falling off the sheer peak in alarming numbers–whether from panic or desperation, I could not tell) were also life-sized.

At the urging of the sibyl, I pick up one of these new sex aids. It is a hand held battery-operated device with a small , soft plastic cup, which, according to the instructions, is to be placed over the clitoris. When the product, called the Eros, is switched on, it creates a gentle vacuum that increases the blood flow to the clitoris. The instructions inform me that the Eros is one of the treatments of choice for women suffering from Female Sexual Arousal Disorder. Upon further examination of the material included in the sales packet, I find that FSAD is the probable diagnosis of women who notice any decrease in their customary desire, lubrication, genital sensation, or orgasmic response patterns.[4]

The Eros, which costs $375, is only available by prescription. Curious about its reverse reflection, I hold it up. The mirror shows me a myriad of such devices. Called "clit pumps," they are available over the counter for one fourth the cost of the Eros. But this is only the beginning of the counter reflections. When I hold the informational packet that comes with the Eros in front of the mirror, queer sex expert, activist, and author, Fairy Butch (a.k.a., Karlyn Lotney) scrolls into view. Trumpeting the virtues of clit pumps, she announces that they can be used for orgasms, genderbending, or all round kinky adventures. Her exuberance about the myriad pleasures of clitpumping contrasts dramatically with the discreet, rehabilitative tone of the Eros instructions.

"Some pumping aficionados enjoy the process as a stand-alone thrill, while others prefer to include it as one part of a combination of sexual activities," Fairy Butch explains. "Clit pumping can be readily integrated with strap-on sex, oral sex, clitoral, vaginal, or anal stimulation"(Lotney, 2000, p. 109). The reflection of Fairy Butch continues: "Some female-bodied people such as transmen and stone butches who do not identify with their female genitalia find that oral sex is transformed after clit pumping; because the size of the clitoris may increase dramatically, fantasies of fellatio are easily accommodated" (p. 117).

Hmmm.

I look from the old map to the new: From pricey remedial device to playful sex toy, from monolith to profusion, from inadequacy to enhancement, dysfunction to pleasure. I'm still musing over the contrast between the maps when I feel a gentle tug on my sweater. It is the sibyl. She looks pointedly at the mirror and then at me. There is no missing this less-than-subtle directive. Now it's my turn to look at myself. Terrified, I glance quickly into the mirror. Too quickly. All I can make out is the vaporous contour of a cloud. I look again, more slowly this time.

Then they come into focus, faceted images of myself/not-myself. All different, they are skinny, fat, black, white, young, old. Each of these women, marshalling her own personal data and choosing her preferred theme and scale, is creating her own map. I watch, amazed, as these user-cartographers grow in number, as the scope and influence of their maps stretches to the edge of the mirror and beyond.

NOTES

1. The sibyl is, in part, the crystalization of my years of practice as a sex therapist, in part the distillation of theory imbibed from a number of social constructivists. Prominent among these muses are Leonore Tiefer, Liana Borghi, and Beatriz Preciado.
2. The inspiration for the profusion of sexual sites on the map comes from Annie Sprinkle's work. See Sprinkle, 1996.
3. For a full account of the counter map, as well as specific ways it can be used in lesbian couples' therapy, see Hall, 2001.
4. Urometrics, the manufacturer of the Eros, has a link on its website that connects visitors with a website called Women's Sexual Health (also sponsored by Urometrics). On this site, a 10 item quiz helps visitors determine if they are suffering from Female Sexual Arousal Disorder. Questions are limited to the quiz-takers' perceptions of sexual desire, genital sensation, and lubrication. Any decreases in these areas, signified by an affirmative answer to any of the ten questions, is a diagnostic indicator of FSAD.

REFERENCES

Hall, M. (2001) Beyond forever after: Narrative therapy with lesbian couples. In P. Kleinplatz (Ed). *Innovations in sex therapy.* New York. Brunner Mazel Press.
Lotney, K. (2000) *The ultimate guide to strap-on sex.* San Francisco: Cleis Press.
Sprinkle, A. (1996) 101 uses for sex–or why sex is so important. In M. Hall (Ed.), *Sexualities.* New York: Harrington Park Press

What's in a Disorder: A Cultural Analysis of Medical and Pharmaceutical Constructions of Male and Female Sexual Dysfunction

Jennifer R. Fishman
Laura Mamo

SUMMARY. This paper analyzes the emergence of two FDA-approved products to treat "sexual disorders": Viagra, a drug prescribed for the treatment of erectile dysfunction, and the Eros, a device prescribed for the treatment of female sexual dysfunction. Through an analysis of advertising and promotional materials for Viagra and the Eros, we argue that these pharmaceutical devices and the discourses they circulate reinforce normative gender ideals by enacting dominant cultural narratives of masculinity, femininity, and male and female sexuality. These cultural narratives of normative gender structure sexuality in such a way that reinforces certain kinds of masculinity, femininity, and (hetero)sexuality, thereby rendering "atypical" gender and sexual expressions, desires, and appearances invisible and marginal. We argue that these constructions reify cultural ideologies about "what counts" as legitimate and appropriate sexuality and that these con-

---

Jennifer R. Fishman and Laura Mamo are affiliated with the University of California.

Address correspondence to: Jennifer Fishman, Doctoral Candidate, Department of Social and Behavioral Sciences, Box 0612, University of California, San Francisco, San Francisco, CA 94143-0612 (E-mail: lmamo@itsa.ucsf.edu or jfishma@ itsa.ucsf. edu).

Selections of this paper are drawn from "Potency in all the right places: Viagra as a technology of the gendered body," Mamo and Fishman. *Body & Society,* 7(2), 2001.

[Haworth co-indexing entry note]: "What's in a Disorder: A Cultural Analysis of Medical and Pharmaceutical Constructions of Male and Female Sexual Dysfunction." Fishman, Jennifer R., and Laura Mamo. Co-published simultaneously in *Women & Therapy* (The Haworth Press, Inc.) Vol. 24, No. 1/2, 2001, pp. 179-193; and: *A New View of Women's Sexual Problems* (ed: Ellyn Kaschak, and Leonore Tiefer) The Haworth Press, Inc., 2001, pp. 179-193. Single or multiple copies of this article are available for a fee from The Haworth Document Delivery Service [1-800-HAWORTH, 9:00 a.m. - 5:00 p.m. (EST). E-mail address: getinfo@haworthpressinc.com].

179

structions have profound implication for social actors, sexologists, and therapists. *[Article copies available for a fee from The Haworth Document Delivery Service: 1-800-HAWORTH. E-mail address: <getinfo@haworthpressinc.com> Website: <http://www.HaworthPress.com> © 2001 by The Haworth Press, Inc. All rights reserved.]*

KEYWORDS. Sexuality, gender, medicalization, sexual dysfunction, discourse, pharmaceuticals

INTRODUCTION

This paper analyzes the emergence of two FDA-approved products to treat "sexual disorders": Viagra, a drug prescribed for the treatment of erectile dysfunction (ED), and the Eros, a device prescribed for the treatment of female sexual dysfunction (FSD). Through an analysis of promotional materials for Viagra and the Eros, we argue that these pharmaceutical devices and the discourses they circulate reinforce normative gender ideals by enacting dominant cultural narratives of masculinity, femininity, and male and female sexuality. These cultural narratives of normative gender structure sexuality in such a way that reinforces certain kinds of masculinity, femininity, and (hetero)sexuality, thereby rendering "atypical" gender and sexual expressions, desires, and appearances invisible and marginal.

The appearance of Viagra and the Eros on the market as treatments for sexual dysfunction signals a shift away from psychotherapeutic interventions toward pharmacological ones (Tiefer, 2000). Of concern here is that this "magic bullet" approach to sexual problems both effaces larger cultural and social phenomena and reinforces dominant ideals of gender. Thus, this paper provides a close reading of the promotional materials for these products in order to make explicit the normative cultural ideals embedded in these discourses–ideals which construct and reinforce uneven power relations and dominant scripts about gender and sexuality. We argue that Viagra and the Eros, as new technologies for the treatment of sexual dysfunction, re-invoke normative assumptions about heterosexuality, what counts as "appropriate" sexual activity, and the desired outcomes of sexual expression. However, in addition, we find that beneath these dominant scripts exist others that allow for alternative readings by potential users to reconstruct these assumptions, therein creating new uses and new discourses about sexuality.

THE MEDICAL LABELING OF SEXUAL DYSFUNCTION

It has been well established that biomedical knowledge, practices and techniques have found their way into people's daily lives, labeling more and more aspects of social life as "illness" or "dis-ease." Sexuality has not escaped medicalization. Since the nineteenth century, biomedicine has placed what it terms "perversions" under the medical gaze; recently, however, a wider range of sexual "problems" have also been placed under medical jurisdiction. These include reproduction, infertility, and now, sexual dysfunction. This shift represents a move to enroll previously "normal" populations into biomedical discourses and treatments. Sexual dysfunction has become one such example, with Viagra and the Eros representing this trend. It should be noted that this is not as simple as it seems, for in many of these cases, it is the "patients" themselves who request such designations, diagnoses, and biomedical solutions.

Sildenafil citrate, developed, marketed, and sold by Pfizer, Inc. under the brand name Viagra, is an oral therapy for the treatment of male erectile dysfunction (ED). Viagra, approved by the Food and Drug Administration (FDA) in March 1998, is considered the first noninvasive, non-surgical medical treatment for this health problem. A medical device called the Eros-CTD ("clitoral therapy device") received FDA clearance in April 2000. It is the only FDA-approved device for the treatment of female sexual dysfunction (FSD), and is available by prescription only. It is a hand-held battery-operated device with a suction cup to be placed on the clitoris that works as a vacuum to enhance blood flow to the genital area. Clinical study results indicate that the device can measurably increase blood flow, which is important for both vaginal lubrication and clitoral sensation (Billups et al., forthcoming).

The emergence of these products at the turn to the twenty-first century takes place in light of FDA regulation changes regarding the advertising of pharmaceuticals, and the increased penetration of pharmaceutical and chemical devices into many aspects of modern life. In 1997, the FDA loosened its regulations for marketing prescription drugs to allow pharmaceutical companies to advertise their products directly to consumers through print advertisements in mainstream magazines and television commercials (Terzian, 1999). In fact, the bulk of pharmaceutical advertising money has shifted to direct advertising to consumers themselves (Meyer, 1998). Prescription drugs are fast becoming popular consumer products, a capitalist fetish, where one is encouraged to think of such drugs as a means through which to improve one's life. The shift to the biomedicalization of life itself is indicative of a cultural and medical assertion that one's life can *always* be improved.

The pharmaceutical industry, one of the most profitable and competitive industries in the U.S. today (Angell, 2000), increasingly relies on lifestyle products like Viagra and the Eros in an attempt to bolster profits and market share. That Viagra has been so profitable most certainly impacts the research priorities of pharmaceutical companies who are now intently interested in *women*'s sexual health. The increasing privatization of biochemical and biotechnological research through pharmaceutical companies has meant that which research gets funded and supported is determined by the profitability of the end product, rather than by what is perceived to be most needed (Bloom, 1994; Muraskin, 1996), most lacking, or most overlooked. In addition, many of these drugs are most likely to appeal to a certain demographic segment of potential consumers, commonly thought of as "aging baby boomers," (see, e.g., Terzian, 1999) who are more likely to try these drugs in an effort to maintain youthful appearances, activities, and lifestyles. It is these intended users that we think the developers and marketers had in mind with Viagra and the Eros. Once aging is redefined in medical terms, a large-scale market becomes available to ensure the success of the next up-and-coming "lifestyle" product.

CULTURAL STUDIES AND DISCOURSE ANALYSIS

In this paper we centrally place biomedical developments within the rubric of cultural studies in order to expand current conceptions of the ways in which cultural discourses of gender, sexuality and biomedical technologies (in this case Viagra and the Eros) mutually shape one another. Since these drugs are linked to gendered, sexualized users, they raise important questions regarding sex, sexuality and gender, as well as issues of "what counts" as legitimate behaviors, expressions, and identities.

Cultural studies is an interdisciplinary field that examines cultural texts, products, and discourses in an effort to reveal ideologies and linguistic arrangements which structure the meanings embedded in the products and practices of social institutions (e.g., mass media, medicine). It looks critically at the ways in which the cultural practices of these institutions are used to support dominant ideologies of powerful social groups and reinforce social inequalities. Medicine, and its concomitant industries, is a social institution that is both informed by and *produces* "culture" through its products and discourses. A discourse is a social artifact that provides a coherent way of describing, categorizing, and "making sense" of the social and material worlds and the objects, persons, and interactions within them (Foucault, 1981). Discourses, in turn, have effects on the constitution of both subjects and objects of knowledge through this description and categorization, which is understood as the exercise of power through numerous, diffuse points and relations. It is our task in this paper to analyze discourses as patterns of ideologies that structure meanings and are produced through the development and promotion of medicine's latest sexual dysfunction treatments.

For our purposes, discourse analysis is useful for exploring how authority on the subject of "sexual dysfunction" is enacted (Terry, 1999) and for locating the *ideologies-in-progress* that produce common knowledge and accepted truths concerning its make-up and subjects. In other words, we explore biomedical constructions of sexual dysfunction, particularly those found in the promotional materials for Viagra and the Eros, as "truth productions" that reveal cultural assumptions, anxieties, and norms. Furthermore, we are suggesting that gendered norms and assumptions are both "inputs" and "outputs" of the social and cultural construction of Viagra and the Eros. Our already inscribed attitudes and understandings of sex, gender, and sexuality influence the manufacturing and diffusion of the drug. With Viagra and the Eros come preconceived ideas about the appropriate (heterosexual, partnered) users and (intercourse-based) uses of these devices thereby reinforcing such normative standards in the promotion of their use.

We analyzed the initial promotional pamphlet about Viagra for distribution by sales representatives, medical personnel, and pharmacists (Pfizer, 1998) and the UroMetrics, Inc. patient information video for the Eros (Urometrics, 2000). As marketing sites to potential consumers, these texts reveal the "ideologies-in-progress" of these technologies.

In our analysis of these texts we ask: What is appropriate (and inappropriate) sexual response and sexual expression? Who are constructed as the "ideal" consumers of the technologies? Under what conditions should these devices be used? And finally, what dominant and subordinate ideologies of gender and sexuality are invoked?

ANALYSIS:
DE-SCRIPTING[1] VIAGRA AND THE EROS

Viagra

Viagra (Re)configures Masculinity, or Viagra as Desire. One of the dominant cultural narratives that Viagra reinscribes is a hegemonic masculinity that relies on normative ideas about male sexuality. The scripts of the Viagra user embody many of the valued characteristics of masculinity, including virility, sexual mastery and control, and unhampered sexual desirousness for women, thereby appealing to potential users' aspirations of attaining (or maintaining) such ideal standards (Potts, 2000). This contributes to a codification of knowledge claims about what is sex, how the male (and female) body "works," and the parameters of appropriate male (and female) sexuality.

The dominant model of male sexuality relies on notions of omnipresent sexual desire. The traditional script of male sexuality is that men always want sex–desire is never the problem (Zilbergeld, 1999). Viagra "works" because desire is taken to be unproblematic for the male user. Promotional materials are careful to posit that Viagra is not an aphrodisiac, but will only work to produce an erection with sexual stimulation. In other words, Viagra is only a techno-assisted erection, not techno-implanted desire. The efficacy of the drug is never measured as whether men want to be sexual after taking the drug, only that they are able to be. This not only assumes men possess omnipresent sexual desire, but Viagra's effectiveness requires it. By extension, it therefore assumes that women are the object of men's sexual desires, thereby constructing normative gendered sexuality for both men and women.

This is evident in the closely linked assumption that the *desired* sexual activity is sexual intercourse or at least penetration. The clinical testing of the efficacy of the drug itself relied almost exclusively on the measurement of whether or not "successful" sexual intercourse could be achieved after administration of Viagra (Pfizer, 1998). An erection itself was measured through self-reports by subjects as to whether or not it was "sufficient" for sexual intercourse. In determining whether Viagra "is right for you," the pamphlet asks: "When you have an erection, is it usually hard enough to enter your partner?" This script reflects and reinforces dominant cultural narratives about appropriate and legitimate male sexuality.

Potency in All the Right Places. A photograph in the pamphlet depicts a middle-aged white couple in bed, smiling and snuggling in each others' arms. It carries the following caption underneath it: "There's more to a good relationship than sex. But if you love someone, you want to be able to show them [sic]. Viagra has helped us feel close again." As in this example, the pamphlet is generally careful to use gender-neutral terms for the sex of a man's sexual partner, even if it means being grammatically incorrect. Yet this seeming political correctness is belied by both the accompanying photographs of exclusively heterosexual couples and by other floating narrative quotes supposedly from Viagra users. For example, the following quote on page 11, "My wife helped me see that the problem wasn't that I was getting old. It was diabetes . . . " is accompanied by a picture of a middle-aged heterosexual couple taking a walk (Pfizer, 1998).

However, this may be a discursive strategy to appeal to traditional values while simultaneously alluding to alternative lifestyles. The use of the term "partner" instead of spouse raised anxieties among conservative "family values" representatives. Lou Sheldon, chairman of the Traditional Values Coalition, wrote a letter to Bob Dole, a spokesman for Viagra, objecting to Dole's statement that Viagra can "help millions of men and their partners" rather than "their spouses" (Garchik, 1999). The use of the term partner instead of spouse could be used to signal the possibility of heterosexual infidelity, a recognition of the high rates of divorced men (and women) in U.S. society, or potential consumers who are men who have sex with men. Enrolling Bob Dole as a spokesperson for Viagra is an ingenious marketing move, as Dole is seen to represent all that is "right" in masculinity–courage, strength, success, and heterosexuality. Because Dole represents the hegemonic ideal of masculinity, the use of "partner" instead of "spouse" seems acceptable. It barely even registers as "alternative."

This juxtaposition of the representation of heteronormativity (normative sexuality), and hegemonic masculinity with an opening available for "alternative lifestyles," indicates how the marketing relies on, and is perceived to need, the social legitimacy of Viagra as a drug for monogamous, heterosexual couples without limiting its potential consumer base. On one hand, the profitability of Viagra demands attracting as many customers as possible. On the other hand, the popularity and social acceptability of a drug for recreational sex in our current political and social climate depends on its alignment with cultural standards of "appropriate" sexual behavior. It is a delicate situation in which the discourse reinforces normative behaviors and relationships, yet also leaves open the possibility for other types of users.

As striking as the heteronormative scripts of Viagra is the recurrent emphasis of Viagra as a relational and coupled technology. As we discuss below, this is strikingly different from the discursive scripts found in the Eros. Another deeply engrained script of Viagra is an assumption that Viagra is going to be used during sexual activity with somebody else. The assumption of relationship use is revealed throughout the text of the pamphlet, and most prominently in the section entitled, "Facing ED [erectile dysfunction] as a couple." This section emphasizes the necessity of "open and honest communication between partners." It is nearly unfathomable to imagine a man taking Viagra for auto-erotic purposes within the context of the pamphlet. Viagra is then constructed as a device that is not only sexually therapeutic but also therapeutic for the overall health and well-being of the relationship. Viagra "fixes" erections and relationships too! There is a further assumption about the nature of a Viagra user's relationship with his partner. The repetitive emphasis on communication and "good" relationships carries with it a script about not only appropriate sexuality, but also appropriate relationship conduct. In many ways, the relationship between a Viagra user and his partner is assumed to be monogamous. Consider the following text:

> If you're the partner of a man with ED, you may need to take the first step. Men with ED are often willing to try treatment options suggested by their partners . . . Understanding ED and knowing that there is a convenient, oral treatment available, can help the two of you to see a doctor and put the worry of ED behind you. (p. 13)

This construction of Viagra as a drug for the "two of you" conveys a script about the appropriate Viagra user as monogamous, in a relationship where he has a partner with whom he wishes to and can discuss these problems, and having a partner who wishes to accompany him to the doctor's office. Alternative constructions of relationships (for example, men with a male partner, men with more than one partner, men without a regular partner, men without any partners, or men who do not wish to tell their partners about their sexual dysfunction) are suppressed in favor of the normative ideas of impotent men. *Impotence itself is constructed as a coupled phenomenon.*

Nowhere is this more evident than in the print campaign for Viagra. In the print advertisements for Viagra, the recurring image is of a late-middle aged, heterosexual couple dancing, with the woman in the man's arms as he dips her across his body. The hint of sex appeal in a scene of an otherwise upstanding couple in a public space is a strategically perfect representation of appropriate conduct and the "ideal" users (i.e., the couple). Furthermore, it illustratively shows the hegemonic promises of Viagra. He is firmly in control of this "dance," indicated by his right arm placed firmly behind her back. The spinning movement captured in the ad lets us know that he still has a "spring in his step" and is still able to take his wife (note the large gold band visible on his left hand) for a spin and put a satisfied smile on her face. The intimacy conveyed through their close bodies and the gazing into each others' eyes reveals the effectiveness of Viagra not only for erections, but also for bringing couples closer together.

THE EROS

Through our analysis, the Eros likewise emerges as a gendered technology, transmitting cultural scripts which serve as enforcers of normatively gendered expressions of sex and sexuality. Similar to Viagra, these scripts include normative assumptions of female (and male) sexuality, femininity (and masculinity), heterosexuality, and ideas of "appropriate" sexual relationships. However, the scripts found in the Eros rely on traditional notions of femininity which construct women as the primary actor in the emotional/relational aspects of a relationship, but not the sexual aspects, thus also maintaining hegemonic masculinity and the appropriate place for male potency.

Gaining Legitimacy: The Eros as Therapy. "Forty-three million women or four in 10 women experience some type of sexual disorder." This is how the patient information video for the Eros-CTD device begins. This statistic, taken from a study recently published in JAMA (Laumann et al., 1999), has been used to justify biomedical research and treatment for the widespread "disease" of "female sexual dysfunction" (FSD). The video, entitled *An Answer to FSD,* proposes that the Eros may help women suffering from FSD symptoms which include decrease in vaginal lubrication, pain during intercourse, difficulty achieving orgasm, and decreased sexual satisfaction. In its promotion and information of its product, the Eros video also promotes certain normative discourses about female sexuality, sexual pleasure, and "appropriate" sexual behavior in its instructions for use and claims of "successful" treatment. It encourages consumer use of the Eros (which costs approximately $375 by prescription and is covered by some insurance plans) by invoking and therefore reifying dominant cultural ideologies. First of all, it promotes FSD as a medical problem and therefore in need of a medical solution. The Eros is offered as just such solution. Secondly, the Eros reinforces the idea that there is a universal, homogeneous female sexual response cycle. By depending on this model, the video claims its product to be effective. Thirdly, the Eros, like Viagra, relies on discourses that promote certain forms of appropriate sexual activity, that is, heterosexual intercourse, as the desired outcome of FSD treatment. The following cultural analysis reveals that, similar to

Viagra, these cultural ideologies rely on and reinforce cultural narratives of normative gender.

After we learn about the scope of women's sexual "problems," the video switches to an interior setting with a woman, seemingly a doctor, in a white coat who tells us that the Eros-CTD is the first and only FDA approved treatment for female sexual dysfunction. While the device itself seems to resemble an over-the-counter sex toy in shape and function, it is carefully constructed as a device for "treatment" rather than for "pleasure" (Urometrics, 2000). This definition is important in a number of ways. First of all, the Eros-CTD is a "recreational" device, just as sex is (mostly) a recreational activity; however, in order to market it as a prescriptive product, it, like Viagra, had to be packaged through medical terminology. Just as female sexual dysfunction has itself been medicalized (see Tiefer in this issue), the Eros follows similar prescriptive patterns, billing itself as a "safe and effective" treatment such that "with regular use" a woman will see "an improvement in overall sexual satisfaction . . . within several weeks." With your Eros device comes detailed instructions for use which tells a woman "how often to use the device and for how long" (Urometrics, 2000). In other words, just as drugs come with a "take two pills every four hours" prescription, the Eros too has prescriptions for use–"the Eros may be used daily." (This begs the obvious question, can it be used more often?) Therefore, the Eros, while capitalizing on the medicalization of women's sexual problems, contributes to this very process through prescriptions and proscriptions for its use.

This brings to light an interesting paradox within the Eros' promotional campaign. On one hand, it wishes to make itself a marketable product, appealing to a broad consumer base (at least 43 million women!) in order to turn a profit. On the other hand, its legitimacy as a consumptive device depends upon its alignment within the medical discourses of other restricted, prescription treatments. Its producers must find a way to market the Eros widely, yet simultaneously be taken seriously as appropriate for clinical treatment. In this sense, it seems to wish to differentiate itself from fetishized sex toys that look remarkably similar and function in similar ways to the Eros (and sell for about one-tenth of the cost). This is accomplished through medical language as well as through alluding to the Eros as a device for "stimulation" but not for direct sexual satisfaction. The Eros video is careful to claim that with prolonged use it will allow for an "enhanced *ability* to achieve orgasm," rather than being able to produce techno-assisted orgasms *through* its use. This may seem like a minor difference, but a "clitoral therapy" device needs all of the social legitimacy it can get.

Use the Eros: No need for foreplay! If we look carefully at this difference, the Eros differentiates itself from sex toys therein assuring its potential consumers (and their husbands) that the device is not intended to replace one's partner, but rather to "ready" oneself for the "main event"–that is, intercourse. The Eros then is purposely designed and promoted to fit into popular cultural understandings of "appropriate" (hetero)sexual activity and the "appropriate" roles and behaviors associated with it. These are developed through dominant discourses about the sequence of events of the sexual response cycle, which activities produce this sequencing of events, and who is responsible for which events. Although it seems rather daring for a product to market itself as a "clitoral therapy device," this can actually be read as a way of assuring that it is not interpreted as a penis replacement. Men are still constructed as necessary for women's sexual fulfillment. Within dominant discourses of female sexuality, while the clitoris has been mostly accepted as a site for sexual stimulation and arousal, it is still perceived as an organ which allows for sufficient arousal for *other* forms of stimulation and activity to take place. The Eros is a "treatment" which allows for the "gold standard" of (hetero)sexual satisfaction–that is, orgasm through "normal" sexual intercourse with a male partner. The Eros campaign, assuring us that it is not trying to rock the heteronormative boat, instead reifies this refrain in making the clitoris an organ for foreplay (an essential step in promoting lubrication), rather than for satisfaction in and of itself. The recommended use for Eros is either "for before intercourse or as self-stimulation" (but not satisfaction), therein curtailing other possible uses, for example with intercourse, instead of intercourse, for use on a woman *by* one's partner, in between or in conjunction with other activities. In fact, it is unclear what the Eros can do that a partner's mouth cannot.

Unlike Viagra which is touted as a technology for couples' use, the Eros' instructions are for use *without* (but not instead of) one's partner. Where ED in general is constructed as a coupled phenomenon, FSD is a "woman's" problem, and likewise her problem to "fix." The Eros is used on one's own time or before sexual activity, such that *then* one can achieve sexual satisfaction and satisfy one's partner through traditional means, namely intercourse. This assures the hetero-couple that the problem was not one of his sexual performance, but a physiological, medical problem of her own. Once a woman "fixes" her "arousal problem," and blood is flowing to the appropriate places, he can still "give" her sexual satisfaction. A quote appears on the screen at the end of the video, purportedly by a "patient's husband": "This is a great device and my wife is now as happy as I am." She, in turn, fulfills her feminine and wifely role of satisfying her partner through traditional means and by extension, healing their relationship. In another text quote at the end of a video, a "patient" says, "After 40 years, I'm so glad that there's finally a solution to the problem that ended my marriage."

CONCLUSIONS

Viagra and the Eros emerge as gendered technologies, active in the construction of male and female sexuality and appropriate male and female behaviors. In fact, the promotional materials both rely on ideologies of masculinity and femininity for their legitimacy as medical treatments. In other words, Viagra constructs appropriate masculinity via its relationship to femininity and the Eros performs the same discursive move in the reverse. Our analysis reveals that both technologies employ similar ideologies-in-progress through their use of cultural scripts about the nature of (hetero)sexual relationships and heteronormative sexuality.

Viagra relies on hegemonic masculinity in such a way that appeals to potential users' aspirations of attaining (or maintaining) ideal male omnipresent sexual desire and reaffirms the *desired* sexual activity as female receptive sexual intercourse. Viagra provides men with a techno-*assisted* erection, not pharmaceutically-derived desire. The Eros is similarly promoted as a product to enable sexual intercourse. But what is important for women's roles in this activity is her receptivity, or "readiness." This is evident in the construction of the Eros as a device for private "stimulation" preceding sexual satisfaction, not as satisfaction. Finally, while both of these technologies are constructed as a coupled phenomenon, unlike Viagra, which is touted as a technology for couples' use, the Eros' instructions are for use *without* (but not instead of) one's partner. This is an interesting discursive move in that the Eros, like Viagra, is constructed as a technology that can save relationships with women's use of it. The distinction is not unimportant; the technologies reaffirm the dominant gendered meanings of masculine sexuality as omnipresent desire and feminine sexuality as fulfilling relational responsibilities.

While these more dominant constructions are obvious, it is also true that alternative readings of these scripts are available and construct additional types of users and uses of these devices then envisioned by their developers. For example, we believe that on the flipside of the heteronormative ideologies of the marketing materials are possibilities for new representations to emerge. Both technologies can fulfill transgressive possibilities even though they are co-constituted with gendered inscriptions that long preceded them. It is not hard to see transformative possibilities created with the use of these devices, altering our understandings of "appropriate" sexual activities, compulsory heterosexuality, and masculinity and femininity. In fact, there is much evidence to show that the destabilization of Viagra's normative scripts is happening already. We have all heard rumors, anecdotes, and media stories (e.g., Trebay, 1999) of: Viagra used for male performance enhancement, or in conjunction with, illicit drugs; women and gay men using Viagra; and of course, older men using Viagra to return to the hetero-social scene. The Eros is a newer product and thus popular stories have not yet surfaced. However, alternative readings are possible. It is not difficult to imagine alternative uses for a product like this: sex toy, engorgement for clitoral insertion, nipple stimulator, oral sex enhancer, penile pump. These stories indicate that while the promotional materials enact certain truth effects on our patients, they are not the only "truths." Therefore, the potential resistance to and liberation from normative scripts of sexuality lies in the heterogeneous users and uses of the technologies themselves. In order to uncover this potential, important questions to ask include: who are the alternative users of Viagra (e.g., gay male users, disabled users, transsexual users, interssexual users, female users, etc.); and under what circumstances is Viagra used and for what purposes (e.g., recreation, procreation, intimacy, performance enhancement, penile penetration, masturbation, size, clitoral insertion, etc.).

Discourse analysis is one strategy that can be employed in an effort to read the ideologies-in-progress at work within particular texts and social institutions. These have consequences for patients, sexologists, and therapists. As we move into the twenty-first century, biomedical innovations designed to "treat" sexual dysfunction will continue to flood the marketplace increasing consumption "choices." These will continue to promote and rely upon standard measurement tools and dominant cultural constructions of what counts as appropriate sexuality, and by extension, as ideal users. This type of analysis, then, plays an important role in evaluating and countering such constructions through uncovering the "scripts" that lie just beneath the surface.

NOTE

1. The term "de-scripting" is from Akrich (1992), and effectively describes the process by technoscience studies scholars of deconstructing the inscripting mechanisms of technologies on the bodies of users.

REFERENCES

Akrich, M. (1992). The de-scription of technical objects. In W. E. Bijker & J. Law (Eds.), Shaping technology/building society (pp. 205-224). Cambridge: The MIT Press.

Angell, M. (2000). The pharmaceutical industry: To whom is it accountable? *The New England Journal of Medicine, 342*, 1902-1904.

Balsamo, A. (1996). *Technologies of the gendered body*. Durham and London: Duke University Press.

Billups, K. L., Berman, L., Berman, J., Metz, M. E., Glennon, M. E., & Goldstein, I. (Forthcoming). Vacuum-induced clitoral engorgement for treatment of female sexual dysfunction. *Journal of Sex & Marital Therapy*.

Bloom, B. (1994). The United States needs a national vaccine authority. *Science, 265*, 1378-1381.

Conrad, P. (1992). Medicalization and social control. *Annual Review of Sociology, 18*, 209-232.

Conrad, P., & Schneider, J. W. (1980). *Deviance and medicalization*. St. Louis: The C.V. Mosby Co.

Dreger, A. D. (1998). *Hermaphrodites and the medical invention of sex*. Cambridge, MA: Harvard University Press.

Ehrenreich, B., & Ehrenreich, J. (1978). Medicine as social control. In J. Ehrenreich (Ed.), *The cultural crisis of modern medicine* (pp. 39-79). New York: Monthly Review Press.

Foucault, M. (1980). *The history of sexuality: An introduction, volume I*. New York: Vintage Books.

Foucault, M. (1981). The order of discourse. In R. Young (Ed.), *Untying the text* (pp. 48-78). London: Routledge.

Garchik, L. (1999, April 19). Dole knuckles rapped. *The San Francisco Chronicle*, pp. C12.

Groneman, C. (2000). *Nymphomania: A history*. New York and London: W.W. Norton and Co.

Laumann, E. O., Paik, A., & Rosen, R. C. (1999). Sexual dysfunction in the United States. *JAMA, 281*, 537-544.

Law, J. (1987). Technology and heterogeneous: The case of Portuguese expansion. In W. E. Bijker, T.P. Hughes and T.J. Pinch (Ed.), *The social construction of technological systems* (pp. 111-134). Cambridge: The MIT Press.

Meyer, H. (1998). The pills that ate your profits. *Hospital and Health Networks, 18*.

Muraskin, W. (1996). Origins of the children's vaccine initiative: The intellectual foundations. *Social Science and Medicine, 42*, 1703-1719.

Pfizer, Inc. (1998). *What every man (and woman) should know, VIAGRA Pamphlet.*

Potts, A. (2000). 'The essence of the hard on': Hegemonic masculinity and the cultural construction of 'erectile dysfunction'. *Men and Masculinities, 3*, 85-103.

Terry, J. (1999). *An American obsession: Science, medicine, and homosexuality in modern society.* Chicago and London: University of Chicago Press.

Terzian, T. V. (1999). Direct-to-consumer prescription drug advertising. *American Journal of Law & Medicine, 25*, 149-167.

Tiefer, L. (1994). The medicalization of impotence–normalizing phallocentrism. *Gender & Society, 8*, 363-377.

Tiefer, L. (2000). Sexology and the pharmaceutical industry: The threat of co-optation. *Journal of Sex Research, 37*, 273-283.

Trebay, G. (1999, November 2). Longer, harder, faster: From sex parties to raves, for both men and women, It's not Bob Dole's Viagra anymore. *The Village Voice*, 36-44.

Urometrics, Inc. (2000). *An answer to FSD.* St. Paul, MN: Urometrics, Inc.

Zilbergeld, B. (1999). *The new male sexuality.* New York: Bantam Books.

Zola, I. K. (1972). Medicine as an institution of social control. *Sociological Review, 20*, 487-504.

Female Adolescent Sexuality: An Argument for a Developmental Perspective on the New View of Women's Sexual Problems

Deborah L. Tolman

SUMMARY. In this paper, I explore the resonance between experiences that are labeled "sexual problems" among adult women and adolescent girls' normative descriptions of their sexual experiences. Noting that female adolescent sexual dysfunction is an oxymoron, I review the feminist phenomenological research on female adolescent sexuality to support this claim. This review demonstrates and underscores the ways in which becoming sexual as an adolescent girl within the confines and constructs of patriarchy lays the groundwork for the kinds of "sexual problems" that are most evident in the female adult population. A developmental perspective on female sexuality is suggested as a way to support and extend the New View of Women's Sexual Problems. *[Article copies available for a fee from The Haworth Document Delivery Service: 1-800-HAWORTH. E-mail address: <getinfo@haworthpressinc.com> Website: <http://www.HaworthPress.com> © 2001 by The Haworth Press, Inc. All rights reserved.]*

KEYWORDS. Adolescent sexuality , sexuality development, narrative research, adolescent girls, sexual desire

Address correspondence to: Deborah L. Tolman, EdD, Center for Research on Women, Wellesley College, 106 Central Street, Wellesley, MA 02487.

[Haworth co-indexing entry note]: "Female Adolescent Sexuality: An Argument for a Developmental Perspective on the New View of Women's Sexual Problems." Tolman, Deborah L. Co-published simultaneously in *Women & Therapy* (The Haworth Press, Inc.) Vol. 24, No. 1/2, 2001, pp. 195-209; and: *A New View of Women's Sexual Problems* (ed: Ellyn Kaschak, and Leonore Tiefer) The Haworth Press, Inc., 2001, pp. 195-209. Single or multiple copies of this article are available for a fee from The Haworth Document Delivery Service [1-800-HAWORTH, 9:00 a.m. - 5:00 p.m. (EST). E-mail address: getinfo@haworthpressinc.com].

Imagine a young woman entering a therapist's office with the following complaints: She is in a committed heterosexual relationship in which she engages in protected sexual intercourse and other behaviors (fellatio, mutual touching) with her male partner. However, she is not sure whether she feels sexual desire and is not sure whether she is orgasmic. Despite the fact that she does not find these experiences particularly pleasurable, she often has them anyway, because she does not want to disappoint her partner and worries about repercussions in their relationship. She has considered the possibility that she is not sexually attracted to men, but is sure that she is heterosexual. She does not recall any history of childhood sexual abuse. How might the average therapist make sense of this case? First off, a judgment about the normalcy or dysfunction of this young woman's experience will likely be made, whether explicitly or not. It is reasonable to conclude that this story is not an account of healthy female sexuality. The dominant paradigm of physiological explanations for sexual problems might lead to a diagnosis of a sexual desire disorder or an orgasmic disorder. It is possible that sexual pain could be responsible for her lack of pleasure. Her compliance with her partner's wishes in contradiction to her own could be attributed to other psychological dysfunctions. If the therapist is dutifully following the direction of the American Psychiatric Association (1994): *Diagnostic and Statistical Manual of Mental Disorders-IV,* this patient is likely to be seen as experiencing multiple forms of sexual dysfunction that demand attention and correction.

Now imagine this same young woman's story told in a different context. Rather than coming to a therapist's office to seek help with sexual problems, imagine this sixteen-year-old, white, middle class adolescent girl walking down the corridor of her high school. Rather than identifying her own experience as problematic and seeking help, she has simply described what sexual experiences are like for her with her current boyfriend in a research interview. Would it occur to her—or to most adults she might encounter in her relational world—that she has sexual "problems"? That this description of sexual experience constitutes sexual dysfunction? That medical factors are the root cause of what sounds like an impaired experience of her sexuality? As a researcher, I have been privy to many stories like this one. While it is possible that the absence of sexual desire, pleasure and orgasm could have organic sources or be the result of drug usage or sex-related conditions, this story is so common that we would then have to believe that there is an epidemic of medically-induced sexual problems among adolescent girls. This story, which, if told by an adult woman, would be interpreted as one of sexual problems, when told by an adolescent girl is in some ways normative–that is, it is not an uncommon story about sexuality for a girl to tell.

Female adolescent sexual dysfunction is an oxymoron. Who has even heard of the notion of adolescent girls having "sexual problems" that have to do with their sexual feelings rather than the social or material repercussions of their behavioral choices? There are no *Newsweek* cover stories about adolescent girls not having desire or orgasms. There is no newspaper coverage about how girls are not even sure of what an orgasm is. In fact, many adults might find it quite disturbing to learn that their physically-mature adolescent daughter does in fact have orgasms. It is widely believed in this society that adolescent girls do not have strong sexual feelings–well, "good" girls that is (yes, the double standard is still well entrenched in the landscape of adolescence). The supposed absence of sexual desire among adolescent girls constitutes the firewall against the supposed raging, uncontrollable hormones of adolescent boys. It is still not "normal," not acceptable and in some corners considered immoral for girls to believe that they can or should have their own sexual desire and pleasure–and therefore can or should think of questioning its absence.

As is pointed out in the New View, it was listening to women describe their experiences of sexuality that shed light on the limits and male-centeredness of models for health and normalcy that had been taken for granted regarding female sexuality. The growing body of phenomenological research on female adolescent sexuality offers a convincing case in support of the New View of Women's Sexual Problems, while at the same time informing it. Every single reason for women's sexual problems that is articulated in the New View can be found in the lives of adolescent girls, with some obviously more potent and relevant than others (i.e., lack of information about how gender roles influence men's and women's sexual expectation is likely more salient and more frequent than inhibitions in arousal or spontaneity due to partner's health status or sexual problems). The research on adolescent girls illuminates in particular the interplay between these various dimensions of female sexuality and arenas of challenge for women's sexual health. I will offer some of the most compelling findings and examples from the experiential studies that have been done to substantiate this claim.

GIRLS' SEXUAL SOCIALIZATION
IN (WHAT REMAINS) A MAN'S WORLD:
A FEMINIST VIEW ON THE DEVELOPMENT
OF FEMALE SEXUALITY

A key premise of the New View is that, in a patriarchal society, women's sexuality is constructed and positioned not in terms of women's own desires, needs, satisfaction, health or happiness, but in the service of men's needs. As Adrienne Rich said so eloquently, "compulsory heterosexuality" is not simply sexual desire for the other sex, but "a political institution which disempowers women"–the bedrock of patriarchy. Rich articulated and thus drew attention to the ways in which heterosexuality as an institution constitutes the primary form of women's oppression, including the objectification of women, the socialization of women (and men) to feel that male sexual 'drive' amounts to a right, the idealization of heterosexual romance, the denial or denigration of female sexual pleasure or agency, rape, pornography, sexual harassment, and the erasure of lesbian existence from history and culture.

It is at adolescence that girls hit "the wall of patriarchy" (Gilligan, 1990, p. 503) as they develop women's bodies and begin making their way into the world of romantic (and not so romantic) relationships organized by ideologies of masculinity, femininity, and sexuality that are anchored in patriarchy. Race and class variations in this process are pronounced, and those structural differences in how women become sexualized by others have significant implications for sexuality in the lives of women and girls (Caraway, 1991; Collins, 1990; Dill, 1988; Thompson, 1995; Wyatt, 1997). In operating through socialization, compulsory heterosexuality systematically and thus seamlessly constructs "normal" female sexuality as passive and oriented to the desires and pleasures of a girl's (assumed) male partner, yielding "feminine" women and "masculine" men, and silence about, and denigration of, female embodied experiences (Tiefer, 1995).

Thus, one of the first key features of girls' developing sexuality is what Nancy Lesko (1988) has called the "hidden curriculum of girls' bodies" (p. 124). Lyn Brown and I (2001) have noted that

> the primary curriculum of girls' bodies is not that they learn that they will be or discover that they are menstruating; the most pervasive curriculum . . . is what feminist philosopher Sandra Bartky calls "the disciplinary project of femininity . . . [that] [w]oman lives her body as seen by another, by an anonymous patriarchal

Other" (1900, p. 72). As Simone de Beauvoir observed, when the adolescent girl's body becomes a woman's body, she "becomes an object and she sees herself as object; she discovers this new aspect of her being with surprise . . . instead of coinciding exactly with herself, she now begins to exist outside." (de Beauvoir, 1961, p. 316)

Of the many lessons of patriarchy, learning to objectify one's own body is one of the first, and one of the most insidious, pervasive and effective. This perspective becomes codified in idealized romance. When one is treated as an object of the desires of others and treats oneself as such, the ability even to know one's own needs and desires is undercut. The effects of this process of disembodiment reverberate throughout the research on female adolescent sexuality—if a girl does not occupy but only looks upon her own body, feeling her own sexual feelings becomes difficult at best.

Karin Martin (1996) conducted a qualitative study of the experience of puberty with 55 white working class and middle class boys and girls aged 14 to 19 in the United States. She found girls to be ambivalent and anxious about their developing bodies and that girls had little subjective (that is, experiential) knowledge of or even interest in their bodies, except for "their work on appearance–jewelry, hair, make-up, clothes . . . as one girl said, " 'my hair is my accomplishment' " (p. 21). Having so little subjective knowledge and also often distorted information about menstruation, gender relations and sex, going through puberty was rarely a positive experience for girls, "associated with sexuality, and sexuality and the female sexual body became associated with dirtiness, shame, taboo, danger, and objectification. As girls internalized these meanings, they began to feel bad about their new bodies and themselves" (p. 27).

In listening to Lily, a seventeen-year-old Latina whom I interviewed in a study on girls' sexual desire (see below), Elizabeth Debold, Lyn Brown and I (1996) heard evidence that Lily had internalized the dictum of the splitting of herself (her mind) from herself (her body) demanded by enacting femininity. When asked what made her feel sexy, she told me how her boyfriend evaluated her appearance every morning: " 'when he says that I look sexy, that's one of my sexy days.' . . . she knows herself in the realm of 'sexy' as the object of male desire" (p. 109). Even after I persisted in trying to learn how Lily herself felt, she continued to report what her boyfriend thought. Lily did not know her own sexiness in terms of her own feelings, only as his observations. We noted that "at this point, the incorporation of the Other's view of herself is so thorough that Lily herself acts as the thief. Listening to her, we hear a cultural discourse uncritically emerging from and creating her with the full force of its authority" (p. 109).

However, the phenomenon of girls' self-objectification, and subsequent passive construction of their own sexuality, is not monolithic. While the press to dissociate from their bodies is powerful for girls, it is not necessarily successful. Janet Holland and her colleagues in the Women, Risk and Aids Project (WRAP) collected accounts about heterosexual relationships from 150 young British women, aged 16-21, from diverse cultural and class backgrounds. This feminist collaborative documented girls' strategies for negotiating safer sex and obstacles to girls making safer choices (Holland, Ramazanoglu, & Scott, 1990; Holland, Ramazanoglu, Scott, Sharpe, & Thomson, 1991, 1992; Holland, Ramazanoglu, Sharpe, & Thomson, 1992, 1994; Holland, Ramazanoglu, & Thomson, 1996). They report "overwhelming documentation" of inequalities of power in sexual relationships and sexual experiences that are organized around boys' needs, desires, and interests in conjunction with an absence of a positive conception of female sexuality. While they noted that in girls' interviews, "reference to and discussion of the body is almost absent from the interview transcripts; female sexuality is present in the interviews but is largely disembodied," they also found that "[t]he young women's accounts do indicate points of tension in which physical bodies interrupt idealized relationships in ways which may be violent, disappointing, sensual, surprising, boring, lovely, disgusting" (pp. 23-24).

In each of the studies, there are always a few girls who resist conventions of compulsory heterosexuality and, at least in some ways, sound more "healthy." These girls tend to be in some fashion "on the margins" of white, middle class heterosexual life: they are Black adolescent mothers (Thompson, 1990a), Latinas (Tolman, 1996), lesbians (Thompson, 1990b), students in a disadvantaged urban public school (Fine, 1988), white girls with complicated class and personal histories (Tolman, 1994). I conducted a study of early adolescent sexual health in which 148 white and Latina poor, working class and middle class girls were surveyed about their sexual experiences and conceptions and how conventional were their beliefs about femininity, and 46 of these girls participated in in-depth interviews on these topics (Tolman, 1999). Some articulated their resistance to complying with conventions that render them passive or position them as potential victims of male sexuality. For instance, one 13-year-old Latina described her resistance to being objectified: "You need to worry what your breast size is. How your butt is formed . . . First it's like the way you act around them [boys], then it's your body, and THEN comes like what's inside . . . I don't like that" (p. 136). She refused to tolerate promiscuous behavior from her boyfriend, which she knew was culturally condoned. "I was straight up with my boyfriend with that too. I was like, 'If you think you're gonna be going on like from me to another girl and then another girl and stuff, you must be buggin, cause it ain't gonna be like that with me.' " She identified and rejected a double standard that enables boys to treat–and mistreat–girls as objects. She understood and was willing to live with the consequences of possibly losing her boyfriend by taking this stand. Yet, the question of whether these experiences are pleasurable for her, incite her desire, or provide space for her to make safe and responsible sexual decisions is not in her lexicon of adolescent relationships. She is too busy monitoring the situation outside of her body to have concerns about what is and is not happening inside.

Conventional romance as the organizing frame for girls' sexuality leaves little room for their own sexual desire or pleasure (or for other forms of desire and satisfaction). In her interviews with white, working class girls, Sharon Thompson observed that these girls organized their relationships and their lives around what she called "the quest romance" (Thompson, 1992). Among the heterosexual girls whom she interviewed, she heard "the same old story" of sexual progress and male pressure, of these girls trying to hold onto what they had to trade–their virginity–for a man who would ultimately marry and protect them and provide the life for which they hoped. She found that in this "bargain," girls gambled for commitment in having sex with the hopes that they would be found "worthy," enacting the construction of their bodies as sexual objects for the approval and enjoyment of boys who were romanticized rather than desired. Their expectations were not associated with sexual pleasure, but with winning the lottery for a committed relationship. It was extremely rare for a teenage girl to tell a story about wanting to go farther sexually than her partner, and nonexistent for white working class girls. This same pattern was less audible in the narratives told to her by lesbian girls, perhaps because they must develop relationships in spite of and in opposition to compulsory heterosexuality.

Thompson asked heterosexual girls to tell their stories about first heterosexual intercourse (Thompson, 1990a, 1992, 1995). She found that these experiences, which one girl described as "putting a big thing in a little hole" (Thompson, 1990a, p. 341), were rarely pleasurable: "It really hurt a lot. The pain was like I couldn't take it" and "I was expecting it to be much nicer than it felt. It didn't hurt or anything. It just didn't feel really good" (p. 365). The absence of girls' sexual desire–or even the expectation of it–can leave girls vulnerable to the needs and narratives of boys with whom they desire relationships. Only a quarter of the heterosexual girls with whom Thompson spoke talked about the experience in terms of pleasure, having expected and having had pleasure. These girls, whom she calls "pleasure narrators," had primarily white, middle-class feminist mothers who talked to them in positive terms about female sexuality, inspiring in their daughters a sense of entitlement to pleasure and desire, anchoring a resistance to the terms for sexuality set by compulsory heterosexuality.

In her now classic article, "Sexuality, schooling and adolescent females: The missing discourse of desire," Michelle Fine (1988) found, in a year-long ethnographic study of an urban public school peopled by low-income African-American and Latina/o adolescents, occasional introductions of a discourse of female desire by young women themselves into classes organized around "superficial notions of male heterosexuality" (p. 36); these attempts were inevitably snuffed out by adults, conveying their own and society's anxiety about female adolescent sexuality. For instance, Opal, a young Black woman, responded to her teacher's solicitation of topics for sex education by asking, "What's an orgasm?" When the other students' laughter died down, the teacher offered a contradictory and confusing answer, in which not people but organs appeared, "Sexual response, sensation all over the body. What's analogous to the male penis on the female?" A boy answered "Clitoris." The teacher, who seems to be trying to encourage the young women to become familiar with their own bodies, suggested that they "go home and look in the mirror . . . [because] it's yours." When the teacher then inquired why it is important for a girl to know "what your body looks like," Opals's response that "you should like your body" is immediately covered over by a warning that girls need to be able to recognize "problems like vaginal warts."

Across the studies and inquiries into female adolescent sexuality, girls do not talk about their own sexual desire or pleasure *unless they are specifically asked*; as I have suggested, it would be crazy for girls to offer this information without explicit assurances of safety (Tolman, 1996; Tolman & Brown, in press). In a study of 30 girls who were juniors in an urban public school (Black, Latina and white, working class and low income) and a suburban one (with one exception, white, upper middle and middle class), and also from a gay and lesbian youth group, I asked girls explicit questions about their sexual feelings, inviting descriptions and narratives about sexual desire. While 27 out of 30 girls described their own desire as part of their experience of their sexuality, overall I discerned a dilemma in how these girls described their own desire and how they felt about and responded to these feelings: How is it possible for a girl to know about and respond to her own sexual feelings and still think of herself, and have others think of her, as a good, normal, appropriate girl? (Tolman, 1994a, 1994b, 1996).

Framed in these terms, the dilemma of desire can be understood as securely located in compulsory heterosexuality, straining and undermining girls' relationships with themselves, with boyfriends or girlfriends, with peers, family and community–although these girls, with some notable exceptions, understood this "problem" as simply the way things are. As one girl in the recent AAUW report on girls complained: "I wish that every girl who enjoys her sexuality was not considered slutty, and dirty. I wish that all the girls could walk around all schools with all the pride guys have" (Haag, 1999, p. 27). In their narratives, the girls in my study described attempting individual solutions to what is in fact a social problem, such as trying to hide their desire by drinking in order to be able to "blame it on the alcohol," having "my mind tell my body no" and "not dancing reggae" to avoid getting aroused. I observed a continuum of embodied sexual desire in the narratives told by this group of girls, from "silent bodies" to being confused about whether they felt desire, to resisting their own desire, to hiding desire from others, to a sense of entitlement to desire within the confines of sanctioned situations (i.e., a "long-term" relationship), to a politicized claim of entitlement to desire (Tolman, in press). Most of these girls struggled either to stay in connection with their bodies or to disconnect from their bodies, with little awareness of the institutionalized and in most cases internalized constructions of femininity, passive female sexuality and appropriate gender relations producing these "problems."

For example, Ellen, an African-American seventeen-year-old, understands her own desire as dangerous, because it could threaten her educational aspirations. Poor girls and girls of color have articulated the pressure they feel to choose between their education and their sexuality, while middle class girls (and I have listened primarily to whites) do not experience their sexuality as a material threat but do ascribe other forms of danger to their desire. A gendered relational context emerges as most salient in many girls' narratives. Rochelle, another African-American urban girl, observed that after having sex in a dissociated state with a former boyfriend that "just happened," in the context of feeling "as though I had to conform to everything he said," facing fears of getting a bad reputation and getting pregnant, and after this boyfriend "flattened

[her] face," she refused to tolerate such treatment from her current boy-friend. While Rochelle has a keen knowledge of her body's hungers, comparing the ebb and flow of her sexual desire to how she feels about eating cake: "if I like go a long period of time without havin' it then, it's really good to me . . . say I don't eat cake a lot, but say, like every two months, I had some cake, then it would be real good to me, so that's like the same thing" (Tolman, 1994a, p. 329), she experienced sexual desire only when alone.

Gendered violence–or fear of it–does not always have a man's face on it. Melissa, one of three lesbian and bisexual girls in the study, was very aware of how her sexual feelings make her vulnerable to harm, in particular other girls' anger and physical violence, because her desire violates compulsory heterosexuality. She manages these well-grounded fears by attempting to restrain her desire: "Whenever I start, I feel like I can't help looking at someone for more than a few seconds, and I keep, and I feel like I have to make myself not stare at them or something" (Tolman, 1994a, p. 336). In contrast, Lisa Diamond (2000) has identi-fied how some sexual minority adolescent women demonstrate fluidity in their sexual feelings, evidencing enough comfort with their sexual desire to engage in a range of relationships as they explore their sexual identity, defined by whom they desire, and in some cases reject the very categories available to contain their sexual desire for girls and/or boys.

A very few girls in my study described resistance to the double stan-dard which entitles boys to sexual desire and sexual agency while deny-ing an active sexuality to girls. Paulina, a recent immigrant from Eastern Europe, is aware of how she is punished for sexuality while "it's okay for a guy to have any feelings or anything . . . the girl has to be this little virgin who is obedient to the men . . . usually a guy makes the first move, not the girl, or the girl's not supposed to do it, the girl's sup-posed to sit there going, no, no you can't. I can't do that" (Tolman & Higgins, 1996, p. 219). Paulina's sense of entitlement to her sexual de-sire serves her well in her ability to make active sexual decisions, to have pleasurable and desired sexual experiences, and to know when she is being violated: "And he just like kept touching me, and I was just like, just get off me. He goes, you know that you want to, and I said no I don't. Get off me, I hate you" (Tolman & Higgins, 1996, p. 220).

Holland and her colleagues (1992) also found that a small group of young women in their study stood out from the rest of the sample by evi-dencing a sense of empowerment about their own sexuality. More of the girls exhibited intellectual power–enlightened beliefs about female en-titlement–rather than experiential power–actually implementing what they knew. They found that, in practice, trying to take control and resist a passive model of female sexuality did not suffice for effective sexual empowerment; a recognition and challenge to *male power* was also required to enable girls to exert control and choice in their sexual experiences. In conclusion, they identify women's conceptions of masculinity and femininity and broader social pressures, as well as men's behavior, as sources of challenge to a positive female sexuality.

They specifically identified "femininity" as "an unsafe sexual strategy" (Holland et al., 1994, p. 23). In the narratives told in their study, they heard girls describe the double bind of needing to take initiative in sexual situations in order to protect themselves (i.e., asking a young man to use a condom), which requires that they admit that they are being actively sexual, while wanting to maintain a sense of themselves as feminine, which requires sexual passivity and (at least the appearance of) sexual inexperience. In listening to this diverse group of heterosexual young women, they noted that girls are dealing with a spectrum of male coercion, ranging from verbal sexual pressure or persuasion ("it wasn't sort of physical, I mean, but in a way it was sort of like mental" [Holland et al., 1992a, p. 655]), to verbal sexual pressure ("he was . . . older, he was very very persuasive and very pushy, and I was so frightened of him at the time that you don't want to say no" [p. 656]), to physical sexual pressure, primarily intimidation ("He told me, 'whatever I do, don't say no, just say yes' and . . . 'you have to say yes, you have to listen to me' . . . I was scared . . . But every time I pushed him, he pulled my hair" [pp. 657-658]), or the use or threat of force, in which young women described abusive relationships and being raped. They conclude that young women may be "very active in resisting men's power, but their resistance may not necessarily be effective. It is clear from our respondents' accounts that young women are actively engaged in constructing their femininity and sexuality, but it is also clear that the negotiation of sexual encounters is a contradictory process in which young women generally lack power" (Holland et al., 1990, p. 341).

TOWARDS A DEVELOPMENTAL PERSPECTIVE ON WOMEN'S SEXUAL "PROBLEMS"

Adolescent girls do not go to sex therapists. The criteria that are generally held to identify sexual difficulties for adult women characterize much of female adolescent sexual experience, based on the current body of research. The empirical work on female adolescent sexuality illustrates how social processes intertwine with psychological and relational ones to produce lived experiences of sexuality in adolescence that could easily be diagnosed as "sexual problems"–yet never are. While sexual feelings are likely normative among adolescent girls, girls rarely get the message that such feelings are normal, to be expected and respected. Very few girls hear from anyone that they should be concerned when they do not feel sexual desire or pleasure.

How, then, are we to make sense of adolescent girls' "diminished" or "lack" of sexual desire or arousal, their "inorgasmia"? In a way, adolescent girls constitute a kind of "special population" of women. As Tracy Higgins and I (1996) observed

> The cultural anxiety precipitated by unbounded female sexuality is perhaps most apparent with regard to adolescent girls. Coming under scrutiny from across the political spectrum, girls' sexuality has been deemed threatening either to girls themselves (potentially resulting in rape, sexually transmitted diseases, unwanted pregnancy), or to society (as evidenced by the single mother, school dropout, welfare dependent). Although none of these issues is limited to teenage girls, all frequently arise in that context because of society's sense of entitlement, or, indeed, obligation, to regulate teen sexuality. (p. 206)

Thus, what is defined as "deviant" for adolescent girls transmogrifies into "normal" sexual function–and thus "dysfunction"–as soon as women cross the threshold into adulthood (Tolman & Diamond, in press). In a time of federally-funded abstinence education which teaches girls how to say no to sexual intercourse and nothing about alternative forms of sexual expression, ways to have sexual pleasure that are safe, or even basic knowledge about their bodies and sexuality, why should we be surprised that over a third of adult women report low sexual desire and/or arousal? (Laumann, Paik, & Rosen, 1999).

For girls, "healthy" sexuality is often positioned as no sexuality, the avoidance of negative consequences by avoiding it altogether. What are the implications of this "no sexuality is good sexuality" model for adolescent girls' development into sexually mature women? Fine has argued that in silencing a discourse of desire and positioning young women only as potential victims of male heterosexuality, "public schooling may actually disable young women in their negotiations as sexual subjects. Trained through and into positions of passivity and victimization, young women are currently educated away from positions of sexual self-interest" (1988, p. 42). She outlines a genuine discourse of desire as an invitation for adolescents "to explore what feels good and bad, desirable and undesirable, grounded in experiences, needs, and limits. Such a discourse would release females from a position of receptivity, enable an analysis of the dialectics of victimization and pleasure, and would pose female adolescents as subjects of sexuality, initiators as well as negotiators" (p. 33).

Adolescent girls' descriptions of how they experience and negotiate their sexuality demands consideration of a developmental framework for how to understand adult female sexuality. While the ever-present physiological model of female sexual disorders applied to women is highly impoverished when it comes to adolescent girls, essentially leaving them out, the New View easily incorporates the various ways in which adolescent girls have described their sexual selves and, sometimes consciously, sometimes not, the sociocultural, political, economic, relational and psychological barriers that they more often than not seem to confront. The adolescent girls in these studies do not construct their struggles with sexuality as problematic. Since they rarely have expectations of pleasure or desire, and they have been socialized to identify and meet male sexual needs, their narratives are told as just the way things are. It is an interpretive framework anchored in the kind of conception of female sexual health offered by the New View that renders their narrative plots of discomfort, distress or dismay problematic, revealing missing story lines of desire and pleasure.

NOTE

1. In the same spirit as the New View, I have offered a model of female adolescent sexual health premised on the nested contexts in which girls develop, explore, experience and construct their sexuality: their individual qualities, their romantic relationships, their social relationships and the sociocultural contexts in which these individual and relational experiences occur (see Tolman, 1999).

REFERENCES

Bartky, S. L. (1990). *Femininity and domination: Studies in the phenomenology of oppression.* New York: Routledge.

Caraway, N. (1991). *Segregated sisterhood: Racism and the politics of American feminism.* Knoxville: University of Tennessee Press.

Collins, P. H. (1990). *Black feminist thought: Knowledge, consciousness, and the politics of empowerment* (Vol. 2). Boston: Unwin Hyman.

de Beauvoir, S. (1961). *The second sex.* New York: Bantam Books.

Debold, E., Tolman, D., & Brown, L. M. (1996). Embodying knowledge, knowing desire: Authority and split subjectivities in girls' epistemological development. In N. R. Goldberger, J. M. Tarule, B. M. Clinchy & M. F. Belenky (Eds.), *Knowledge, difference and power* (pp. 85-125). New York: Basic Books.

Diamond, L. M. (2000). Sexual identity, attractions, and behavior among young sexual-minority women over a two-year period. *Developmental Psychology, 36,* 241-250.

Dill, B. T. (1988). The dialectics of black womanhood. In M. R. Malson & E. Mudimbe-Boyi & J. F. O'Barr & M. Wyer (Eds.), *Black women in America: Social science perspectives* (pp. 65-77). Chicago: The University of Chicago Press.

Fine, M. (1988). Sexuality, schooling, and adolescent females: The missing discourse of desire. *Harvard Educational Review, 58* (1), 29-53.

Gilligan, C. (1990). Joining the resistance: Psychology, politics, girls and women. *Michigan Quarterly Review, 29*(4), 501-536.

Haag, P. (1999). *Voices of a generation: Teenage girls on sex, school, and self.* Washington, DC: American Association of University Women Educational Foundation.

Holland, J., Ramazanoglu, C., & Scott, S. (1990). *Sex, risk, danger: AIDS education policy and young women's sexuality.* London: The Tufnell Press.

Holland, J., Ramazanoglu, C., Scott, S., Sharpe, S., & Thomson, R. (1991). Between embarrassment and trust: Young women and the diversity of condom use. In P. Aggleton, G. Hart & P. Davies (Eds.), *AIDS: Responses, interventions and care* (pp. 127-148). Bristol, PA: The Falmer Press.

Holland, J., Ramazanoglu, C., Scott, S., Sharpe, S., & Thomson, R. (1992). Pressure, resistance, empowerment: Young women and the negotiation of safer sex. In P. Aggleton & P. Davies & G. Hart (Eds.), *AIDS: Rights, risk and reason* (pp. 142-162). Washington, D.C.: The Falmer Press.

Holland, J., Ramazanoglu, C., Sharpe, S., & Thomson, R. (1992). Pleasure, pressure and power: Some contradictions of gendered sexuality. *The Sociological Review, 40*(4), 645-674.

Holland, J., Ramazanoglu, C., Sharpe, S., & Thomson, R. (1994). Power and desire: The embodiment of female sexuality. *Feminist Review, 46,* 21-38.

Holland, J., Ramazanoglu, C., & Thomson, R. (1996). In the same boat? The gendered (in)experience of first heterosex. In D. Richardson (Ed.), *Telling it straight: Theorizing heterosexuality.* Buckingham: Open University Press.

Laumann, E. O., Paik, A., & Rosen, R. C. (1999). Sexual dysfunction in the United States: Prevalence and predictors. *Journal of the American Medical Association, 281*(6), 537-544.

Lesko, N. (1998). The curriculum of the body. In L. Roman, L. Christian-Smith & E. Ellsworth (Eds.), *Becoming feminine* (pp. 124-142). Philadelphia: Falmer Press.

Martin, K. A. (1996). *Puberty, sexuality, and the self: Girls and boys at adolescence.* New York: Routledge.

Rich, A. (1983). Compulsory heterosexuality and lesbian existence. In A. Snitow, C. Stansell & S. Thompson (Eds.), *Powers of desire: The politics of sexuality* (pp. 177-205). New York: Monthly Review Press.

Thompson, S. (1990a). Drastic entertainments: Teenage mothers' signifying narratives. In F. Ginsburg & A. L. Tsing (Eds.), *Uncertain terms: Negotiating gender in American culture* (pp. 269-281). Boston: Beacon Press.

Thompson, S. (1990b). Putting a big thing into a little hole: Teenage girls' accounts of sexual initiation. *The Journal of Sex Research, 27*(3), 341-361.

Thompson, S. (1992). Search for tomorrow: On feminism and the reconstruction of teen romance. In C. S. Vance (Ed.), *Pleasure and danger: Exploring female sexuality* (pp. 350-384). London: Pandora Press.

Thompson, S. (1995). *Going all the way: Teenage girls' tales of sex, romance and pregnancy.* New York: Hill and Wang.

Tiefer, L. (1995). *Sex is not a natural act & other essays.* Boulder: Westview Press.

Tolman, D. L. (1994). Daring to desire: Culture and the bodies of adolescent girls. In J. Irvine (Ed.), *Sexual cultures: Adolescents, communities and the construction of identity.* Philadelphia: Temple University Press.

Tolman, D. L. (1994). Doing desire: Adolescent girls' struggles for/with sexuality. *Gender and Society, 8*(3), 324-342.

Tolman, D. L. (1996). Adolescent girls' sexuality: Debunking the myth of the urban girl. In B. J. R. Leadbeater & N. Way (Eds.), *Urban girls: Resisting stereotypes, creating identities* (pp. 255-271). New York: New York University Press.

Tolman, D. L. (1999). Femininity as a barrier to positive sexual health for adolescent girls. *Journal of the American Medical Women's Association, 54*(3), 133-138.

Tolman, D. L. (in press). *Dilemma of desire: Teenage girls and sexuality.* Cambridge, MA: Harvard University Press.

Tolman, D. L., & Brown, L. B. (2001). Adolescent Voices, Resonating Resistance. In R. Unger (Ed.), *Handbook on the psychology of women and gender.* New York: Wiley & Sons.

Tolman, D. L., & Higgins, T. (1996). How being a good girl can be bad for girls. In N. B. Maglin & D. Perry (Eds.), *Good girls/bad girls: Women, sex, violence and power in the 1990s.* New Brunswick, NJ: Rutgers University Press.

Wyatt, G. E. (1997). *Stolen women: Reclaiming our sexuality, taking back our lives.* New York: John Wiley & Sons, Inc.

Orgasms for Sale:
The Role of Profit and Politics
in Addressing Women's Sexual Satisfaction

Amy Allina

SUMMARY. Medical experts are promoting a corporate medical model for addressing women's sexuality. Without public funding for a diversified sexuality research agenda, the market driven research of the private sector will continue to dominate the scope of the so-called knowledge acquired about women's sexual experience. In addition, conservative political activism has generated fear and discomfort with discussing sexuality that is a barrier to developing positive, healthy sexual relationships for adults as well as for adolescents and youth who need information to aid them in sexual decision-making. Medical professionals, too, lack reliable and independent sources of information about sexuality. There is a need for appropriate information about sexuality to be made available and accessible in diverse communities for all ages. Both corporate control over sexuality research and conservative control over sexuality education policy must be challenged by activism demonstrating public support for a constructive sexuality policy agenda. *[Article copies available for a fee from The Haworth Document Delivery Service: 1-800-HAWORTH. E-mail address:*

This paper was written by Amy Allina, Program & Policy Director of the National Women's Health Network, with input from Wendy Sanford of the Boston Women's Health Book Collective.

Address correspondence to: Amy Allina, National Women's Health Network, 514 Tenth Street, NW, Fourth Floor, Washington, DC 20004.

[Haworth co-indexing entry note]: "Orgasms for Sale: The Role of Profit and Politics in Addressing Women's Sexual Satisfaction." Allina, Amy. Co-published simultaneously in *Women & Therapy* (The Haworth Press, Inc.) Vol. 24, No. 1/2, 2001, pp. 211-218; and: *A New View of Women's Sexual Problems* (ed: Ellyn Kaschak, and Leonore Tiefer) The Haworth Press, Inc., 2001, pp. 211-218. Single or multiple copies of this article are available for a fee from The Haworth Document Delivery Service [1-800-HAWORTH, 9:00 a.m. - 5:00 p.m. (EST). E-mail address: getinfo@haworthpressinc.com].

211

KEYWORDS. Female sexual dysfunction (FSD), feminist, health, policy, sexuality education, sexuality research

In 1971, when the Boston Women's Health Course Collective wrote the chapter on sexuality for the first edition of *Our Bodies, Our Selves (OBOS),* they offered a fundamental challenge to the idea that women's feelings and concerns about sexuality could be explained or addressed by books or doctors or courses that focused exclusively on "How-To-Do-It." The widely accepted assumption at the time was that women who didn't enjoy sex were frigid, but this assumption ignored many of the important factors that affected women's sexual experiences. The authors of *OBOS,* the classic feminist text on health, asserted that " 'Frigidity' or inadequacy in bed is not divorced from the social realities we experience all the time" (Boston Women's Health Course Collective, 1971). Instead of defining women's sexual problems in terms of repression or failure to reach orgasm, they explained, women's relationship to sex and their bodies needed to be considered in the context of the social, political and economic forces that affect all aspects of women's lives.

Thirty years later, more than 4.5 million copies of *Our Bodies, Our Selves* have been printed and sold worldwide (Boston Women's Health Book Collective, 1998), but feminist health activists are still fighting a twenty-first century version of the same battles over how to approach female sexuality. These battles are both political and economic, and they are taking place in research institutions, clinical settings and in legislatures and policy-making bodies nationwide.

MAINSTREAM MEDICAL EXPERTS DEFINE "FEMALE SEXUAL DYSFUNCTION"

Medical experts in 2001 are promoting a way of thinking about women's sexual problems that is based on a corporate medical model. Fueled by the overwhelming response to the introduction of Viagra, the drug for male impotence, medical researchers and health care providers, pharmaceutical companies and medical device manufacturers are all looking for the next blockbuster sex-enhancing product–the one that will solve the problem they call "female sexual dysfunction" (FSD).

By using such medical terms to describe women's sexual dissatisfaction, these health experts steer those who are concerned about women's problems with sex toward solutions that can be manufactured, marketed and sold to women, solutions that will make money for companies and medical institutions that offer treatment to women experiencing FSD. In doing so, they also steer us away from a consideration of approaches which incorporate the understanding that for many women who experience sexual dissatisfaction, cultural, political and relational forces contribute as much, if not more, to their problems.

This bias of the corporate medical model has a controlling effect on the research conducted and programs implemented. More broadly, it also affects the public discourse taking place regarding women's sexual experience.

PRODUCT DEVELOPMENT
DRIVES THE RESEARCH AGENDA

Pharmaceutical industry research budgets are so large in comparison to other sources of financial support for health research that the corporate agenda inevitably drives the topics of research pursued. This is true not just with respect to research on sexuality but across the field of health. Research into questions that do not lend themselves to product development, such as the impact of environmental pollutants on health or the role of diet in disease prevention, is much harder to find funding for in comparison to an investigation into the possibility that a patented or patentable chemical compound might offer some previously unproven health benefit. In the field of sexuality research, this means that many interesting and important questions which might well shed light on the socio-cultural, economic or political factors contributing to women's sexual dissatisfaction are less likely to be examined. Yet many women might benefit from a more developed understanding of such questions as:

- what are effective strategies for couples who are dealing with the impact that major life crises (e.g., serious illness of a child, parent or self, job loss, etc.) can have on sexual desire?
- how does an economic power imbalance in a relationship affect women's sexual satisfaction?
- what is the effect of exercise on sexual desire and does it differ by gender?

- are there differing levels of sexual satisfaction between women with male partners and women with female partners?
- what is the effect on women's sexual satisfaction of narrow media images of feminine beauty which emphasize an unattainable ideal?
- what is the range of ways that women define and experience sexual satisfaction?

Unfortunately, industry funds do not go to such work because it is not likely to lead to development of a new product. And public funding for consideration of these questions is often limited by the fear of legislators and government officials that support for sexuality research may expose them to political attack.

It is telling that at the major national meeting of female sexuality researchers and clinicians in 1999, half the participants identified themselves as being from industry and many papers and presentations were uncontrolled studies on the effects of sildenafil (Viagra), but there was no paper presented on the relationship between social class and genital pain or between sexual dissatisfaction and knowledge about bodies, feelings, and gender socialization (Loe, 2000). Occasionally, someone mentioned domestic violence or sexual assault, but there was no acknowledgment of the widespread nature of these experiences or of their significance to medical experts who are attempting to treat women's sexual dissatisfaction. This conference was sponsored by Pfizer (the manufacturer of Viagra), Schering Plough and several other pharmaceutical companies.

Until we are able to generate the political will to provide public funding for a more diversified sexuality research agenda, market driven research of the private sector will continue to dominate the scope of the so-called knowledge we acquire about women's sexual experience, and women's own knowledge of our experiences will continue to be undervalued.

POLITICAL HYPOCRISY AND NARROW-MINDED MORALITY UNDERMINES EFFECTIVE PROGRAMS

Lack of political will is also a significant problem when it comes to education and information sharing on the topic of sexuality. The policy issues come into play most directly around school-based sex education programs, but the problem is much broader than that in reality. The level of fear and discomfort with discussing sexuality that is prevalent in the United States is a barrier to developing positive, healthy sexual relationships for adults as well as for adolescents and youth who need information to aid them in the decision-making they will inevitably face around sex.

Comprehensive, age-appropriate sexuality education programs for children and youth have been shown to be effective in preventing unintended pregnancy and sexually transmitted disease (STD). They can also play an important role in laying the foundation for the development of positive and satisfying sexual relationships. In the United States, however, such programs are all too rare. On the contrary, federal and state governments are spending millions of dollars every year on abstinence-only education which promotes sexual abstinence outside of marriage as the only acceptable choice and does not include information on contraception, STD prevention, masturbation or homosexuality.

The political support for, and government commitment to, abstinence-only education demonstrates a lack of courage on the part of policy makers, many of whom are aware that such programs have not been proven effective. The World Health Organization reviewed 35 programs from a number of different countries and found that abstinence-only programs were less effective than programs that promoted safer sex practices as well as delay of first intercourse (Baldo et al., 1993). The government focus on abstinence-only education also reflects, however, a lack of awareness of the reality that the majority of parents do not support this approach (Henry J. Kaiser Family Foundation, 2000). Raising the volume on the public demand for effective sexuality education is critical to the effort to turn around the misguided policy approach that has been followed in recent years.

Moreover, the need for accurate and confidential sources of information about sexuality is not limited to school-age children. In addition to school-based education programs, there is a need in the United States for better sources of information about sexual health from a wide variety of sources and for a wide variety of audiences. Almost half the pregnancies in this country each year are unintended (Henshaw, 1998) and 15 million people become infected with an STD each year, roughly half of whom contract a lifelong infection (CDC, 2000). Despite the public focus on teen pregnancy, these problems are not limited to adolescents. Syphilis rates, for example, are highest among women in their twenties and men 35-39 in spite of the fact that this is a curable disease (CDC, 2000).

The high rates of unintended pregnancy and STD infection are the most visible indications that access to information and services about sex is inadequate, but sexual dissatisfaction is also there lurking under the public radar. For most people, women's magazines with their sensational headlines and stories that are often very thin on accurate, evidence-based information are the most accessible source of information on how to deal with sexual questions and problems. Sex advice columns and programs run in many newspapers and magazines and on radio and television, but their quality varies widely and they only reach a small minority of the population. Making appropriate information available and accessible in diverse communities for all ages would be a giant step forward in this country.

The situation in Europe is notably different. There, television ads promote condoms and contraception; sex education is widely available throughout the school years. In Holland, young people are taught to use both a condom, for STDs, and the Pill for pregnancy–this dual protection strategy is referred to as "double dutch." Condoms are sold in vending machines on street corners. Here, companies promote Viagra on television, but the networks refuse to air condom ads. (Ads for Viagra, as for all prescription medications, are not permitted on European television.) And what are the consequences of these different approaches? Two significant measures strongly support the European strategy: in the countries where this sexual health information is widely available there are far fewer unwanted pregnancies and fewer abortions. The contradictions and hypocrisy of the U.S. system work against the development of healthy sexual behavior and contribute to sexual problems.

Even those with access to health care providers do not necessarily have access to good sexual health information. Medical professionals, too, lack reliable and independent sources of information about sexuality. Just as pharmaceutical companies influence the research agenda, they also control much of the information flowing to health care providers through advertising, sales visits and medical education. Pharmaceutical companies spend between $8,000-$13,000 per physician per year to affect drug prescribing practices. Drug company salespeople regularly visit the offices of physicians, nurse practitioners, midwives, nurses and physician assistants and work to provide them with drug samples, gifts and information about the company's products. A study of these sales presentations found that 11 percent of the statements made by company representatives on such visits was inaccurate (Ziegler et al., 1995).

Education programs and information that is not provided directly by companies which might be assumed to be more accurate is subject to corporate influence as well. Health care providers are required by state law to obtain continuing medical education credits every year to keep their licenses, and those credits are now almost entirely provided by drug company sponsored conferences and lectures. In the sexuality field, Pfizer's speaker's bureau dominates the landscape, producing teleconferences, Internet courses, and professional journal inserts, as well as panels that crisscross the country, presenting the same selective information in all venues. Marcia Angell, former editor of the *New England Journal of Medicine,* has become a formidable critic of these developments, reminding readers, in her editorials, that academic medicine should not be "for sale" (Angell, 2000).

A CONSTRUCTIVE SEXUALITY POLICY AGENDA

Success of efforts to address women's sexual satisfaction has been limited by the strong and active support that has existed for the narrow political and economic agendas of those who oppose a comprehensive approach. As long as drug prices remain exorbitant in this country, there will be plentiful financial resources available for research oriented toward product development and large investments in drug promotion. Conservative activists have been more highly organized and effective to date in putting forward their short-sighted agenda with respect to sexuality education. Feminist health activists, public health advocates and educators on the national, state and community levels have been forced to devote their resources to fighting defensive battles against funding for abstinence-only programs instead of working to build public demand for better approaches.

Both corporate control over sexuality research and conservative control over sexuality policy making must be challenged by activism demonstrating public support for a constructive sexuality policy agenda. This agenda includes:

- implementation of comprehensive sexuality education curricula;
- increased access to accurate and confidential sexuality information in communities; and
- expanded federal resources for a diversified research agenda on sexuality.

Parents, educators, public health advocates and feminist health activists will have to work together to build the political will to make the needed changes.

REFERENCES

Angell, M. (May 18, 2000). "Is academic medicine for sale?" *N Engl J. Med*, B42 (20): 1516-1518.

Baldo M, Aggleton P, Slutkin G. *Does Sex Education Lead to Earlier or Increased Sexual Activity in Youth*? Presented at the IXth International Conference on AIDS, Berlin, 6-10 June, 1993. Geneva, Switzerland: World Health Organization, 1993.

Boston Women's Health Book Collective, *Our Bodies, Our Selves for the New Century*. New York, NY: Simon & Schuster, 1998.

Boston Women's Health Course Collective, *Our Bodies, Our Selves*. Boston, Massachusetts: 1971.

Centers for Disease Control and Prevention (CDC), "Tracking the Hidden Epidemics: Trends in STDs in the United States." U.S. Department of Health and Human Services, Atlanta, Georgia: 2000.

Henry J. Kaiser Family Foundation, "Sex Education in America Survey." September 26, 2000.

Henshaw, Stanley K. "Unintended Pregnancy in the United States," *Family Planning Perspectives*, 30, January/February 1998, 24-29, 46.

Loe, Mieka. "Female Sexual Dysfunction: For Women or for Sale?," *The Network News*. National Women's Health Network, Washington, DC: January/February 2000.

Ziegler MG, Lew P, Singer BC. "The Accuracy of Drug Information from Pharmaceutical Sales Representatives." *Journal of the American Medical Association* 1995; 273: 1296-1298.

Fat Oppression and Psychotherapy, edited by Laura S. Brown, PhD, and Esther D. Rothblum, PhD (Vol. 8, No. 3, 1990). *"Challenges many traditional beliefs about being fat . . . A refreshing new perspective for approaching and thinking about issues related to weight." (Association for Women in Psychology Newsletter)*

Lesbianism: Affirming Nontraditional Roles, edited by Esther D. Rothblum, PhD, and Ellen Cole, PhD (Vol. 8, No. 1/2, 1989). *"Touches on many of the most significant issues brought before therapists today." (Newsletter of the Association of Gay & Lesbian Psychiatrists)*

Women and Sex Therapy: Closing the Circle of Sexual Knowledge, edited by Ellen Cole, PhD, and Esther D. Rothblum, PhD (Vol. 7, No. 2/3, 1989). *"Adds immeasureably to the feminist therapy literature that dispels male paradigms of pathology with regard to women." (Journal of Sex Education & Therapy)*

The Politics of Race and Gender in Therapy, edited by Lenora Fulani, PhD (Vol. 6, No. 4, 1988). *Women of color examine newer therapies that encourage them to develop their historical identity.*

Treating Women's Fear of Failure, edited by Esther D. Rothblum, PhD, and Ellen Cole, PhD (Vol. 6, No. 3, 1988). *"Should be recommended reading for all mental health professionals, social workers, educators, and vocational counselors who work with women." (The Journal of Clinical Psychiatry)*

Women, Power, and Therapy: Issues for Women, edited by Marjorie Braude, MD (Vol. 6, No. 1/2, 1987). *"Raise[s] therapists' consciousness about the importance of considering gender-based power in therapy. . . welcome contribution." (Australian Journal of Psychology)*

Dynamics of Feminist Therapy, edited by Doris Howard (Vol. 5, No. 2/3, 1987). *"A comprehensive treatment of an important and vexing subject." (Australian Journal of Sex, Marriage and Family)*

A Woman's Recovery from the Trauma of War: Twelve Responses from Feminist Therapists and Activists, edited by Esther D. Rothblum, PhD, and Ellen Cole, PhD (Vol. 5, No. 1, 1986). *"A milestone. In it, twelve women pay very close attention to a woman who has been deeply wounded by war." (The World)*

Women and Mental Health: New Directions for Change, edited by Carol T. Mowbray, PhD, Susan Lanir, MA, and Marilyn Hulce, MSW, ACSW (Vol. 3, No. 3/4, 1985). *"The overview of sex differences in disorders is clear and sensitive, as is the review of sexual exploitation of clients by therapists. . . . Mandatory reading for all therapists who work with women." (British Journal of Medical Psychology and The British Psychological Society)*

Women Changing Therapy: New Assessments, Values, and Strategies in Feminist Therapy, edited by Joan Hamerman Robbins and Rachel Josefowitz Siegel, MSW (Vol. 2, No. 2/3, 1983). *"An excellent collection to use in teaching therapists that reflection and resolution in treatment do not simply lead to adaptation, but to an active inner process of judging." (News for Women in Psychiatry)*

Current Feminist Issues in Psychotherapy, edited by The New England Association for Women in Psychology (Vol. 1, No. 3, 1983). *Addresses depression, displaced homemakers, sibling incest, and body image from a feminist perspective.*

Index

Abuse, history of, 34-36
Adolescent sexuality
  as compared with adult, 196-197
  developmental issues in, 195-209
  developmental perspective on,
      205-207
  socialization and, 198-205
AIDS/HIV. *See* Sexually transmitted
      diseases (STDs)
American Psychiatric Association.
      See DSM
American Urological Association
      (AUA), 66
American way of life, as sexuality
      issue, 150-153
AMES (Associación de Mujeres en
      Salud) (Costa Rica), 53-57
An Answer to FSD (video), 187-188
Apomorphine (Uprima), 70-72
Appearance. *See* Body image
Arousal
  female problems with, 156
  male problems with, 154-156
  partner-focused problems with,
      156-157

Bias
  experimenter, 79-82
  subject selection, 78-79
Body image, 53-57,198-200
Boston Conference of 1999, 68-69,
      88-90
Boston Women's Health Book
      Collective, 211-218
Breastfeeding, medicalization of,
      129-130

(University of) California (San Fran-
      cisco), 179-193
Centers for Disease Control and
      Prevention (CDC), 39-42
Childbirth
  medicalization of, 128-129
  orgasm in, 128-129
Circumcision, female, 50
City University of New York (CUNY),
      43-46
Clinician's role, 14-15
Costa Rica, 53-57
Cultural issues
  in adolescent sexuality, 200-201
  in Central America, 53-57
  in Israel, 47-52
  Latina sexualities, 33-37
  in Muslim communities, 50-52
Cultural studies, as discipline, 182-183

Desire
  in adolescent girls, 201-204
  double standard and, 204
Desire discrepancy, 151-153
Developmental issues
  adolescent sexuality, 195-209. *See
      also* Adolescent sexuality
  in sexual orientation, 117-119
*Diagnostic and Statistical Manual of
      Psychiatric Disorders. See
      DSM* entries
Direct-to-consumer advertising,
      75,181-182
Dole, Bob, 185
DSM. See also Medicalization
  alternative classification system, 5-7.
      See also New View; Sexual

Homosexuality, 111-121. *See also*
Lesbian sexuality; Sexual
orientation
Homosexuality in Perspective
(Masters and Johnson), 165
Human Sexual Response (Masters &
Johnson). *See* Masters and
Johnson

India, 59-62
*International Journal of Impotence
Research,* 67
Interpersonal Exchange Model of
Sexual Satisfaction, 23-26
Inversion model, of sexual
orientation, 112
Israel, sexology in, 47-52

John Jay College-City University of
New York, 43-46
Journal of Sex & Marital Therapy,
68

Lactation, medicalization of, 129-130
Latin America, 53-57
Latina sexualities, 33-37
"Lesbian bed death," 162-165,
170-172
Lesbian sexuality, 36-37,43-46,
111-121,161-172,173-178.
See also Sexual orientation
Life-cycle events, as related to
sexuality, 126-130
Lifestyle issues, in sexuality
expression, 150-153

Madonna/whore imagery, 125
Male sexual dysfunction, 65-66
Marginalized women, 39-42
Marriage practices, in India, 59-62

(University of) Massachusetts Medical
School, 9-15
Masters and Johnson
comparison with *DSM,* 77-78
"effective sexual stimulation" concept, 81-82
experimenter bias in, 79-82
homosexuality and, 167-170
Homosexuality in Perspective, 165
as model of female sexuality, 126
subject selection biases in, 78-79
Medical factors, family physician's
view, 13
Medicalization, 64-68,127,187-188. *See
also* "Female sexual
dysfunction" (FSD)
of childbirth, 128-129
"FSD" consensus statement, 68-70
gendered technologies and (Viagra
and Eros), 179-193
of lactation, 129-130
Masters and Johnson influence on,
77-82
men's, 64-65
of pregnancy, 127-128
women's, 66-67
Multiculturalism. *See* Cultural issues
Multi-variable model, 43-46

National Women's Health Network,
211-218
(University of) New Brunswick
(Canada), 23-26
New View
Costa Rican therapist's perspective,
53-57
developmental perspective and adolescent sexuality, 195-209. *See
also* Adolescent sexuality
family physician's response, 9-15
feminist perspective on, 17-21
historical background, 63-98. *See
also* Historical background